Royal College of Physicians of London

Seventy Years of Life in the Victorian Era

Royal College of Physicians of London

Seventy Years of Life in the Victorian Era

ISBN/EAN: 9783742820150

Manufactured in Europe, USA, Canada, Australia, Japa

Cover: Foto ©ninafisch / pixelio.de

Manufactured and distributed by brebook publishing software (www.brebook.com)

Royal College of Physicians of London

Seventy Years of Life in the Victorian Era

T. FISHER UNWIN
PATERNOSTER SQUARE
MDCCCXCIII

LIST OF ILLUSTRATIONS.

	PAGE
SYDNEY ...	151
TOWN HALL, SYDNEY ...	158
ZIG-ZAG RAILWAY, BLUE MOUNTAINS, LITHGOW VALLEY, N.S.W. ...	160
FERN TREE VALLEY, SCOTSDALE, TASMANIA ...	169
NEW ZEALAND CHIEF ...	202
NEW ZEALAND VEGETABLE CATERPILLAR ...	208
AUCKLAND YOUNG LADY ...	214
SEALS ON THE ROCKS AT SAN FRANCISCO ...	227
SALT LAKE CITY ...	234
THE ROYAL GORGE, PASSAGE OF THE ROCKIES ...	240
RAILWAY OVER THE ROCKIES ...	242
NIAGARA FALLS ...	255
THE BRIDGE OVER NIAGARA RAPIDS ...	258
NEW YORK ...	265
TERMINUS, ELEVATED RAILWAY, NEW YORK ...	267
BROADWAY, NEW YORK ...	278

SEVENTY YEARS OF LIFE IN THE VICTORIAN ERA.

CHAPTER I.

I AM one who has just commenced to traverse his seventy-first year, and can look backward over a life more or less of a checkered character, involving as it does a time spent in actual warfare, as well as in a struggling civil life passed in the metropolis and the provinces of England, with intervals of travel extending over Europe, the Australian colonies, and America. A review of the experiences of such a life may, perhaps, prove to be interesting and even instructive, and I make no further apologies for printing these reminiscences.

My father was a country rector, who had three sons, of whom I was the youngest. The rectory was not a very rich one, and the income was not supplemented to any great extent by private means. Consequently there was no hesitation as to what was to be done with "our boys:" we were early impressed with the fact that we must work for our own living, and be the architects of our own future position, hence we were to select the three learned professions respectively, and Physic fell to my lot, my brothers choosing Law and Divinity. My father, fortunately for us, was a good classic, having been elected, as a young man, to act as coadjutor with the head master of Rugby School; hence we were well founded in what was then deemed the *sine quâ non* of a gentleman's education, and the pater kept pegging away at us till we reached the age of thirteen, when we were sent off to a public school to continue our plodding with varying success. Our mother was one in a million, and no sacrifice was too great for her to make for the well-being of her sons. She was very beautiful, and descended from an old family beginning with the Crusaders' times. She gave up the world for the sake of her children. She was the grand home peacemaker, and her sons " grew up and blessed her." Our parents were indulgent to a certain extent, but they had their hard-and-fast line, which was firm and unyielding, and which we were taught to respect. We were allowed our fill of field sports as young lads, and took a practical interest in all the work connected with the cultivation of an extensive glebe-land. This laid the foundation of vigorous health. Cricket, tennis, and croquet were not to the fore in those days.

Play over, our schooling was work—work and no mistake—it meant business, serious and attentive, and we were taught to sing in harmony:—

> " When a weary task you find it,
> Persevere, and never mind it."

Whether at work or play there was no nonsensical familiarity permitted, and a gulf of respectful distance was always maintained at such times, and it never entered our heads to nickname either of our parents to their faces or behind their backs—our father as the "Gov.," or our mother as the "Old Lady." In these very enlightened and very much civilised days such a reverential attitude would, I take it, be considered by Young England as too old-fashioned!

When we become men, that is, when we leave behind the restraints of schooldom and pass on to college life, we are supposed to put aside childish things; but that, in too many cases, is only an assumption by freshmen, who air their littlenesses in strutting about bedecked in full-fledged attire of the most approved fashion, to the sweet delight of the artistic tailor, who will wait patiently any length of time for his extortionate bill, which, when presented after the lapse of two or three years, shocks and confounds the self-denying parents at home, who are in blissful ignorance that such an indebtedness exists; and yet the young hopeful can face his loving ones, vacation after vacation, without a blush, consoling his conscience that that is the way young fellows act who would assume the right tone and do credit to their college. They are too weak-kneed to resist the temptation of having a change of trousers for every day in the week, &c., and thus to assume the appearance of wealth which they have not. From the stand-point of my bringing up I could see no fun in this sort of foppishness, nor any feeling of satisfaction in strutting up and down High Street in cap and gown, the observed of all observers, especially of the fair sex. My father, if he had been in the commercial line, would soon have convinced me in technical language that that style of thing would "not pay." Therefore, without further ado, I tackled to, and though the harness chafed me a little at first, I soon found it became easier in the wearing, and that regular systematic work for every hour of the day as it came round was a grand stay against the inclination to swerve from the right track and to join in the pranks of the pleasure-seeking lot, who would do their best to bring you down to their level, and do no hard work till the last year of their curriculum, with the risk of being "plucked," cramming notwithstanding. In order to secure a good place in the estimation of the professors and stand fairly well with college authorities I determined to succeed if labour and plodding would do it. I could not command success of course, but I resolved not to have it on my conscience that I did not do my best to deserve it, and laying to heart the principle of the old fable that the tortoise will overtake the hare if it keeps pegging away long enough, and does not faint and get down-spirited on the way, I determined to rise up at 5.30 A.M., light the fire, make my coffee, and get an hour's start at thinking and plodding before my more lively antagonists were awake. This early rising made it easy to be punctual at chapel parade at 7.30 A.M., which I never failed to attend, as it seemed to sanctify and encourage the day's employment; it was a bright, cheerful service, so rendered by the students' quartet part singing, of which I was bass. I seldom went into society during my first summer's session, which was assiduously given up to the study of botany, and a good standard of health was kept up by roaming over the country in all directions in search of specimens, of which I made a useful, practical selection, and arranged four hundred dried ones for the examination, which I passed, and which resulted in my obtaining the certificate of honour, an old student taking the silver medal. Thus I made my first mark, and secured the smile of approval of one of the professors at least. And what was more encouraging, this, my first trial trip in science, pleased a relative of mine, a double-first classman at Oxford, who had risen entirely by his own unaided efforts to an eminent position in Christchurch, that he invited me to spend a portion of the long vacation at his house in Peckwater Quadrangle. There I met some of the greatest intellects of the day—all now gone to their rest. From their conversation I frequently gathered many useful hints, which roused my ambition to rise and go ahead if industry would do it. I was much amused one day by observing that their enjoyment of a good dinner did not interfere with the mental labours of these great men. My cousin, a bachelor, was celebrated for his excellent *cuisine*, and dinners *a la Russe* were just then coming into vogue, and one evening, during my stay, twelve of the great dons were invited to meet round the hospitable board, when sixteen courses were served; the constant changing of plates was amusing, if not bewildering, and one celebrated, but humorous guest, who sat next to me, had his plate removed thirteen times out of the possible sixteen, and, what is more, managed to keep talking all the time, cracking jokes and reciting telling anecdotes, reminding one rather of the gifts of the late Bishop Wilberforce in this respect.

Having now to return to college for the winter session, the crucial question that had to be put to myself was how much working power I had in me, and how many prizes were there within measurable distance of a first-year's student's chance of getting. I had the hardihood and presumption to decide to compete for four of these, which were open also to second and third-years' men. The first was a gold medal and money, the interest of £1,000, given by a well-known philanthropist, for the best essay on a chosen subject bearing on science, with a view to exemplify the Power, Wisdom, and Goodness of God—somewhat after the style of the Bridgewater treatises. The next plum was a gold medal for the best report of cases taken at the bedside of the sick poor in their own homes, being out-patients of the hospital which we all walked.

Another gold medal was awarded by authorities to that student who could pass the best examination in all the subjects taught during the winter session; but for this " good-all-round " prize it was laid down as an essential that the student should have been a regular attendant at morning chapel. This *sine quâ non* reduced the numbers who wished to compete *considerably*; but it goes without saying that this medal was the great cynosure of all eyes!

The fourth prize in contemplation was a medal for

the best examination in practical chemistry; and as the professor had selected me as his assistant to help him in the college laboratory, I stood a good chance of securing this, though the work was very dirty, the furnaces making one's hands like those of a blacksmith; but the analysis (organic and inorganic) were very fascinating and deeply impressive, never to be effaced from the memory. I had, as I say, the hardihood to try and gain these alluring rewards held out to the young men. Some of the elder fellows deemed me very impertinent to dream of such an ambitious scale of work; but I had made up my mind and set to, undaunted and even uninfluenced by their sneers and gibes. Up early, and closing at 11 P.M., shunning society, and resisting gaieties of all kinds, I determined to plod on and win the lot, if self-denial and hard work would do it. But I may remark here, come what may, I had determined not to do any secular work on the Sunday. I closed my books at midnight on Saturday, and did not open them again till Monday morning.

CHAPTER II.

I NEED not dwell on the trials and opposition I encountered during my first winter's campaign—it was gloomy indeed, but it all ended in sunshine in the spring. When it was decided that I had been the successful competitor for the four aforesaid prizes, then human nature asserted herself, and those who had been my bitterest enemies generously came forward with their congratulations, and, in the slang of even that time, dubbed me a "brick," and said I was a credit to the college. But the most gratifying day was still to come, when the sessional prizes were to be distributed among the successful students; and when I was called up for the fourth time to receive a medal—and that in a town hall crowded with ladies and gentlemen—the applause was unmistakable; and to enhance the delight of the reception, the prizes came from the hands of a chairman, a peer, and himself a double-first class-man. I could not help feeling rather staggered, as it was such a revulsion of position—from a retired ascetic life in a college room to be the central mark in such a splendid gathering—but if for a time I felt a pardonable degree of elation, it was quickly suppressed by my father's manner when I took the medals home. Of course he was pleased with my acquisitions, but he very quickly gave me to understand that I must not stay my hand, but go on working—in fact, must be content to be a student all my life if I would hold my own in the world. Much to my great grief, my poor mother had gone to her rest in heaven before these honours had been conferred on her "dillin," otherwise it would have been a pleasurable moment to prove to her that her self-sacrifices and her self-effacement for the well-being of her family were bearing fruit. Our sorrow was shared by the poor people especially, for she had constituted herself for years the parish doctor (we being six miles from the regular one), dispensing medicines and surgical appliances and medical comforts to the sick and needy with a willing and liberal hand unaided, for there was no rich squire's house to draw upon in emergencies, the community being made up of small farmers and miners. The mouldy, dilapidated state of the church was a constant fret to her highly wrought moral sensitiveness, for in those days of religious indifferentism it was most difficult to get money even to make the necessary repairs. I recollect when the tower was giving way under the weight of its eight bells, my father had no end of trouble to collect £10, having to supplement the rest of the cost out of his own pocket—and this for to keep this portion of the sacred edifice from collapsing altogether. When I reflect upon and compare the condition of the national churches of that period with that of the present day, even in obscure districts, I am struck with astonishment at the great change for the better. On entering one of these, open only once a week, the smell was like that of a mildewing vault, damp and stuffy, with fungi growing out between the flagstones on the floor; the woodwork of the seats worm-eaten and decaying, and the three-decker itself hardly safe to mount. Those were the days in which dissent made much headway with the lower illiterate classes, roused to a high pitch of enthusiasm by itinerant preachers chosen from themselves, and who could speak to their hearts in a phraseology peculiar to themselves the grand truths in the good old Book.

Passing on from this bit of digression, we arrive at the second winter session, which commenced under most auspicious circumstances. I had made my mark, and was something more than the mere numeral on my college room door. Our warden (the chancellor of a diocese and the son of a bishop who had married a peer's daughter with a nice dowry)—a man who knew what hard brain-work meant, having edited three large volumes on Ecclesiastical Law—was so exercised in his mind over the fact that any student could manage to monopolise four college medals in one year that, at one of his wine parties which he gave to a select few every week, he surprised us by saying that he would be pleased to confer £50 on any student who could accomplish the same feat again. We forgot the dignity of his position for the moment, and gave him a hearty cheer for his liberal offer; £50 was great in our eyes in those days, magnified to the extent of £500 to what that sum would be to us in after life. It must be confessed that I felt much disappointed that I was out of the running; but, pillowing the matter over that night, I reflected over the principle of the proposal, and, calling upon the warden the next morning, asked him if he deemed it an essential to the gaining of his £50 that the prizes should be actually and despotically four medals. His reply thrilled me with hope. "Certainly not," he said. "All I bargain for is, that they should be first class." Then I replied, "Perhaps you would permit the Scholarship on Divinity to stand as one?" "Not only so," said he, "but, being a clergyman, I should feel rather inclined to make that count as two." "Oh, no," I replied; "pray keep to your original agreement." But he said, with a twinkle in his eye, "Are you going to try?" "Certainly so, if you will allow me." A cordial shake of the hand was his answer, and we parted, he saying it would be fearfully hard work; but there was an encouraging "God help you," unexpressed save in his benevolent face. Well, the winter months were passed in right down hard plodding, on which I relied rather than upon any superior talents I had been blessed with. Those of superior intellects would persist, as usual, in putting off coming into the struggle and the fight till the season was half spent, and then in their flurry got nervous, sleepless, and dyspeptic, and, with brains *suddenly* overstrained, the staying powers of the memory would fail just at the finish. In all my anxiety to win I still kept to my resolution not to do any secular work on the Sunday, but I drew a line there which did not include the study of divinity and philosophy; these I set apart for that day as recreative, peaceful, and inspiring. Butler's "Analogy," Paley's "Evidences of Christianity," and Fénélon's works were the books for the examination to get the scholarship which was good for £20 a year.

To make a long story short, and not to weary the attention of the reader, I will at once jump to the conclusion of the session, which ended in my being the successful competitor for the Chancellor's Prize of £50, which involved, happily for me, the much-coveted scholarship. These secured to me £70 in cash, which for the moment made me feel passing rich, and the vacation would have been spent in undimmed pleasure but for a very heavy black cloud which came across my sunny sky. My father was suddenly taken away from us at this critical time of my career in life, and with him was gone our old home at the rectory, and, what was worse, I was now thrown on my own resources practically to continue and finish my studies and obtain my diplomas.

CHAPTER III.

The real tug of war began in my third and last year, and it was very doubtful at its beginning whether I could find sufficient financial help to remain in college and finish the necessary course of lectures and secure my hospital certificates. As to my very dear relations, some of them boasting of their thousands, I soon found that they could flatter with their lips, but they did not feel disposed to fork out much from their purses. "Put not your trust in princes, nor in any child of man." Assistance came in the nick of time from most unexpected quarters, from strangers, in fact, and it roused the feeling that the loving Father was just chastening, but not forsaking, the newly-made orphan. Circumstances soon proved this as plainly as if an angel from heaven had spoken. I had my £70 intact, and my "commons" in the college hall would only cost me £24. I therefore had a fair balance in hand, but to supplement this I got £10 for acting as tutor to a junior class which the good warden had instituted, and which he entrusted to my supervision. This was very cheering, and a great compliment to an undergraduate. He also confided to me as umpire a prize of £6 to be given to the student whom I considered had passed the best examination in these two subjects—ditto, another compliment. Feeling quite safe as to getting through my final exams. for the diplomas when the time arrived for such, I did not stick now so close to work, but went out to enjoy a little musical society, but what I greatly yearned for, and had set my heart upon, was to get if possible a stained glass window at the east end of the college chapel. This I set myself out to accomplish, and having first obtained a beautiful design—the subject being our Saviour healing the sick at the Pool of Bethesda, which was given to me by a rising young artist as a gratuitous contribution—I found that the cost of putting in the window would be £120, the manufacturers waiving their claim to any trade profit. So far so good. Now began my first begging-letter experience, and as my application was a good and disinterested one, it gave me boldness to persevere. Subscriptions came in nicely, and in order to square the deficit I gave a demonstrative course of lectures on chemistry in the college hall, to which outsiders were admitted by payment. This was also a success, and ended with a surplus, which delighted the professorial staff, who were in fears that the hat would have to go round among them after all. And though they considered me in an irresponsible position, the whole affair from beginning to ending was a striking proof to them and to all the students what could be done by pluck and perseverance, provided the object to be attained had sound moral and religious bearings, and this even by an individual poor and humble who had only made his mark by taking a few medals, &c.

Nothing very worthy of note took place till the end of the session, when all my certificates, necessary for my final exams., were filled up and signed by the respective professors, and I was ready, with feelings unruffled, to undergo those trying ordeals so fearfully dreaded by the student who has become perhaps nervously and tremblingly anxious because his accusing conscience whispers to him that he has not made the best use of his time and opportunities, and has put off till the third year, and to his trust in " coaching," to cram into an unprepared and an unexpanded mind and memory that amount of knowledge which ought to have been *gradually* acquired over the course of the three years allotted to him. Sleeplessness and sinking dyspepsia overtake him at the eleventh hour, and as the solemn day arrives he throws up the sponge in sheer fright at the idea of being " plucked," so he retires into private life and private study for six or twelve months, involving additional expense to his self-sacrificing relations or friends, whom he has cajoled into believing that he has broken down from a legitimate strain of over-work—a deception his tutor could at any moment prove to the contrary. The above description is truly typical of those young men who have been cursed with a little independence of their own, and which they have magnified in their worldly inexperience into something of tenfold its value, and have been induced under this false notion to lead a life of *dolce far niente* during the first two years of their college life, and have thus trifled with opportunities which can never be recalled. Such instances are very pitiable and sorrowful when the subject is a married man who is trying to enter the profession later in life than ordinary. An instance of this kind I recollect very well. I was coaching a gentleman whose wife had the means of starting him in a profession, and she was very ambitious that he should succeed, and he, on his part, was equally anxious to show her that she had not married a fool, but one who could soar far above the mental calibre of a tradesman, from whom she had originated; consequently the man's mettle was up, and I must admit he made the most courageous efforts to succeed. He was a strong, athletic fellow, and loved practical surgery, in which he was well up, having been an assistant to a surgeon in the " Black Country " for several years, but when we came to abstract theories and abstruse occult subjects, he was stupidity itself, and my labours to drill him into something like decent shape was prodigious, and my stock of patience was sorely tried ; but what annoyed me much was this—when he stumbled a little in his replies he used to get so guiltily red in the face, which was of the full-moon size, and made him look so intensely stupid and deficient. I was consoled, however, by the knowledge that he really was thoroughly well up in practical surgery, and that it was to the College of Surgeons he was going for a diploma, but I knew the examiners there were not content with manual skill only—they will have a man liberally educated in the bothering 'ologies as well; so I kept pegging along steadily until the awful day arrived, and I actually coached him up to the very doors of the college, and as he entered its gloomy portals wound up with one final warning, viz.: " Should the examiners tackle you on a subject you are not quite at home in, pray go on talking, and don't blush and hesitate as if you did not know, and in the confusion the question may be changed to one your jabbering has suggested. Of course you were a little deaf and did not hear exactly what was asked, do you understand?" "Oh, yes," said he, " I twig your meaning." I waited in some trepidation till his examination was over, and when he presented himself with a beaming countenance redder even than usual, I plainly perceived that all was well, and that he had passed the fiery ordeal, he remarking, " But for your last warning at the entrance I really do believe that I should have been 'ploughed.' The examiner took me on the hip, and I began to feel I was getting hot and confused, when, remembering your hint, I stumbled on and said something about the femoral, when the examiner, smiling, said, ' Oh, yes, what about the femoral? Do you mean the artery or the hernia?' 'Either,' said I, promptly. 'Very well, let us see what you know?' Thanks to you, I was at my ease directly, and getting through the descriptions satisfactorily, I gained confidence and passed the remainder comfortably." "Now," I replied, equally gratified, "won't your wife be pleased, and won't she give you such an affectionate hug as you have never as yet experienced, and if she never prayed heartily before I am sure she did to-day for your success. And now you deserve her respect as well as her love. Go forth and prosper, my dear fellow, and don't forget the cheerful saying from the good old Book : ' Oh rest in the Lord, and wait patiently for Him, and He shall give thee thy heart's desire.' "

As my last session was closing in upon me, and everything was prepared for my examination, the only difficulties which stared me in the face were those of a pecuniary character. I could not see where the money was to come from to pay the necessary fees for the diplomas; £35 would be required for the degree of M.D., reducing the expenses to the lowest figure. But taking a retrospective view of the past three years, and the wonderful way in which I had been upheld by so many unforeseen and unexpected interpositions, I did not lose faith in the continuous mercy of a kind overruling Providence, nor yet in the power of prayer, which my good mother never ceased to instil into us. I was not kept very long in anxious suspense. Our good warden, and his equally good countess, with whom I had been staying for some weeks to recoup my energies, which had run down from too close teaching, informed me that the founder of the so-called Bridgewater Treatise, which I had succeeded in gaining, hearing of the fix I was in, very kindly offered to pay my M.D. fees as soon as I had passed, which I did at once. This benevolent act of a person I had never seen was so unlooked for that I was astonished beyond measure, and it so exercised my thoughts that it implanted in me more than ever a very lively faith in the Divine ruling, and Heaven's supervision of the orphan, who was evidently not going to be deserted. About this time I was introduced to an honourable and reverend divine, who came to my aid by advising me to apply to the "Sons of Clergy Corporation" for assistance to pay the fees of the College of Surgeons, which that admirable institution of bicentennial goodness agreed to do, and I became a full-fledged surgeon.

CHAPTER IV.

WITH the aid of my prize-money and that of the scholarship my cruse of oil was again replenished, which enabled me to accept a pressing invitation from my old professor of chemistry who was staying in Paris, to pay that lively city a visit. This I did by taking a river steamer at Havre and going up that lovely portion of the Seine between that town and Rouen, where I got off and took the train for Paris, which I crossed from west to east to reach the students' quarters. Here I found the professor located in a cheap hotel, the whole expenses of which were met by an expenditure of thirty francs a week. Those were palmy days when the prices for everything had not been run up to the same extent as they are now by crowds of rich Americans and wealthy English merchants, aggravated by an increased octroi in consequence of the expenditure of many millions for Hausman's improvements—the wholesale sweeping off of the old rookeries, and in their place the erection of huge highly decorated mansions which have made everything cent per cent dearer for every class of lodgment in this gay city. I did not pass my time in amusements only. I was advised by the professor to take a two months' course of practical surgical operations on the dead subject at Clamart, where a public certificate would be given as soon as the pupil could perform the whole series of operations as quickly and skilfully as the teacher, authorised and selected by the French Government, could do them. This boon I acquired at the end of the two months. I also attended the practice at the Hôtel Dieu, a Government chemical laboratory, and other public educational establishments open gratuitously to the student, where I picked up some useful crumbs not easily got at in England. I may here state that Paris was at that time the resort of men in pursuit of science from all parts of the world. There were five different languages spoken in the saloon of our hotel, each nationality seated at separate tables. They were a godless lot, and one French count, a more zealous infidel than the rest, was exerting his talents to show, by the chemical experiments he was making, that the Mosaic order of creation was a series of scientific blunders from beginning to end. However, it served to arouse my interest on the subject so far that when I returned to England I spent much time and some expense in exploring the matter for my own satisfaction, which involved some delicate manipulations to show the influence of light on the surface of vegetation, and the wonderful circle of interchanges between that world and the animal creation through the medium of the atmosphere. It took several months to complete, and in the end it convinced me more than anything I could have gleaned from the most logical abstract theories, however plausible, that the order of creation as laid down by the unscienced mind of Moses was, on the whole, a marvel of accuracy and replete with truths which modern man, with all his wonderful aids from the perfect instruments for research in the eighteenth century, could not upset or gainsay!

This analysis, though wearisome and trying to one's patience, resulting in regulating and setting my thoughts and convictions on the two grand cardinal points—my faith in the Scriptures, and the Omnipresence of the Deity. Therefore I am thankful for my first visit to Paris, now forty-four years ago, for implanting in my heart these deep religious impressions which have never forsaken me.

The last of the "three days' *fêtes* of July" at the public expense which had been annually held to commemorate the restoration of the monarchy under Louis Philippe took place when I was in Paris, and the contemptuous way in which everything of a Napoleonic character was treated was quite remarkable—for instance, plaister casts of Napoleon in his cocked hat and riding coat, and Marshal Ney and such like noted personages connected with their glorious wars, would be set up, like so many Aunt Sallys in the booths to be shot at for a sou. But this *fête*, in which the people seemed to run wild, was not powerful enough to divert the attention of the populace from certain wrongs which agitators kept dinging into their ears, and the king would not budge an inch from those privileges which are supposed to hedge him about by divine right, notwithstanding, it is said, the intercession of Madame Adelaide, his daughter, who prayed to him on bended knees that he would make some concession to the people before it was too late ; but the king was stubborn, and could not realise the truth of the position till he heard shots fired into the windows of the Tuileries, when he fled almost penniless to the coast and took refuge in an English yacht and made his way to England, the safe refuge for those in political trouble.

Before this crisis, the undercurrent of murmuring discontent among the democracy was apparent to every one except to those in the palace. I could—every one could—see in every street and in every café, knots of men collected together talking politics and discussing openly the situation. The fire was smouldering for months and giving fearful warnings, but the executive took no heed—none are so blind as those who won't see.

I now took my leave of the gay metropolis of fashion, and having some cash to spare I returned home by way of Belgium, visiting Brussels, Antwerp, Maline, and doing the Rhine from Cologne to Strasbourg, which previous hard work enabled me to enjoy the more. On reaching London I got a letter from one of my old college professors requesting me, if I had made no other engagements, to join their staff as tutor, offering me one hundred a year, with rooms and free commons, and any fees I could pick up by private coaching. This offer came upon me quite as a windfall, and I gladly accepted the appointment, as it gave me an opportunity of prosecuting my studies in order to get the license to practice medicine from the Royal College of Physicians of London which, at that time, required one to submit to five or six days' examination, and to have reached the age of twenty-six years. The winter session passed off uneventfully, saving the materialistic impression which began to prevail among the more advanced students, and which I endeavoured to combat with all the forcible arguments I could muster, and having made an unusual mark myself as a thinker and practical demonstrator, I perhaps exerted more influence and weight in counteracting this deadly influence. At least, our relative positions as tutor and student were such that we could unreservedly and dispassionately discuss the metaphysical arguments together without quarrelling and without compromising our independence.

In April I went up for my examination at the College of Physicians, and as the windows overlooked Trafalgar Square we had a full view of the celebrated Chartist meeting which took place on one of the days. We were much amused at the fussy attitude of the hundreds of special constables who, " bedecked with a little brief authority, played such fantastic tricks " by shoving about defenceless women and children; while the Duke of Wellington had had secreted in St. Martin's Church the Guards and some shotted cannon, and in the Strand the sacred buildings near Somerset House were ready to rake that thoroughfare from end to end in case of a popular uproar, and the risk of looting the shops; but the scare collapsed quietly and peace was not disturbed, and it all ended in the classes learning a lesson from the masses!

Though our time and attention was much diverted from our examining papers during this day's excitement, we finally satisfied the censors that we could be entrusted with the lives of Her Majesty's subjects, and our diplomas were duly handed over to us, headed by the signature of old Dr. Paris, a physician of eminence of a bygone generation, and whose knowledge of the then progress in science, especially analytical chemistry, was rather foggy. My health gave way about this time, and I spent several months at the seaside to recruit it. And as I rallied picked up a five-pound note now and again by giving a practical lecture on chemistry and botany to young men at mechanic institutes.

As another phrase of my life will soon commence, I will defer the same till we are *en route* to the next chapter.

CHAPTER V.

WHEN recruiting at the seaside, I heard of a vacancy in the medical staff of a large infirmary in a midland county town. A physician was required to fill the post of attending, not only to this infirmary with its hundred beds, but also to a fever hospital with another fifty. As there were only two physicians to do the work, the duties seemed rather onerous even to me, but I was pressed to try my luck, as a lady voter said. And on visiting the town for the first time as a perfect stranger to every one, it was discouraging to learn that there were already four candidates in the field, three being well-known local practitioners, and the fourth an elderly physician from London, a stranger like myself. It seemed rather a hopeless sort of struggle, especially so with the three former, but a clergyman of position and influence in the county, and a large subscriber to the funds of the institution, was won over by his wife to my side, and he surprised me by saying that there was a great deal of political feeling in connection with the election, that there was in fact a Whig and Tory side in the matter. I being a clergyman's son was regarded as necessarily belonging to the Conservative section, though I had no political bias one way or the other, for my mission in life was one of mercy to all ranks and conditions of men. I chartered a dog-cart, and canvassed the county thoroughly, and was introduced to about sixty good families, but a great duke and the founder of the infirmary were hot against me, but I was told not to lose heart for all that. On the day of the election the three local candidates retired, because the body of governors present unanimously decided that the appointment would not allow them to continue in general practice.

The choice then rested between me and the elderly physician from town, and when it came to this narrow pass one of the local doctors handed over to my side twenty-four ladies' proxies, which he held blank in reserve, and filled them in with my name, this astute movement brought me in at the head of the poll with a majority of sixteen, much to the vexation and disappointment of the founder and his rich Whig party, including his Grace, the high and mighty duke. When the chairman complained of my youth, a popular clergyman present retorted by saying that it was just possible a man might be a wee bit too old, alluding, of course, to the elderly candidate with his bald head and grey hair, who was said to be seventy, clenching his remarks also with the further one that we should have lost the services of Pitt, the prime minister of England, if we had rejected him on account of his age, which was only twenty-one years when the king made him his premier.

However, the legality of the disposal of the twenty-four proxy papers in my favour cropt up, and it was finally decided, after a very stormy discussion, to put us to the trouble and expense of another canvass, and poll the county once more; but my party insisted that I should be acting physician at the infirmary during the interval of two months, which gave me a very good innings, and I lost no opportunity of ingratiating myself with every person concerned, so that when the anxious day at last arrived I came in with a triumphant majority of two hundred in lieu of sixteen. Thus only good came out of an apparent evil. Friends rallied around me in every direction, and the second election diverted much attention to me as a persecuted individual, which tended to rouse a sort of general sympathy, very beneficial to a young physician making his way among strangers in a strange land.

The result was what might be expected. I rapidly got into a practice, and in two years had set up a pretty little phæton with a pair of ponies, backed by a smart "tiger." Financially I was aided by taking three young men into my house, who were preparing for their examinations, and who were very useful to me in taking down a report of my cases at the hospitals and enlivening my evenings.

I think the above record of difficulties and trials and depressing circumstances ought to encourage young professionals to keep a good heart and never to say die, even when the outlook seems very black indeed!

For the first time in my life I began to feel what it was to bask in easy circumstances, and the pleasurable repose from anxiety involving ways and means was the none less enjoyable because the change was the outcome of my own exertions. The only thing I had now to fear was the danger of becoming too much of a diner out, as the county families were over kind and pressing, and the constant acceptance of their courteous invitations would lead me into expense, and withdraw my mind from study and close attention to practice. It required no little tact to steer clear of giving offence when so much disinterested kindness was being shown towards me on all sides, but very often I could plead that the distances were too far, and the nights too dark to venture out; thus by one excuse or another I managed to keep my social pleasures within reasonable and conscientious limits. I was perfectly convinced that a society man was not the one to gain the professional confidence of the people; hence I defined my boundary and kept to it.

I was startled one morning at breakfast by one of my pupils saying that he and his fellow students had been scheming how they could get up to see the Great Exhibition (1851)—the one grand novelty and talk of the whole civilised world, being the first of its kind ever organised on such a prodigious scale; but Prince Albert had set his heart upon its accomplishment, and the glittering work was done. I had been contemplating the possibility of getting to see it, but the expense of lodgings deterred me. I had heard of a party of Germans taking a beautiful West-end suite of drawing-rooms, and paying twenty-five guineas a week, which were surreptitiously occupied by thirty or forty men, who huddled together on the floors, cooked, slept, and smoked in them, and left at the end of the season, leaving the decorations, carpets, and furniture in a filthy state. After a little correspondence, we, that is, myself and three pupils clubbing together, negotiated for rooms in a small public in High Street, Kensington, close to the Gardens, where the charges were moderate for the occasion, being those of a first-class hotel in ordinary times. We had a high gala life of it for three days. The wonderful sights in the world's fair served us as a topic of conversation for several months. We were amazed at the two huge elms, one hundred and twenty feet in height, inclosed in the glass roof of the transepts, and the birds flying about and chirping in their branches. Then came the life-like statuary of the renowned Gibson, especially his Greek slave and tinted Venus.

Then our attention to the rows of bottles with the lovely aniline dyes of every conceivable colour, all extracted from sticky, stinking coal tar!

Amid the din of voices of thousands of people, nothing startled us so much as to hear the numerous languages spoken as coming from all nations under the sun, and the quaint picturesque costumes of every hue and from every clime. These elbowed one in every direction, and when the scene was viewed from the galleries a most charming sight was presented— a restless, surging panorama of heads and bodies clothed in every conceivable fantastic form, and glistening under the sunlight with all the dazzling colouring of a rainbow. It was a fascinating wondrous display of shape and colour, and only to cost one shilling! Yet the committee cleared £200,000 after all expenses were paid. We had heard previously a great deal of French and Belgian lace and Lyons velvets, but the first prize for these exhibits were taken by Great Britain. Much of this success was doubtless owing to the schools of design which had been started in our country by Prince Albert.

CHAPTER VI.

Nothing very eventful occurred till the summer of 1854, when an opportunity presented itself of a trip to New York. A steamer of 2,000 tons, shiprigged, with an auxiliary of 200 horse power, was chartered to make its first voyage to commence an Anglo-American trade in opposition to the Yankee clippers which were very jealous of any competition. We had a very rough passage, occupying nineteen days, the sea running mountains high, and I thought we should have lost a young girl of sixteen, who was such a bad sailor that she could not retain anything fluid or solid from the beginning to the end of the voyage, and the application of large hot poultices was the only thing which gave her any relief at all. This girl with her two elder sisters were returning to their home on a slave estate in South America, and were in charge of a black woman who had been entrusted to go all the way to Paris to fetch them. I never saw such devotion as I witnessed in this negro woman. She was unwearied in her attendance night and day, and the salvation of her young mistress was, humanly speaking, due to her loving-kindnesses. I had read some harrowing tales of the cruelty of the Southern slaveholders towards their people; but after what I had seen on board that ship I began to doubt much of the truth of such statements. We had as a passenger a celebrated black woman called the "Black Swan," who sang divinely, giving us now and again a treat in the saloon. She had been to London, where the Queen and Prince Consort had taken her up and patronised her with a pecuniary result very satisfactory to herself. When she was singing in her cabin it was difficult to believe that such sweet thrilling sounds could issue from the throat of such a repulsive looking individual.

On nearing what is called the "Banks of Newfoundland" we got into fog of white cloud, and we slowed our engines to two miles an hour, and just as we had passed safely through the mist we saw facing us a brig at anchor, about a cable's length, and we had just time to port our helm and clear her stem; it was a close shave indeed, and I shall never forget the consternation depicted upon our good captain's pale face; he seemed petrified for the moment to see danger so near, for had the fog not been cleared, he said, we must have sent the brig to the bottom, and probably come off with a hole in our bows. Why this vessel was anchored at this particular spot was this—immediately in the vicinity, fishing for cod, were a number of boats, and the brig was present acting as their depôt to receive their catchings. As the sea was calm the skipper sent one of his boats with some cod, and asking for some beef in exchange, which the said crew were out of. One of the Yankee passengers said we Britishers did not know how cod should be cooked, and very officiously demanded that he should go to the ship's galley and give instructions to the *chef*, which the steward good-humouredly allowed; but when the fish was placed on the saloon table very few would touch it, it was so flabby, tasteless, and slimy, hence the connoisseur got pretty well joked by the English party. Another fellow of the same bumptious type vowed we slow-going ones from the old country did not even know how to enjoy the luxury of tobacco in a proper way, and began at once to show us how this was to be done, first by taking a quid from the hollow of his cheek and clearing his throat of its dark nauseous saliva, secondly by taking a pinch of snuff from an elaborate gold box, and thirdly producing a Havannah cigar which he began to smoke with great gusto, thus illustrating the three ways the weed may be used and enjoyed (?) by the same individual. I need hardly say that the European ladies present turned away in disgust from this vain display of our brother Jonathan, but I am writing now of what occurred thirty-seven years ago, the rising generation of young people in America though still rather fast are not vulgar withal. After the war between the North and the South a crowd of Americans overran Europe and picked up in their travels some most useful lessons which mollified their manners immensely, and they returned to their country wonderfully toned down and less offensive in their style of address, and with a gradual dropping of their constant impertinent interrogatives. One never hears now in anything like decent society such salutations as, " Well, stranger, your hat shineth gloriously; I guess that beaver cost a lot, where does it hail from?" Or if in a train they would be quite restless till they found out where you were going. "I am steering south," one would say, "and I calculate you are on the same track? Where shall you cast anchor to-night?" And they would gradually worm out of you whether you were going to join a ranch, or bent on speculation in pork and lard at Chicago, or whether your inclinations were in the corn or oil line; and it is an easy transition from the quality to the quantity, from which it would be soon found out whether you had a large pile or not to foot up with. Now if you were wide awake and endowed with much patient tact a quarrel would be avoided, and all would end well with the usual invitation to cement the passing friendship by liquoring up.

As we were nearing Sandy Hook, and the sea calmed down, we were enabled to carry up our little sufferer and place her flat on a mattress on the deck and give her a sun bath which seemed to revive her much, and the knowledge that her dear native land was in sight still more so. With our auxiliary screw we did not get on very fast, and we were not warped up to the quay till near midnight; it was a dark night, and no one was allowed to go ashore before the mails were delivered, and these were not to be disturbed till the morning, and so we betook ourselves to our berths to sleep the rest of the thankful in heart, for I don't think there was a soul on board but who was most grateful to a kind Providence for preserving us and the vessel from foundering in the bottomless deep. It was a most boisterous trial trip, though perhaps not a prolonged one for those days of comparative slow steaming. I for one awoke refreshed the next day, though the heat and smells were anything but agreeable. I was anticipating a pleasant ramble in the world-renowned Broadway and its side avenues of huge mansions, but when I presented myself on deck I saw there was an unusual commotion among the officers of the ship with the captain in their midst, holding a most vociferous harangue with two or three Yankee officials; and on coming to inquire into this turmoil I found that a dead negro had been placed in a boat alongside our vessel during the night, and no one was allowed to disembark till an inquest had been held on the body. Of course the verdict of the jury was in our favour, for it was readily proved that no one on our ship had anything whatever to do with causing the death of the black body, and it was made very clearly apparent by what came out at the inquiry that the disgusting annoyance originated in an opposition set up by the American marine to English interference with their shipping trade. A sort of revenge and spite in fact, which we had to put up with as an instance of their narrowmindedness in those illiberal days. Afterwards we were left at peace, and I roamed over the busy and money-making city, teeming with a restless excitable people whose one sole aim and object in life seemed to be business, eternal business, for which they have the keenest eye, the men leaving to their womenkind the acquisition of all the refinements of art and literature, and to whom they instinctively turn for all the current information whether social, political, national, or European, and all other topics not directly connected with trade which engrosses all their attention. Thus the American women took a high position at that period, especially the young girls of the family, who were very liberally educated and indulged in foreign travel, and who acted quite the queen in their mother's drawing-room. These were they who were thoroughly well posted up in all passing events at home and abroad, and thus did away with the necessity of any reading or study by their fathers, who cared for little beyond the limits of business transactions in which they were absorbed morning, noon, and night. Here I think lies the explanation why the young American ladies are such charming society in these days and so much sought after by English noblemen and other men of position and brains, though, I dare say, many of them being linked to a pile of dollars have this to thank perhaps for playing no secondary part in the drama of life!

I had a few letters of introduction to some good families who treated me with marked hospitality, and I was surprised at the extreme abstinence at the dinner table, no wine or spirits were present, and I understood the young ladies never took anything of the kind, hence I could easily understand why they had such beautiful complexions.

The atmosphere was, at this time, most oppressive, the thermometer registering on the shady side of Broadway 105° F., and as my time was limited I had to be about in it a good deal. The smells near the quays were very offensive, and I should say that the air was fully charged with microbes, at least there were more than I could contend against, and I was knocked down suddenly with an acute attack of dysentery, which so prostrated me that I could not rise from bed, and no remedies seemed to have any effect in checking it; and getting alarmed I ventured on an heroic dose of chloroform, which sent me into a sleep lasting off and on for twenty-four hours, and when I came to my senses again the complaint had gone and did not return. I was so bad for a time that I had given up all hopes of ever seeing dear old England again, hence I was only too glad to be well enough to return home in the same vessel which took me out, besides I felt quite an attachment to our good captain, who was not only very skilful, but was a man of strong religious sentiments, and who preserved an unspotted character among his officers and crew. His Sundays at sea when he conducted his own services was a sight to see. Every man who could be spared was regularly cleaned up and present, and the whole day was kept as sacred as possible, most refreshing to those who had any serious feelings at all.

Nothing worthy of note supervened on the passage home, and the sensation of seeing again the shores of our dear country can only be realised by those who have been away from them for the first time and returned in safety.

CHAPTER VII.

I HAVE now arrived at a very important epoch, not only in my life, but in the history of Europe also. War was declared in this year of grace 1854 against Russia by England and France, who joined their forces to those of Turkey who had been fighting on the Danube single-handed against the great Autocrat of the North, and subsequently Italy joined the Allies with some thirteen thousand of her picked troops. The origin of this bloody war may be very briefly described. The Greeks disputed the exclusive rights of the French to twelve "Holy Places"—the four principal of which were the great Cupola of the Holy Sepulchre, the Tomb of the Virgin, the great church at Bethlehem, and part of the Garden of Gethsemane. The French Government instituted a commission of inquiry into the dispute, and the verdict of this commission was in favour of the French Catholics, who considered their claim established because the Sultan had specially confirmed their rights by a firman, and here probably the row would have ended if the Emperor of Russia had not interfered, and in a very despotic manner sent the Sultan an autograph letter claiming for the Greeks all their ancient privileges in Jerusalem, and condemning the Turkish ministry for countenancing the pretensions of the French Catholic party. The Sultan got alarmed, and fearing to offend his great domineering neighbour, dismissed the "mixed" Commission, and got a new one formed composed of Turks only. While this commission was sitting the Emperor Nicholas proposed to Louis Napoleon that they should settle this question themselves, leaving the Sultan to carry out their wishes only. To this request Napoleon returned a decided negative. Well, the Turkish Commission sent in their report proposing that the great Cupola should be common property, and that the French Catholics should have access to the Tomb of the Virgin, and a key to the church at Bethlehem. This decision the French accepted under protest, but Nicholas demanded that the firman should be published throughout the Sultan's dominions, which gave great offence to the French, who demanded the recall of the firman unless it was promulgated with as little publicity as possible. On, however, the Turkish official in charge of the document arriving at Jerusalem, the Greeks clamoured for a public reading of the firman with the usual pomp and parade, and on receiving further instructions, the document was read publicly. Then arose the question whether the French Catholics should have a key to a side door or enter by the great portal of the Church of the Holy Sepulchre, which the Latins could not but feel to be humiliating. Nicholas was not the man to brook resistance to his wishes, so he sent to Constantinople Menschikoff as a special ambassador with specific demands, and he acted so insolently towards the Sultan that he claimed a Russian protectorate over the whole of the Greek subjects of the Ottoman Empire, who constituted four-fifths of the entire nation, so that from one squabble to another matters assumed such a pitch that England, France, Austria, and Prussia, felt compelled to interfere, especially when Nicholas ordered an Army Corps to take possession of Moldavia and Wallachia as "material guarantees." The four Powers tried hard to make a treaty of peace at Vienna, which, however, proved a nullity, for the Turk would not concede an inch, and declared war on the 5th of October, 1853, sending their celebrated general, Omar Pasha, with 120,000 troops to defend the Danube against the passage of the Russians, thus showing how—

"From very small beginnings sad issues did arise."

It was an illustration of the old fable of the wolf and the lamb, or rather the Bear and the Lamb, which wanted an excuse, however flimsy, to attack an innocent victim, and then overrun and annex its country. The great Northern Bear had been for a long time casting longing eyes on the possessions of the "Sick Man," and yearned to fulfil the prophecies of Peter the Great, that sooner or later Russia would be master at Constantinople. Active fighting had been going on at Shoomla on the Danube during the winter of 1853-4, the Turks displaying their usual courage behind their breastworks, and keeping in check the attacks of their powerful foe—the weak against the mighty—thus rousing the indignation and sympathies of the nations of Europe, in the expression of which feeling the Englishman was most demonstrative, hence our Queen came forward on the 27th of March, 1854, and announced to both Houses of Parliament, "that she felt bound to afford active assistance to her ally the Sultan against unprovoked aggression," and war was declared against Russia by the English. The Emperor Napoleon about the same time made a similar announcement, and the fleets of both nations anchored in Besika Bay at the entrance to the Dardenelles—part of our flotilla going to block the ports of the Baltic. The English and French land forces were on a large scale, and considering that we had been at peace for forty years, our contingent was magnificent, and to all appearances well appointed. The command was given to Lord Raglan, a Peninsular officer, and a pupil of the "Iron Duke," who was supported by such bravos as Sir Colin Campbell and Sir George Cathcart. The war was a popular one, the people being exasperated beyond measure by the publication of the remarkable "Secret Correspondence," in which Nicholas proposed that the Turkish Empire should be partitioned off—England and Russia to take a division. And the anger of the public was not lessened when they heard that the same proposition had been made to Louis Napoleon, in which bargain England was carefully left out in the cold. Hence the departure of our troops was hailed with the greatest enthusiasm, English and French standing side by side, forgetting completely their old hereditary feud. Parliament suspended its hostilities, and the "opposition" its grievances when its members heard that the Czar Nicholas had tried to bribe English statesmen, in order to get them to conform to his wishes. They unanimously denounced this Russian aggression as dead against European freedom and civilisation. Little Lord Russell, a scion of an old historic house of liberty, quite surpassed himself with heroic grandeur when he took up the challenge so insolently given, and cried, "God defend the right!" which Englishmen of all ranks echoed most heartily.

Having now finished a description of how this vexatious and bloody war originated, I will devote several separate chapters to a rehearsal of the manner in which it personally affected my life.

CHAPTER VIII.

HAVING obtained letters of introduction from Sir Andrew Smith, Director-General of the Army Medical Department to Sir John Hall, Chief of the Medical Staff in the Crimea, I took passage with the 46th Regiment on the unfortunate steamer *Prince*, a beautiful new transport, this being her voyage out for the first time. We had a splendid time of it till we reached the Morea, when having to change our course for the north we encountered a regular mistral, against which our good ship could make no headway, as she had only a small auxiliary screw power, so we had to lay to till the morning. The sea ran mountains high during the night, and our deck getting washed with some heavy seas, the stabling, with eleven chargers on board, got shaken from its fastenings, and the horses getting frightened, began to plunge and tumble about. The colonel's horse, a valuable thoroughbred, fell and began kicking the others, to save which the colonel himself cut the animal's throat and had him hauled overboard. We all thought this a plucky thing to do, especially at night time, with the ship rolling and tossing in a downpour of rain. The next day it calmed down somewhat, and we were able to proceed slowly through the lovely Greek islands, passed Athens, and then we were compelled to pull up again in a bay off the island Negropont. From the deck we could plainly see the natives ploughing with the same primitive machine described by Virgil, and drawn by an unequal yoke, an ox and an ass. The head wind moderating we were enabled to steam northward once more, and soon found ourselves passing up the Dardenelles, which Byron swam across, though the current is very strong in its centre. Then came our passage through the sea of Marmora, with its picturesque Prince's Islands, and our entrance into the Bosphorus at seven in the morning, when we beheld one of the most glorious sights in the universe—surpassing anything the imagination of the most lively mind could picture to itself, namely, a brilliant morning sun shining upon Constantinople with its gilded minarets, and many white palaces rising one above another, interspersed with domes, and gardens, and cemeteries, with the everlasting cypress peeping out everywhere. We were all on deck enjoying this brilliant and never-to-be-forgotten scene, which to us, hailing from sunless England, looked like fairyland! We cast anchor off Scutari, and I disembarked to get orders, and these were to proceed to the Crimea; but as I was returning to our steamer, the channel had taken on a rough aspect, and the boat could not proceed but slowly, and I could not catch up the *Prince*, which, having a patent windlass, weighed anchor quickly, and steamed away without me, to my no little chagrin. I had no idea what the future would bring forth, for this very circumstance saved my life, because had I remained on board I should most likely have gone down with the vessel when she foundered in the bay of Balaclava on the 14th of November, when she and seventeen other craft were wrecked. The *Prince* had on board a most valuable cargo of warm winter clothing and a fresh supply of electric apparatus. The captain, crew, and some military not yet landed, were drowned, only six were saved out of 150, and these were drawn up the cliffs with cords. After this digression I will hark back to Scutari, where I experienced my first great shock arising from the horrors of war. While I was conversing with the medical superintendent, who should come in but Dr. F——, with a very distressed face, saying that he had just arrived with a large cargo of wounded from the Crimea; that in the Black Sea they had encountered a fearful gale, and that for three days it was impossible to dress a third of the cases, and that several were delirious with pain and nerve shock. There were about 150 wounded on board, many having died on the rough passage down. In his dilemma he asked the chief for the assistance of two or three surgeons to help him to get this shipload of misery ashore, then to dress them and to operate, as several limbs required to be amputated. To this modest request the perplexed superintendent replied, "I am sorry to say that I cannot afford to give you the aid you ask for, we are so wofully short-handed;" but pointing to me he said: "Here is an experienced hand just out from a home hospital, who will, I dare say, be of great help to you." Then Dr. F—— and I left the office and were soon hard at work till our backs ached again with stooping and carrying and endeavouring somewhat to relieve this mangled mass of humanity. The wounds, not having been dressed for so long, were in a most horrible state, and the foul odours were almost unbearable, even to one accustomed to such. A few more shiploads of like horrors followed, and then the outcome of the wounded from the three battlefields of Alma, Balaclava, and Inkerman, were duly landed and placed in comparatively comfortable quarters in the two huge hospitals at Scutari and the one on the Bosphorus, while the Russian prisoners were accommodated in a hospital at Pera. The two Scutari buildings were of immense size, and were originally intended to hide away 20,000 Turkish troops to suppress instantly any rebellion among the Sultan's subjects in Constantinople. The corridors were very lofty and wide and well lighted, and they made admirable wards for the sick and wounded, which numbered at this particular time 4,600, including the Russian prisoners. Mr. Bracebridge took the trouble to measure the flooring on which they were billeted, and found that it extended nearly four miles!

Miss Nightingale arrived out from England the beginning of November, bringing with her about twenty-four experienced nurses of her own selection, and they were indeed of great service in dressing and attending the wounded, and seeing that they were properly supplied with medical comforts. Miss Nightingale, on her own responsibility, and in defiance of all red-tapeism, ordered over from Constantinople bazaars hundreds of mattresses for the poor fellows to lie upon. And though she was sorely distressed to find that she could not get sufficient laundry work done to give such a crowd of sick and disabled men even one clean shirt a week, she might well look puzzled when the medical chief asked her where she thought four thousand shirts could be washed—even supposing the men had a change of flannels, which scores had not, and many were torn, and would go to pieces if exposed to rough handling. Notwithstanding such drawbacks as these, I soon perceived that she and her aids had produced a great and beneficent reform before I left for the Crimea, which I did in about six weeks, after having shared actively in scenes of distress, disease, and bloodshed, such as it is impossible to depict with pen or pencil, but which Lord Panmure did me the great honour of appreciating by rewarding me with an extra six months' pay amounting to £230. There was a great outcry sent home with respect to the dearth of medical attendants, and then the authorities sent out to Scutari a lot of raw young surgeons, who were of little use in severe cases, and worried one's life out with questions as what was to be done here and what there, they would not take any responsibility on their inexperienced shoulders, and were not of much more use than Miss Nightingale's skilled nurses, but it proved to them an excellent school of instruction. On my arrival in the Crimea I went off to head-quarters to present my letters of introduction to Sir John Hall, the head of the Medical Department, who received me most kindly, and arranged for me to take up my quarters at the Balaclava Hospital, formerly a large Russian Government school, which was filled to repletion with six hundred patients, suffering principally from rheumatism and dysentery, arising from exposure in the trenches, and want of proper nourishment. Here, also, the medical staff were very short-handed, and I sadly overworked. Besides this heavy duty, I was asked to act as a temporary sanitary officer, and while thus engaged I had to condemn a shipload of Turkish loaves of black bread which the Sultan had sent up as a present to our troops, but which had become fermented and mildewed in the hold, and thus rendered unfit for human food, hence I had to condemn this life-giving cargo, and it was ordered out of harm's way by being thrown overboard into the Black Sea. They were so long on the passage, thanks to the sluggish Turk, and on our part we were slow to order the loaves (3,200) out and get them distributed, red-tapery in the shape of check and counter-check being so dilatory. Our regulations for times of peace were not in keeping with the rapid demands of active warfare. Again, I was told off to attend any sick ladies who might arrive in the harbour, and thus I was brought into contact with Miss Nightingale once more, who would come up to see how the nursing was going on in the Crimea. Before she could return to Scutari she was attacked with camp fever, and laid up in one of the transports. For her recovery she relied entirely on good nursing and nourishment, and objected all through her attack to take either stimulants or medicines. When she recovered she was a mere wreck of her former self, and how to get her back to Scutari was the difficulty, as she was a very bad sailor; so I petitioned Lord

Dudley for the loan of his yacht, which was lying idle in the harbour. He received me very graciously, but thought my application rather an astounding one. Miss Nightingale was now however one of the celebrities of the position, and his lordship yielded with a good grace, and not only that, but said the doctor attached to the steamer should accompany her on the voyage, which was a great boon, considering we were so shorthanded. Though her cabin was most luxuriously fitted up with every possible convenience, and the berth was slung by elastic webbing to the roof-floor and sides, and thus every lurch was provided for, she had a dreadful passage, and the doctor had great difficulty in keeping life in her, but, God be thanked, she was spared to do much good work afterwards. How well the following lines apply to her courageous deeds!

> "Oh woman, thou art not the weakly thing some
> Would deem thee, light and wavering,
> Thine is no vulgar strength, thou canst not wield
> The warrior's weapon in the battle-field,
> Thou canst do more than this, it is thine to
> Breathe, without a sense of fear,
> The sick room close and tainted atmosphere."

Though many years have elapsed since that memorable occasion, the warmth of my gratitude has never cooled down when I call to mind the great kindness I received from that inestimable and self-sacrificing lady, when I in my turn was laid low with Asiatic cholera in the Crimea. She supplied me with a continuous relay of experienced nurses, who gave me their invaluable services both night and day, and carried me safely through one of the most fatal of scourges, in which ordinary remedies are of no avail, but close attention to minutiæ is of the utmost importance.

In January, February, and March, 1855, the physical strain on our troops began to show itself in a very marked manner; what with twenty-four hours at a stretch in the cold damp trenches without a wink of sleep, stagnating in the snow and sludge with holes in their boots and similar ventilation in their trousers, with food consisting of too much salt junk and pork, biscuits rather mildewy, with green coffee which few could roast before it burnt a hole in their tins, which rendered them useless for drinking, and though last not least of the evils, too much rum taken on the empty stomach and excited brains. It is no wonder they succumbed to rheumatism, diarrhœa, and dysentery, which filled the hospital marquees in front, from whence they were sent down in batches in snow or sunshine to board ship, for anything was better than keeping them in the atmosphere of these canvas charnel lodgings, the air of which was simply abominable and death-giving. The men thus sent away in the four winter months *hors de combat* were ten thousand in number, the cream of our small army, and the place of these old-seasoned soldiers was taken by raw young recruits from home. It was not till February that tinned milk and arrowroot, and such-like medical necessaries, came out in sufficient quantity to treat these cases properly, for medicines were of no use whatever since the patients were simply dying of starvation. Scurvy was rife from the excess of salt food, and it was impossible to get vegetables at any price. I remember paying myself £2 for a small sack of potatoes given to me as a favour by the captain of a ship I knew, but before I could get them hidden away in my diggings, an army chaplain met me and implored, as I valued his life, that I would allow him to have half, and being an Irishman, his eloquence prevailed, and with many blessings on my head, walked off with many meals of my murphies!

At this time such were the difficulties of keeping body and soul together, and preventing the encroachments of disease among officers and men alike, that to constant inquiries as to what they could do for the best, my reply became a stereotyped one, namely, "Avoid the tendency to death," and this saying became a camp expression among the troops. Such is the hardening influence of the horrors of active warfare on man's heart, that the selfish remark often heard at home, "Every one for himself, and God for us all," would not be inappropriate under such dire circumstances in which heavenly aspirations seem out of place, because man's nature is so thoroughly out of joint! To give an instance of the heartlessness and want of feeling of even the men towards their officers I may mention, that a man who had been shot through the chest had, wonderfully to say, recovered, and I gave him light work to do by making him an orderly nurse at the hospital. A very distinguished Italian general was at that time under my care, and I was very anxious to save him if possible; and one night I could not sleep thinking of him, so I got up at 2 a.m. to see how he was progressing, when to my horror and disgust I found the poor fellow stretched dead on the floor, and the orderly in the bed with his clothes and boots on, drunk with the port wine which he ought to have given to his patient. With this harrowing incident I shall pass on to another chapter.

CHAPTER IX.

Our troops were employed in January, February, and March, in hauling up to the batteries in the front, a distance of six miles, shot and shell, preparatory to another, the second great bombardment. This six miles had no regular road, but a beaten track of loose stones and deep ruts, filled with a sticky sort of compound resembling a mixture of clay and glue which sucked off the horses' shoes with a thud, and had no mercy on the soles and heels of the ill-fitting boots of the men, which were a mile too large, so that it was not an unusual thing to meet a fellow with his soles facing inwards. The drudgery and discomfort, and the wear and tear both for man and beast in the slow process of getting up this ammunition to the front was inconceivably painful to witness day by day. Picture to yourself, fair reader, if you can, a long file of dirty-faced beings with unkempt hair, wearing a close-fitting cap with flaps over the ears to keep out the intense cold, wearing a cat's-skin mufti coat of faded material, and showing no uniform except a pair of patched trousers with the red stripe hardly visible, and walking in a slouching manner like a country bumpkin at home; and you have then the appearance of those engaged in this miserable sickening occupation: What a transformation from the smart and trim aspect of the soldier on parade in Hyde Park. The servant girls in Belgravia would turn up there noses at such unlovable and wretched-looking creatures. Just stop these gallant fighters and ask them what they now think of the pomp and glory and circumstance of war, such as the recruiting sergeant dinned into their ears when enlisting; methinks they would have scorned the proffered shilling with a sneer. If simple Tommy Atkins had been taught Latin, he would have said, " No, no: *Experientia docet.*"

The time at last arrived when it was considered that sufficient ammunition of shot and shell had been stowed away in the magazines to serve the three hundred cannon which were to deal destruction to the devoted town. On the 9th of April, 1855, therefore, Lord Raglan gave orders to open fire. The morning opened with a grey mist, and with a wretched outlook, and one could not see fifty yards in front. Notwithstanding this unsuitable weather, the mandate had gone forth the night before, and the bombardment commenced with a roar of noise never to be forgotten, and the shots were sent haphazard and without aim into empty space, and the ammunition expended recklessly, regardless of the immense labour it took to haul it up. This useless firing went on for two or three hours, till the order to " cease firing " was sent from headquarters. And when the atmosphere cleared up we could not see that we had done much damage. I had obtained a pass to the front from our Quartermaster-General, expecting that there would be a great carnage, and many wounded to attend to, and few to do it; but when I got to the trenches I found that the wiser Russians had reserved their fire, and had not replied to our early morning salute till the atmosphere had cleared and they could see their enemy and his batteries; hence there were no more than the usual amount of casualties. But I was rather horrified at seeing the headless body of an officer carried by me on a stretcher, whom I had previously known as a splendid athlete, upwards of six feet high. This is the way he was killed: he and two other shorter comrades were standing up, chatting away and lighting each other's cigars, when a round shot came over the parapet and took my friend's head clear off, being the taller one. Now had he taken the precaution of sitting down in the trench, this sad accident would not have happened. Many a fine fellow lost his life by thus incautiously exposing himself. In the following month of May took place a most desperate series of sorties on the French left— the scene of these bloody combats being in front of the central bastion, a space of about six square acres, inclosing a cemetery with a church in it, and surrounded by a wall which was loopholed for musketry. These sorties were obstinately persisted in for three nights, and may well be regarded as regular battles, for there were thousands of Russians and French engaged on each side. The onslaught began by several battalions of the enemy taking the French by surprise, by a vigorous rush into the two front parallels, which they actually succeeded in getting into, when a most murderous hand-to-hand encounter occurred for the mastery, and these two trenches became piled up with the dead and the dying. A report soon reached the French reserve forces, distanced about a mile off, ten thousand of whom came up at the double to succour their overpowered comrades, with the result that these sprightly fellows, with their usual dash, soon turned out the Russians, and not only out of the approaches, but pluckily followed them over the parapet into the open ground, honeycombed with rifle-pits, surrounding the cemetery, where, "war to the knife," the most bloody scenes took place, neither party budging a yard. On this small area and in the cemetery itself, "no longer God's acre," now the devil's, a regular series of hard battles were fought between these two sturdy combatants, with their small arms only.

Hearing that the carnage on both sides was something awful, and exceeding that which had as yet occurred during the war, I and a friend obtained a pass from the French commandant, and one of his sergeants as our guide, in order to get safely to the seat of the struggle and to be present at the burying party. When we ascended the front breastwork and looked down upon this field in such a circumscribed space, the sight that met our eyes was something ghastly in the extreme. The heaps of the dead lay thick and high, not only on the open grass sward but between the stone crosses in the peaceful-looking cemetery. Even to me, now an old hand, this small plateau, as an evidence of the fierce and sanguinary contest between two brave peoples, was blood-curdling. To look down placidly on human forms divine, without heads, legs and arms torn asunder; bowels protruding; brains oozing through skulls shattered by musket shots; faces blackened by powder and besmeared by blood issuing from mouth, nose, and ears; human heads mixed up indiscriminately with cannon balls; arms in one place, legs in another—and grim death everywhere! These commingling with broken swords and rifles, and remnants of tattered uniforms, presented a spectacle which some would deem unfit for publication, but which is here given, though as a shadow of the reality, as a warning to those in authority, sitting at their ease at home, not to make war till every other possible means has been exhausted to arbitrate for peace! In contrast to this painful outlook, was such as one would expect to see among a lot of clubmen in Rotten Row. The French and Russian officers met in the most friendly and nonchalant manner, as if a burying party of thousands was a thing of every-day occurrence. They smilingly exchanged cigars and drank each other's health out of their spirit flasks, making witty remarks on the funny aspect of the mangled dead! Such is the hardening effect of actual warfare in deadening the conscience of man, and brutalising his better nature. To mix with this crowd of well-educated, and at other times refined men, one might have exclaimed, "How these Christians love one another!" but such an impression soon vanishes when the bugle recalled the several parties behind their breastworks and the firing commenced as fiercely as ever, and I and my friend were glad to get away in safety; but in turning the angle of the first approach, which was in the line of the fire, we drew back hesitatingly, when the sergeant, seeing us linger, said, "Come along, there is no danger;" and the words were hardly out of his mouth when three balls struck the bank with an ominous thud, which would have taken us in the shoulder if we had unthinkingly followed the advice of our impulsive guide. Thank God, we escaped a wounding which might, or might not, have been fatal. Our past experience was of some avail to us on this occasion.

About this time a little incident occurred. A small streak of silver edging to the dark cloud of horrors which had overshadowed us so long, but brought to the fore the kindly benevolent character of the commander-in-chief of the English army. In describing this circumstance to various groups of ladies in my travels round the world, I have styled it as "the Baby Incident." It came to pass in this way: A mandate went forth to the effect that a certain suburb of Sebastopol was to have a raid made upon it by a select body of our men; the attack to take place at midday, when the enemy were at dinner. The surprise was so complete, and the rush so sudden, that the venture turned out a perfect success. On entering the cottages they found that the occupants had skedaddled, leaving their dinners untouched on the tables, the canaries in their cages, and various articles of domestic use littered about, but in one cottage was left behind, in the heedless flight, a child about six months old, clothed, and asleep in its cradle, wrapped in innocent and blissful ignorance of its future. An officer took up the little one in his arms and carried her out as a prisoner of war. On reporting the success of the raid to headquarters and the capture of the little mite, the question was very naturally asked what was to be done with this helpless prisoner? The reply came back from Lord Raglan ordering a flag of truce to be sent out the next morning, which was responded to, and when the staff-officers met on the neutral ground to have a parley, they were moved to laughter at the novel procedure over so trifling a matter as that of the well-being of a little child, but they politely consented to the demands of our chief, namely, that the mother of the child should be sought for. Hence a careful search was made for the woman, but in vain; no mother was forthcoming to acknowledge her lost babe. Such is war. On the aides-de-camp bringing this fact to the knowledge of his lordship, the next question was what in the world could be done with this little mite of humanity? And here cropped up the benevolent thoughtfulness of good Lord Raglan. "Go," said he, "and make inquiries among the women in the camp, and find out if there be any nursing mothers who would be willing to take charge of an enemy's child." The messenger returned and stated that he had fortunately discovered that the wife of one of the men of the rifle brigade had a baby a few weeks old, and was willing to undertake double duty—and thus relieved us from a perplexing dilemma.

After three weeks had elapsed, the staff at headquarters were startled one morning by Lord Raglan asking them if they had heard anything lately of this now remarkable child, but the incident had vanished clean from their memories, not so with Raglan the Good. "I wish," said he, "one of you would go down and see how the mother and her twins are getting on." The reply received was to the effect that the two children were thriving admirably well, but that the poor woman herself looked weak and thoroughly washed out. "Oh, indeed," said his lordship; then inquired how many cows there were, and on being told that they were all dry except one, "Then," continued our self-denying chief, "send down a bottle of milk to that woman every morning," a requisition which struck them with dismay, as they would have in that case but a scanty supply for their teas. I need hardly say that after this notice the *protégé* of his lordship became quite popular, and might have been styled, not a *fille du regiment* merely, but a *fille de l'armie*, for every fellow in the vicinity of the woman's tent took to nursing with singular delight, in fact, there was quite a *furor* as to who should have the honour of caressing the little enemy. Then an army chaplain took her in hand and christened her Alma, and so renowned had she become at the end of the war that the Queen adopted her and gave her a liberal education, suitable for the position of a governess, which post she took up in a family going out to the Cape, where she in time was married very well to a German, who had been one of our mercenary legion, and had, among others, an allotment of land given to him instead of money, and I believe this German colony did prosper well eventually. And here we will take leave of our dear little Alma.

I may here relate another anecdote in connection with our worthy chief, who was one of the coolest men under fire that ever wore the Queen's uniform. His figure on horseback was well known throughout the camp. Dressed in a plain frock coat, with one sleeveless arm, and wearing a forage cap, he was riding down to see how the batteries were progressing, especially the one on Inkerman ridge, which was such a fearfully contested point at the celebrated battle bearing that name.

One morning, as he was going down as usual, he met an artillery sergeant on his way to the rear, after a night's watch. Just as the man was about to salute his commander, a round shot came over and knocked the busby off his head, and passed over the stern of his lordship's horse, but the sergeant, unmoved, coolly completed his salute, as if his life had been in no danger whatever. Lord Raglan was so struck with the man's wonderful presence of mind under such trying circumstances, exclaimed, "Well, my man, that was indeed a narrow miss;" and the sergeant, with lively promptitude, replied, "Yes, my lord, it was; but a miss is as good as a mile." And so they parted, but our chief was not the man to forget such a splendid and valuable gift even in an uncommissioned officer. Hence we were not surprised to hear that the lucky fellow had been promoted to a commission in the service. Speaking of promotions, some very singular ones took place from the ranks after Inkerman. I was acquainted with a Captain B——, a gentlemanly fellow, who was born in his regiment, became first a drummer-boy, then gradually ascended the scale till he rose to be a colour-sergeant, in which position he entered the battle of Inkerman, where every officer in his company was killed, and he brought the remainder of his men out as their senior officer, and was subsequently promoted to be a lieutenant and captain in the same *Gazette* and in his old regiment.

I will now rest on my oars awhile, as my next chapter will be a heavy one, as it reveals my doings with the Italian contingent.

CHAPTER X.

WHEN the Italian contingent joined us in the spring of 1855, it was brought out in English transports under a pecuniary arrangement with our Government, which guaranteed also to provision them for some time after their arrival; but in consequence of our own defective commissariat we could not meet our engagement so to do in anything like a satisfactory manner. What we wanted so badly ourselves we could not give to them, however much we might sympathise with those new-comers. The Italian troops of all arms of the service numbered about 15,000 all told. They first of all encamped themselves in an unhealthy part of Balaclava valley, and what with this mistake and the short commons we could spare to them, Asiatic cholera attacked these splendid picked men, the very cream of the Italian army, a body of magnificent athletes, but grand physical development was no barrier to the insidious inroads of this black plague—the very scourge of scourges, the effects of which drew tears of agony from their brave and sorrowing general. In this sad and distressing plight La Marmora appealed to Lord Raglan for some experienced English officers to help him out of his dilemma. Hence it came to pass that I was selected to aid them in their sanitary and medical organisation, and a commissariat officer, of considerable experience and aptitude, was sent to do all he could with the limited means then at his disposal. Notwithstanding the improvement in their position and supplies better regulated, cholera of the worst possible Asiatic type attacked them, and continued to baffle all our efforts to check its ravages. A man, for instance, would be, to all appearance, in perfect health at breakfast time, and afterwards be struck down, and in a few hours of awful agony would be dead by the evening, and buried before the morning dawned in solemn silence and secrecy, in order to prevent the knowledge reaching the ears of his comrades and causing depression of mind, a state of feeling certain to invite an attack. Oh! it was indeed a tearful and heartrending sight to behold a long file of these splendid fellows sown up in their blankets, the soldier's shroud, carried off to an ignominious trench to be buried side by side, packed away like herrings in a barrel, then a few inches of soil thrown over them till the next lot came in unwept over by any bereaved mother or sister, *sic transit gloria mundi*.

Thus were disposed of thirteen ~~thousand~~ [1300] men of all ranks from the general to the private in about six weeks. Among the many brave commanders who were lost to the Italian army at this time, none was more lamented than the intrepid, stern-looking Alessandro della Marmora, whose jaw had been fractured during the war of 1849, and who was brother to Alphonso the chief. Alessandro had organised the rifles (Bersaglieri), renowned for their quickness, precision, and powers of endurance, and these fine military qualities he soon began to put to the test in the Crimea by making a reconnaisance to the north side of Sebastopol in order to ascertain the exact strength of the enemy's forces in that direction. Four days' provisions were dealt out to the men and this trying expedition took place with a satisfactory result. They all returned well and in good spirits considering the hardships they had undergone — except their plucky leader who was attacked with acute dysentery which he treated at first with indifference, insisting on marching on foot with the rest of his men till he fainted away from exhaustion; then they lifted him on to a horse, the only one with them when he swooned again, then they were obliged to resort to a stretcher, on which he was brought back much to his great chagrin, for he had boasted that he could outmarch any man in the army. On arriving at his hut I received a telegram from Sir John Hall ordering my immediate attendance at his side. Though he was kept alive for three days, the case was hopeless from the beginning, and he gradually sank from loss of blood, and died in my arms at two o'clock one night; and when I went up to inform his brother of the death he wept over this favourite leader like a child, and his men mourned for him as a friend as well as a general. He had married an English lady, and the frequent muttering of her christian name in his sleep was rather trying to one's feelings reminding me of home. He had a heavy, twisted, long moustache like his king's, which I had cut off and sent to the widow with his Bible; for, wonderful to relate, a large number of Bibles in the Italian language had been given by one of our colporteurs to the troops, and they used to sit round the camp fires when one would read to others who could not the pathetic tales of mercy, forbearance, and love in the grand old Book. Their Roman Catholic chaplains were furious and ordered the men to deliver them up, but they one and all refused point blank to do anything of the kind, and even their officers' commands fared no better, and in fear of a mutiny the subject was allowed to drop and each knapsack contained the precious jewel to the end of the campaign, and how far this wonderful influence had to do with furthering the completion of Italian unity subsequently it is not for me to say, at any rate *their* first battle for *religious* liberty commenced in the Crimea.

On leaving poor La Marmora late one dark night I met a couple of French Zouaves with two horses in tow. I could just see clearly enough to be satisfied that all was not right, for I had heard of their tricks of stealing stray horses, killing them and then cutting steaks out of their loins; so I challenged them, and they pretended not to understand French, mumbling some gibberish between themselves, but when I threatened to summon the Provost-Marshal, they quietly yielded up the animals with a grumble. When I took them to La Marmora's where I got a light I then found one of the horses belonged to an English battery, and so I took him at once within its proper boundary much to the relief of the sentinel on duty, who said he had broken his tether and jumped over the breastwork. The other was a fine racer-looking fellow, a bright chestnut with white stockings, having a smart head collar on, not English or French I knew, so I took him home to my stable, and advertised him in the *Hue and Cry* at headquarters, but only one subaltern came to inquire, saying he had lost a fine brown charger with black points; hearing this my groom allowed him to see the horse, which did not tally with his description in the least. He turned out a most useful companion till the end of the campaign when I sold him for £3, the Government allowing us £40 for each charger not taken to England, so I made a good thing of my friend the chestnut.

The strain upon my mental and physical powers was now very great indeed, inasmuch as all this worry with Italians was additional to my other ordinary duties at the Balaclava hospital where I had a lot of Italian officers under my care, and we were still deplorably deficient in medical aid of the right standard, hence just as the horrid plague was on the wane, having exhausted itself as it were, I fell ill myself with cholera, and placed on board ship in the harbour where I received close and unremitting attention from a regular relay of Miss Nightingale's nurses, and with them and the kindness of my male friends of every class I was in danger of becoming quite a pet patient, and I fear a subject of no little envy to other sick officers on board, for I could boast of a whole cabin to myself with the exception of some huge rats which paid me a visit every night to quench their thirst in my water jug; but I was too languid to heed such trifles, indeed I was so paralysed with pain and weakness that I felt perfectly indifferent whether I lived or died. I had sense enough left, however, to remember how fatal this disease was to all those patients who had drunk regularly their ration of spirit, and more if they could get it, that I begged of my attendants none should be given to me; so I had my way, contrary as it was to the prejudices in its favour in those ignorant times. So I was nursed instead of physicked through the fiery ordeal, and I was one of the very few who ever recovered. God, indeed, was gracious and merciful, and permitted the tree to remain for several years longer to bear its humble fruit. When convalescing I was much cheered and benefited by that good religious officer, Colonel L——, who was on sick leave on the same vessel. On meeting some of the working staff after my recovery, they were rather surprised to see me on my legs again; exclaiming: " Well, old fellow, we prophesied that you would kill yourself sooner or later, the pace was too fast to last you know. For the future you had better be guided by our wise motto." " And pray what may that be?" " Simply this: *Moderate your zeal and draw your pay!* " " But how about your consciences!" I asked. "Oh, our consciences indeed, how can you expect us to have any when the authorities at home show so little?" The reply was not amiss when one recollects how the hearts of many men were then boiling over with indignation at the cruel apathy and neglect with which the troops were treated by the English Government. Such is the low standard of religious aspirations in times of actual warfare!

We have now arrived at the day in which the grand

assault was to be made on the Redan, the 18th of June, 1855. Not that we had the faintest hope of holding it, supposing it could be captured. No, the sacrifice of life was to be made for the purpose of diverting the attention of the enemy. The French were to attack the Malakoff the same day, and we, on our side, were to make the most hopeless of assaults, as our allies had not the remotest chance of succeeding, but were beaten back with the most awful slaughter, while our loss was proportionately great. The strength of the Redan was something prodigious. When I examined it after it was relinquished by the Russians, I found it to be a singular construction. Running the whole length of its earthworks was a subterranean gallery supplied with a plank platform for the soldiers to sleep upon, and in the floor were sunken ships' tanks to hold water, which were replenished every night by women; thus the enemy were in comparative comfort and safety too, while we were exposed in open trenches. We had the same kind of loose chalky ground to work in, and there was no reason why our engineers should not have constructed such underground shelters, but then we were not blessed with having such a skilled scientist as Todleben on our side! After peace was proclaimed General Luders and I became very friendly, and he told me, that when we were hammering away at their batteries and flattered ourselves that we had silenced them because they did not reply, the artillerymen retired for the time into these underground barracks till the firing ceased or we had exhausted our ammunition; and this was the case at the Malakoff as well as the Redan, thus very many lives were saved from the bursting of shells. After the bombardment of the 18th of June, I was very much struck with the unusual number of wounds below the knee, and Luders told me his men were ordered to fire low in order to secure as many as possible of our fellows being put *hors de combat*—not to kill outright, as these wounded would be of no further use in that war, and yet would be an enormous expense and worry to us by crowding our hospitals and transports, thus acting, as our enemy knew only too well, as a most obstructionable impedimenta on the field of battle.

In our hurry to reach the wounded three of us thought we might venture to cross the open between two of the approaches, but we had reckoned without our host the lynx-eyed enemy ever on the alert, a 13-inch shell was sent at us, which came with its usual whistling noise, describing an arc in the sky as visible as a cricket ball. We fell immediately on our faces, the safest position to take, and watched its course. When it sank into the earth and burst up with a tremendous noise, throwing its fragments with stones and soil 200 feet into the air, it was a grand sight, and we were not struck by the descending pieces, wherein lies the great danger at such times; but one portion of the shell did come so near that I brought it home to remind me of another narrow escape from death, and to convince me that a merciful Providence was still guarding me.

Nothing during the summer months particularly occurred except Lord Raglan's death, and, as far as I was concerned, the despatching of the wounded down to Scutari as soon as they were able to bear the voyage, but the whole of the army were secretly sapping up nearer and nearer to the Malakoff and the Redan, especially the former which was now 400 yards in length and seemed impregnable. So that when the 5th of September arrived the French sappers could almost touch the base of abattis of this most formidable earthwork bristling with cannon. When the assault was made they had not far to run. All was kept a profound secret till the morning of the 5th when a fierce cannonade from many hundreds of guns was made upon the Malakoff, which ceased at the dinner hour when the sprightly French took it by surprise and a rush; and a hand-to-hand fight with any weapon went on for some time each side bringing up their reserves till regular battles were fought for this most important commanding point, which had at its mercy the shipping, the forts, the Redan, and the south side of Sebastopol with its churches and mansions. The tricolour flag floating on the Malakoff was to be the sign that the English were to assault the Redan, which they proceeded to do, and failed as before to hold it because our reserves did not back up the assaulting column as they ought to have done. It was the same mistake as was made on the 18th of June. When the French secured a footing in the Malakoff they filled up the trenches and turned the works towards the enemy, but for three days the Russians were employed in vacating the south side and going over the harbour on a poontoon bridge to the north side, blowing up their ships and forts and magazines, making an infernal noise. They left their large hospital with a thousand dead among the wounded for us to take care of. By the ninth they had all gone clean away to the north side. And thus ended this portion of the siege after a most eventful year to ourselves and our allies who had most laboriously excavated 70 miles of trenches, made 60 thousand fascines and gabions, and fired away 1,500,000 shot and shell. We will now rest awhile and then begin our second year with a fresh chapter.

CHAPTER XI.

At the commencement of the second winter's campaign there was a wonderful transformation from the wretched aspect of affairs which prevailed during our first winter. Some remarkable specimens of civil engineering works were brought to our aid. A railroad was made to the army divisions on the front from Balaclava, and the old roadway by its side was properly macadamized, so that the building of wooden huts and the transport of supplies went on merrily. During these operations the English navvies showed the lethargic Turks the right way to use the pick and the spade, and to trundle a wheelbarrow along a plank. Some very amusing scenes occurred at the expense of the sleepy Osmanli. But let us proceed. No one doubted but that we should have to pass another winter on the plateau before Sebastopol. The Russians after the fall of the south side had fortified themselves strongly on the north, erecting huge earthworks and batteries along the Mackenzie heights bristling with hundreds of cannon, which frowned down on the Tchernaya valley and its river, the dividing line between the two opposing armies, which stared at one another, showing their teeth like a couple of bull dogs but never firing a shot.

There was no doubt, at this particular time, that the Russians were in an awful predicament and yearning for the bare necessities of life. They had at least 200,000 to feed, and the provisioning of such a mass of mouths must have been difficult indeed and costly beyond calculation, inasmuch as the country in the war had become denuded of every blade of corn and all the draught animals had been sacrificed months ago by bringing down food and ammunition from the mainland of Russia; while we were receiving supplies comfortably by sea though at exorbitant prices. It is no wonder, then, that the Emperor of Russia when he paid his visit of encouragement to his troops in the Crimea, and saw for himself some of the horrors of war in the overpacked hospitals at Backsheserai, in October, 1855, became convinced that the best thing he could do was to sign a treaty of peace as soon as he could do it without humiliation. He could see that it was impossible his army could carry on the struggle much longer, without succumbing from sheer exhaustion. Soldiers like other men cannot fight without food in their stomachs, and how was this to be conveyed to them if they continued the suicidal process of killing for meat the draught bullocks as they came into camp, and then burnt the arabas for firewood, instead of sending them back for further supplies! The commissariat had requisitioned the farmers for miles and miles up the country till there were no more animals or arabas left to cultivate the soil. It was a crying shame, and men, women, and children must have died from famine if this cruel war had not been brought rapidly to a close in the spring of 1856. The Emperor, too, a man of peace, so different to his father, must have seen on his way down the barrenness of the land—its desolation, its misery, the half-starved looks of the peasantry, and the dead animals lying thick on the roadside, and other signs, enough to bring the tears to the eyes of many a more hard-hearted man than Alexander was. In contrast to all this deplorable picture we, on our side, were basking in the sun of reaction, and revelling in all sorts of luxury supplied by the patriotic and other funds, the generous gift of a loving country which had at last awakened from its slumbering indifference.

At the beginning of the winter 1855 I was transferred from my position at Balaclava, to take charge of the Monastery of St. George, where about a dozen of the old monks' rooms were furnished with single beds, constituting a little hospital for the reception of those home-sick gentlemen, who were pleading all sorts of illnesses with a view of getting back to England on the ground of *urgent private affairs*, an indulgence which was becoming scandalously abused. Hence a mandate had been issued from headquarters that a check should be put to this bit of weakness on the part of some of the officers, who were well known not to relish trench duties, and who were yearning for the flesh pots of Egypt in their own luxurious homes. When, therefore, an officer pleaded some physical infirmity as an excuse for decamping, he was first sent off to the monastery and placed under my care in one of the little wards, in order to test his incapacity for further active duty in the trenches or elsewhere. Various were the dodges practised upon me to get a medical certificate of permanent invalidism which would justify a departure for Scutari or England. The eyes were the favourite organs of complaint, these appearing unaccountably red, and even continuing so, notwithstanding the remedies employed. No amendment taking place in a few days I would put on a savage look and threaten them with all sorts of pains and penalties. An interview would take place somewhat after the following manner: "Now, old fellow, if you cannot keep your fingers from your eyes I shall be under the painful necessity of blindfolding you, and placing an orderly in your room at night to keep watch over you, and to certify to me that justice is done to my remedies." This would stop any further tampering and malingering, and after trying every possible device to get over me would throw up the sponge, and quietly go back to their duties again. It was a very unwelcome and disagreeable position of trust to be placed in, but I was not going to commit a breach of that confidence reposed in me by the commander-in-chief to please any one be he nobleman or commoner.

It must not be supposed that the monastery occupied all my attention at this time. About a quarter of a mile away, a large corrugated-iron building had been erected for stores. It did not long continue occupied with such. A body of troops had been sent off to attack and occupy the Kinburn Fortress, situated on a sandy plain. What with the glare of the sun and the clouds of fine sand which blew over the fort, the garrison became attacked with Egyptian ophthalmia, a most contagious and destructive disease of the eye. Those afflicted were sent back to the Crimea, where it began to spread immediately. I was at once sent for by Sir John Hall our chief, who was in an awful fix. A few were already blind with the complaint and the hospitals were full. I suggested that all the cases should be collected and isolated without an hour's delay. "Just so," said Sir John, "but where can we place them?" I then brought to his notice the store building and recommended that it should be emptied of its contents and beds placed in it. "Go back," said he, with evident relief, "and do what you think is necessary; this is not the first time I have given you a *carte blanche*." Seeing there was a foot of snow on the ground and that it was falling fast he continued, "How can you get them together such severe weather as this?" I replied, "that I should carry them on stretchers covered over face and all, with a couple of blankets. The position was a desperate one, and isolation imperative. The removal or otherwise was a question of sight or total blindness!" We parted, and on my road back in a blinding snowstorm I should have gone over the cliffs into the sea but for the sagacity of my old chestnut, who saw the danger, which I did not, and he would not be urged a step further. The track being obscured by the snow, I retraced till I got to some huts when I found I was a good mile out of my bearings. My compass now helped me home where

I arrived with feelings of earnest gratitude for another providential intervention. Having the command of plenty of labour I soon got the building into shipshape and the patients settled down in their beds. The cold was so intense that some nights it was below zero and the poor fellows suffered dreadfully. There was one small stove in its centre, a sort of make believe which did not prevent the tea and milk, &c., taken from freezing into lumps when spilt on the beards of the men. My own hair became a mass of ice from my breath congealing when passing to and fro from my quarters. It was a hard life doubtless, but one's health, like that of the army generally, was most excellent. Our mortality during the second winter did not exceed ¾ per man per cent. Thanks to a better commissariat, plenty of warm clothing and an abundance of wholesome good food, and though last not least, no nerve excitement from the constant apprehension of an onslaught from a wide-awake and heroic enemy. What a pleasant change from our first winter's experience! Then, again, what work we had was varied with play. There was a great deal of dining out, and where we dined we slept, for it was not safe to pass the different sentries of our gallant allies at night, because if we did not give the pass word rightly they would as soon just put a bullet into one as not—no parley was their order! My friends in the Black Watch had really the only mess worthy of the name, and it was a fine sight to see old Cameron, like a father, seated at the head of the table, surrounded by his sturdy comrades, intermingling the toasts with humorous remarks on the situation. Kamara was their post, and it was conveniently located for a pleasure trip into the Baida valley, which we undertook one day, and entering a Tartar gentleman's house we were hospitably entertained by his wife who said her husband was in prison on suspicion of having supplied us with provisions. She was a beautiful woman, and gave us some sad stories of how the Cossacks robbed them of food, and even violently assaulted them if they were refused; no position was respected by these soldier robbers. The most diverting amusement was the institution of amateur theatricals got up by the officers, and another of a lower grade by the non-commissioned officers. Both parties succeeding in rousing side-breaking laughter by their serio-comic performances. The get-up of the lady-gentlemen being most creditable considering they had not the advantage of a Bond-street milliner in the Crimea. The following bill, which I have preserved and which was printed at the local press of the *Hue and Cry*, gives the names of the play and the actors:—

Theatre Royal, Fourth Division. This Evening, April 10, 1856. Her Majesty's servants will perform—

LITTLE TODDLEKINS!

Mr. Jones Robinson Brownsmith ...	CAPT. EARLE, 57th Regt.
Mr. Barnaby Babicombe	MAJOR GARNET, 46th Regt.
Captain Littlepop ...	CAPT. NICHOLAS, 46th Regt.
Amanthis ...	MR. CLARKSON, 68th Regt.
Annie Babicombe	MR. SAUNDERSON, 68th Regt.
Susan	MR. V. STUART, 68th Regt.

To conclude with—

GOING TO THE DERBY.

Mr. Jeremiah Twiddle	... CAPT. EARLE.
Mr. John James Chucks	... LIEUT. DE LACY LACY, 63rd Regt.
Captain Nobble	... MAJOR LORD A. G. RUSSELL, R.B.
Sam (waiter of Spread Eagle)	LIEUT. HARRINGTON, R.B.

Mrs. Twiddle, Mrs. Chucks, Mrs. Plummy, and Gipsy Woman, by LIEUTS. SAUNDERSON, CLARKSON, and STUART, of the 68th, and LIEUT. PRIOR, 48th.

Doors open at half-past seven o'clock : Performance at 8.

GOD SAVE THE QUEEN.

The foregoing fun was interlarded with some pony races, of which the following is a copy of the "Card of the Races":—

SEBASTOPOL SPRING MEETING.

MONDAY, MARCH 24, 1856.

Stewards:

Viscount Talon and Marquis de Spinola, Major Astley, Major Dewar, Major Brown, Lieut.-Col. Campbell, Capt. Chapman, Col. Hale, Mr. Wilkin, Capt. Connel, Major Nicholson, Col. Hay, and Capt. Ponsonby.

Honorary Treasurer and Secretary—Major Wombwell, 46th.

The first race was a handicap sweepstakes of £1 each, with £25 added, for ponies of fourteen hands and under. Half a mile on the flat. There were forty entries, which Capt. Cornat's gr. p. "Bignot" won. Then came a steeplechase of two miles for £50. This was won by Viscount Talon's "Paddy Boy," ridden by the owner; followed by three other races, won respectively by Capt. Morant's g. g. "Clinker," Capt. Price's, 11th Hussars, "Lillington," and Capt. Brabason's, R.A., "Chutney."

Again, for the benefit of those of a more literary turn of mind, a series of educational lectures were given in the library and reading-hut of the Third Division. The following programme, which I have kept by me for the last thirty-five years, will convey a good idea of the subjects selected to instruct and amuse :—

The "Pursuit of Knowledge under Difficulties," by Rev. B. Harris, Chaplain.

"Places of Interest in Old Testament," by Rev. H. Wheeler, Chaplain.

"Mohammedism," by Rev. H. W. M. Egan, Principal Chaplain.

"On Temperance," by Sir James Alexander, Col. of 14th Regt.

So much for our minds; now to show that our bodies were well cared for at the same time. I will here insert a copy of an old list I have by me which gives the following quantities—they seem large, but then I had five mouths to feed beside myself :— "Bread, 9 lbs.; meat, 6 lbs.; coffee, 6 ounces; rice, ditto; sugar, 12 ounces; rum, 3 gills; potatoes, 1½ lbs.; onions, ¾ lbs.; pepper ¼ ounce; and 3 ounces of salt."

Now I am on the subject of victualling, it may be mentioned that during the second winter I had got from home a man-cook and a cooking range, with a set of tins as fittings, which enabled me to give my friends quite a *récherché* spread of five or six courses, made more dainty-looking by being laid on a white tablecloth, supplemented by the additional refinement of snow-white napkins. Such a civilised appearance had not been seen by us since our departure from board ship, and it drew tears from some of my guests, because it reminded them so forcibly of the happy and luxurious surroundings of their homes in dear old England, where they would be enhanced, maybe, by the sunny smiles of wife and children, or mother and sisters. I need hardly say the Monastery of St. George became not a little popular, and various were the visitors of both sexes who did me the honour of calling in the afternoons, and patronising the luxuries so hard to collect, I being six miles distant from the suttlers' camp, where those landsharks charged a most exorbitant price for everything. When the migratory birds came flocking over from the north, and settled down exhausted in the snow, there was no difficulty in securing a larder full of wild fowl, especially the golden plover, which were as plump as our partridges, and in such crowds did they come that I killed one day eight of them at one shot. This windfall was a welcome addition to one's ordinary diet. My cook made these birds into delicious pies, larding them with fat pork, and placing them over a basis of fresh beef or mutton. These pies were quite a *pièce de résistance*, and while they lasted became quite the talk of my visiting circle for many a day after. My friends came in the afternoons, not only to taste the luxuries I could place before them, but to admire the beautiful view from the Terrace, and to listen to the chime, rung by old Peter in the Greek church. Peter was quite a character, rather crippled in his limbs, and was the only one left behind by the church community, but too fond of rum, which in his sober moments he called "No bono, Johnny."

CHAPTER XII.

THERE were discussions and disputes as to whether we had shattered Fort Constantine at the north entrance of the harbour when it was bombarded on the 17th of October, 1854, by our ships, especially the three-decker *Albion*, which went so close in, and got herself such a battering. Hence, when peace was concluded, we made up a party and rode round by the Mackenzie heights to see for ourselves. We found the fort was occupied by the Russian commander-in-chief, General Luders, who received us very kindly, and treated us most hospitably. When we told him the purport of our visit, he smiled, and said, " Come and see." He acted as our guide, and took us round the whole of the parapets, explaining every circumstance in connection with the attack, and how they were protected by gabions. On a close examination we could not discover hardly a place where the stonework had been chipped. This review of the outside finished, the general asked us to see the inside. Here we found, in a large casemate, a table laid out with sumptuous refreshments, in fact, six delicious courses were provided, to which we did ample justice, and to two or three different wines, finishing up with a glass of that well-known delicacy, Crimean champagne, in which our host drank our healths at the shrine of Peace. The cannon was in position in this casemate, and such a toast struck us as somewhat ironical and seemingly out of place, but we parted most excellent friends, and he promised to return the visit by coming to see me at the monastery, which he did shortly afterwards, coming in a droski drawn by five splendid ponies. So wonderfully drilled were they, that they would start or stop, deviate right or left, by word of command. The general tried to induce some ladies to take a drive with him, but seeing that we had no regular roads, and that the vehicle bumped about unpleasantly on the uneven plateau, they declined; but such trifles not troubling my mind, I took a seat at his side, and was amazed at the wonderfully skilful way in which he handled his team. The heads of the ponies were decorated with foxes' brushes and a regular chime of little bells, which seem to excite them to gallop at a great speed. The general paid the Greek church a visit, and old Peter honoured him with one of his best peals.

My cook, hearing that so distinguished a guest had paid me a visit, tried to surpass himself by laying out as fine a luncheon as his limited supplies would permit of, and my visitor, being an old campaigner, took in the situation, and determined to enjoy himself accordingly. To give zest to the entertainment there was seated at the table, a very handsome lady, to whom he gave a cross of Siberian gold, which hung from his watch chain. This generous act did not arise from his having imbibed too much Crimean champagne, for I had none to give him ; it must have been due entirely to the lady's fascinating appearance and address.

When the genial general took his leave, he carried away with him all our warm good wishes, leaving behind the golden cross to remind us of one of the pleasantest days we had ever spent in the Crimea. Little did we think a few weeks back that we should be spending so soon such a happy time with the commander of our enemy's forces on the north side of Sebastopol—but *tel est la vie.*

When the treaty of peace was signed we heard that each plenipotentiary was desirous of preserving the pen with which he subscribed the important document, but these great men were obliged to yield to the expressed wishes of the Empress Eugénie, who supplied them with a beautifully jewelled eagle's quill which she desired to retain as a memento of the momentous event. When this treaty reached the Crimea it brought with it to some of the old stagers the realisation of hopes long hoped for, namely, an early opportunity of getting home alive, and to tell in person terrible tales of battles and sieges, the loss of some friends and the making of others, while to many who came out at a later date it was a source of disappointment—subaltern officers, for example, who viewed the army as an instrument towards worldly prosperity, trusted that peace would not supervene till they had an opportunity of distinguishing themselves, and winning a place in the records of glory! Oh, vanity of vanities, they did not take to heart the saying in the good old Book, that "they who live by the sword shall die with the sword." I heard an anxious mother on one occasion exclaim, in simple ignorance of what the horrors of actual warfare were like, "Oh! my poor boy, I am so sorry, he had just got to the head of the lieutenants, and I was in hopes of hearing any day of his becoming a captain, and now the war is over he may have to wait ever so long." She, with a mother's natural instincts, did not stop to reflect that her son's promotion would have been accomplished through the further shedding of much human blood and the cruel display of the worst of passions. How thoroughly selfish we are, even when our precious lives and souls are at stake! Talk of Christianity and its peaceful influences, I should like to know how many men were brought to think of the Saviour while this horrid carnage was going on, when, I take it, half a million of lives were ruthlessly sacrificed on both sides in order to gratify the vain ambition of one man, who prosecuted this prolonged warfare under the cloak of religion. Picture to yourself, dear reader, the following incidents associated with the cessation of hostilities. Though thousands of soldiers in the spring were employed in road-making, building of huts, and in drill, there was nevertheless much spare time, which was spent scandalously in drinking, card-playing, and gambling. The English were better paid than the troops of our allies, and they did not know what to do with their money; hence scenes of drunkenness and debauchery prevailed at Kadikoi, where suttlers' booths were kept by most disorderly traders, who encouraged all sorts of vices, winked at acts of violence, and even murder. Night was made hideous with

their brawls, and it was not safe to go near their
squatting ground if you at all valued your life!
It was a blessed day indeed when the post-office
authorities instituted a mode of sending gold to England
by means of money orders. Many men then
availed themselves of this easy means of forwarding
their spare cash to their wives and families, or to
their aged parents, thus securing themselves against
the indulgence in their besetting sins—drunkenness
and gambling. It may well be said that idleness,
backed by riches, is the mother of many miseries.
The time had now arrived when we were to bid farewell
to the Crimea, and the recollection, if that were
possible, of all its horrors, its dangers and worries,
only too thankful that we had escaped with our lives.
The beautiful month of June, 1856, found us on board
a steam transport bound for Constantinople, where I
landed, and went off to pay my respects to my old
patient, Miss Nightingale. I found that noble creature
looking very pale and slender, and delicate in
appearance, with her beautiful black hair cut short,
but still retaining her wonted stock of fiery courage
and activity. She was simply worshipped by the sick
and wounded, who romantically kissed her very
shadow as she noiselessly glided along the corridors,
lamp in hand, when all was silent and quiet at night,
to satisfy herself that all was going on well among
her eyeless, armless, footless, shot, sabred, and
bayoneted devotees. There, within those dismal
walls, was to be seen this refined, highly cultured
lady, going the rounds of her wards two and a half
miles in extent, among thousands of uneducated men,

rough, rugged, bloody, dirty, wounded, sick, hungry, and miserable, undertaking painful and arduous duties with every possible deficiency in the necessary supplies, for she had to deal with men wrapped up in departmental formalism called " red-tapeism," whereby living wounded sick soldiers, the defenders of their country's honour, were treated as so many bales of goods, to be packed aside in heaps and then forgotten. To correct such crying and shameful misdoings was Miss Nightingale's heavy task, almost singlehanded. She might indeed be well defined without any exaggeration a " ministering angel " in these hospitals.

Calling to mind the real luxury of a Turkish bath, I could not leave Stamboul without resorting to that bodily refreshment. The building is like a huge church, with a dome in the centre, in which 150 people can walk about comfortably, and enjoy the delicious balmy heat, and get a good rub down by a small boy, who after lathering you all over, will grinningly show you what an incredible quantity of black scurf he has managed to scrape off your apparently white skin, but there it is on his hands, and you have to believe him. This desquamation will account, perhaps, for the inexpressibly soothing sensations one feels afterwards in the cooling room, where a feeling of heavenly peace and rest takes possession of one. Such a physical and mental paradise you will not find in the puny baths which have been set up in England, and which are a mere sham in comparison with those in Constantinople.

In taking leave of Scutari and its hospitals, I may just mention an incident which presents to us a very forcible picture how warfare with its horrid sequences and debasing surroundings deadens man's heart to all those refined susceptibilities of a moral and religious nature, and suppresses that sympathetic kindliness of feeling which dominates and exercises our minds when we behold our friends and companions ruthlessly snatched suddenly from us in times of peace. Read, and believe if you can, gentle reader, sitting at your ease in these "piping times of peace," the following plain and unvarnished truth. When the sick and the wounded had collected in their thousands at the Scutari hospitals, and even in the cavalry stables near thereto, they began to die off in scores daily, not so much from actual wounds as from dysentery and fever occurring in broken-down, starved constitutions — hopeless cases. An insupportable gloom overspread the place like a black pall, which affected the spirits and courage of the noble nurses terribly, but their heroism was something wonderful to witness. The cemetery, therefore, at such a time, became the centre of melancholy interest. The private soldiers were buried *en masse* as I have already described they were in the Crimea, simply stitched up in their blankets, and laid side by side in a large grave, while the officers were interred in a small cemetery overlooking the sea, each with a wooden tablet at the head of the spot. In this resting-place are lying eight doctors, the victims of hard work and disease! The bodies of the dead were collected together in heaps in an empty ward, then a string of invalid orderlies would form a procession and carry the bodies on stretchers through a long corridor filled with patients who had become so accustomed to this melancholy looking train, that they would go on chatting, reading, or being read to, or any other amusement going on, without their attention being diverted in the slightest degree by this touching spectacle of their dead comrades going to their last home!

Oh! war, war, with all thy pomp, glitter, and glory! How dost thou in thy very bitterness of trial curse our race, sowing penalties and pains broadcast over us, heaping up poverty on the very poor, recklessly deriding the widow in her bereavement, making her husbandless, making her childless; thou begettest orphans; in the very wantonness of thy cruelty dost thou seek victims from every grade; reckless of all social distinctions, bringing down to one dead level the heartbroken and the desolate! Shortsighted, ignorant, and vain men crown thy triumphs with laurel; but the cypress of the cemetery and the yew of the village churchyard would be more fitting emblems of thy accursed work! I will now draw down a veil over this harrowing picture. May the time be not far distant in this era of the world in which the saying in the Book of books shall be verified, namely, "They shall beat their swords into ploughshares and their spears into pruning-hooks. Nation shall not lift up sword against nation, neither shall they learn war any more"!

I now proceeded on my journey homewards, which I hoped to accomplish so as to spend my thirty-sixth birthday in my own country. On board I found an officer whom I had met formerly at Malta on his way up to the Crimea. He, like many others on furlough from India, had diverged and gone to the fighting field to volunteer his services in order to see what war was really like; he never having seen a shot fired in anger while in India. He appeared then very impatient to have a go at the Russians, and was vainly boasting of what he would and could do when he had a chance, flourishing in the air his six-shooter. I had now an opportunity of asking him how he had succeeded, and whether he had left his mark behind him. As soon as I mentioned the subject, his countenance fell and he looked rather gloomy. When I reminded him of his remarks about potting the enemy with his revolver, "Well," he said, "I had my chance, it was at Inkerman, and I will tell you all about it. I got entangled in a *melée* as the duke did, and it was during a hand-to-hand fight when a fellow was about to cut me down, I fired my revolver at and missed him, and then I lost my nerve and self-possession so far as not to let go the trigger for the next shot, and thus was in imminent danger of being killed had not a private soldier come to the rescue and parried the cut with his bayonet. I need hardly tell you that such a narrow escape will never be forgotten, and that it took all the bounce out of me for the future."

> "Man, proud man!
> Dressed in a little brief authority, ...
> Plays such fantastic tricks before high heaven,
> As make the angels weep!"

Nothing of any great moment occurred before we reached Malta, where we landed and were made much of. One officer struggling along on two crutches came in for quite an ovation; he had been shot in the stomach and the bullet had made its exit at the side of the spine, and yet, wonderful to relate, he had survived and was doing well. Another poor fellow, walking on one crutch, was shot in the heel; the bone had become a mere shell, the interior having crumbled away. He was suffering a good deal, and the leg would be eventually shorter than the other. Both these officers would be compelled to give up the service, much against their will, and become pensioners for the rest of their lives upon the nation's bounty. The latter case is still alive but lame, and has been well cared for by a grateful country, and in his old age comfortably berthed by the Queen at Windsor. Our reception at Gibraltar was equally pleasant and agreeable. One vied with another, ladies and all, in showering kindnesses upon us, and introducing for our comfort all sorts of delicacies to make our voyage more congenial and health-giving. I myself, besides suffering from the effects of cholera, had had three scurvy ulcers on the leg, which had exceedingly reduced me, and so shattered my general health, that I should have to look out for a sanitorium on arriving in England where I should have to remain two or three years to re-establish my constitution. As to further service in the army that was quite out of the question. Arriving at Portsmouth, my luggage, which was something considerable, was allowed to pass the custom house without examination and my store of Turkish tobacco was admitted duty free. From Portsmouth I made my way to Brighton, which I had selected as my future headquarters. And here I will stay my hand for the present.

CHAPTER XIII.

EXCEPT to those who have experienced the fiery ordeal of having passed through an active campaign of two years' duration in such a war as that of the years 1854-5-6, none can realise in the faintest degree the blessed calm and blissful peace in which the soul reposes when once more one is safe at home again in the midst of every luxury and refinement, and rejoicing in the congratulations of relations and friends at the many narrow escapes to life; cheered also at being honoured with the country's approval and recognition of one's services under fire. In due course the King Victor Emmanuel forwarded to me through the Foreign Office the Cross of a Knight of the Royal Order of St. Maurice and St. Lazarus, "for distinguished services before the enemy," which I received accompanied with a royal warrant to accept and wear the same, signed by Her Majesty herself. This Order with the English and Turkish war medals enabled me to appear at Court with three decorations on my breast. Such an occasion was glorious enough to elicit a sense of pride and vanity in most men's hearts, but to me all such feelings were swallowed up in the one grand predominating reflection that I had escaped with my life, which idea, at all times, brought to the fore such a deep sense of gratitude to the Giver of all mercies that all the other superficial and mundane thoughts were totally eclipsed. Though many years have elapsed, this condition of mind still exists, and when a gallant volunteer for instance, in the full pride of his new uniform, exclaims, " Oh how I should like to appear at a *levée* with such decorations," I would reply, " My dear fellow, you little know at what a risk to life and health they were obtained, or you would not think so much of them ! "

The first regiment which arrived at Brighton after I took up my residence was the 4th Dragoon Guards which had distinguished itself in the Crimea, hence we soon cottoned together. I became officially attached to the *depôt* there, and thus kept in touch with some of my old campaigning friends. Consequently joined in the festivities which the good town's people were not slow to indulge both to officers and men. The first fancy-dress ball ever held in the picturesque old Pavilion was a grand success, there being upwards of eleven hundred present. Nearly all Shakespeare's characters were represented. It was a part of the programme that all the party should be presented to and passed by the Doge of Venice, who was seated on a throne in the long corridor. This was a very dazzling sight, the glittering uniforms and quaint old dresses were superb. A Queen's Drawing-room reception could not have come up to it. A friend of mine went in as Falstaff, and his broad front was bejewelled to the tune of £2,000, and he was obliged to pay two guineas each for two of Nathan's

men in plain evening dress to safeguard them and
him from loss or robbery. There were three or four
dressed as Shakespeare in silk velvet with point
lace collar and cuffs. Two pretty sisters, beautifully
figured in pink tights and tulle skirts with wings
on the shoulders representing angels, were much
admired. Everything was conducted with the utmost
decorum, and the committee strictly forbad any
objectionable get-up. The return ball by the 4th
Dragoons to their friends was brilliant in the extreme,
and the Pavilion suite of rooms was decorated with
great taste and lavish expense. Dancing was just
possible in the crowded rooms, and when the supper-
room was thrown open at midnight it was quite
impossible to get near the tables sitting or standing,
groaning as they were with every luxury in season
and out of season.

After remaining a few years at Brighton, and my
health having, thanks to its fine bracing air, become
thoroughly established, I came to the wise conclusion
that that pleasure resort was very well for amusement and to spend money in, but that it was not the
place to get into a lucrative practice unless one
obtained a *locus standi* in partnership with some old
practitioner, resident in the town for years. Hence
my ambition was to fix myself in London as soon as
I could afford to settle in some fashionable street in
its West End, for there is no city in the world where
a professional man can get on so well as in London
if he can patiently abide his time, undisturbed by a
sense of fear or favour.

But before this move took place, I had an oppor-

tunity of visiting Italy, where, in consequence of my
having received their order of knighthood, I was
received with distinguished favour. I was present in
Florence when King Victor Emmanuel made his
grand *entrée* into that city, and made it for the time
being the capital of United Italy. There were great
festivities to celebrate the event. I got an invitation to the first royal ball at the Pitti Palace,
when there were present 5,000 of the *élite* of the
nobility of the land, parading its long suite of twenty-
four reception-rooms. The Queen of Portugal was
mistress of the ceremonies. I was permitted to enter
the compartment where the royal quadrille was
being danced, in which were engaged the king's
daughter and three of his sons. When I entered
the refreshment room, I was surprised to see the
tables spread with the most harmless and costless
delicacies. The king said neither he nor the country
could afford to give expensive entertainments—their
war debt was too heavy. There was a huge ormulu
inlaid punch bowl, out of which a servant was
ladling cupfuls of something of a brown colour, and
as it was much patronised by the ladies, I came to
the conclusion that it could not possibly be punch, so
I went in for a cup of it, and lo! behold it was
nothing stronger than clear beef tea—a nice innocent
beverage to dance upon truly. At that time the
cholera was raging at Naples, and nothing would
satisfy the king but he must needs go down, contrary
to advice, and pay the hospitals a personal visit. Of
course it was considered a very brave self-sacrificing
thing to do, and when he returned in safety to

Florence the people were half crazy with delight, and he was received with an uproar of cheers.

Patti was then engaged at the opera house, and though very young was rapidly becoming a great favourite. Hence, on the king's return he went to the opera; Patti had just been before the curtain to receive the applause of the audience three times when the king entered the royal box; then it commenced again more furiously than ever, and poor little Patti, not being aware of the royal presence, came forward again to be applauded, but soon discovered her mistake, but was consoled by receiving a handsome bracelet from His Majesty.

It is not often one finds a foreign order of much service in travelling from place to place, but a very pleasant exception occurred to me on one occasion when visiting the north of Italy. A party of ladies requested my escort from Venice to the river Po. One had been laid up with inflamed eyes, to whom I had been of some little service. They were English, and did not know any other language than their mother tongue; under these circumstances I consented to take a seat in one of their carriages—for two were required. Thus we posted down to the banks of the river. When we arrived our luggage was to be examined at the custom house; but when I showed the official my credentials he very politely permitted our baggage to pass free, and we got at once into the ferry-boat and were taken over to the opposite side before another large party could clear the customs; thus I was enabled to secure the only vehicle standing there, on which our luggage was placed. While I was chatting with the man in charge of the office on the south side, the other party had got over, and had bribed our cabby with a napoleon to take our trunks off and put theirs on. No doubt the wealthy English heiress with her suite of man-servants and maid-servants, courier and doctor, looked very grand and imposing; but when I appealed to the official to give me precedence on account of my order of knighthood, he immediately reversed the position of things, giving the driver a good rating. You can better imagine than I can describe it the looks of this rich domineering English party, when they saw their fine boxes taken down and placed uncere-moniously on the muddy shingle, and watching us drive off to Ferrara, a distance of five or six miles, which we reached in time for *table d'hôte* dinner; while the great lady and her companions were obliged to wait till carriages were sent from the town to convey them to the hotel, which they reached about midnight, when no meals could be had.

One more instance in which I found the Italian order of social service was in Rome. In that city there were at that time several private galleries of painting and sculpture, and valuable libraries, possess-ing ancient collections of manuscripts of great in-terest, in the mansions of the decayed nobility. The old Hôtel d'Angleterre had then a large number of visitors under its roof, by some of whom I was solicited to get them an introduction to see these treasures, which I had no difficulty in doing. When a sufficient sum of money had been collected as a honorarium for the great but impoverished owner, whose scanty income was considerably augmented by these tolls, then, and not till then, would I consent to be the guide to the party.

A rather singular bet was made by some friends in the hotel on the eve of our attending the *levée* at the Vatican. I must first say that the Pope, in those palmy Church days, was temporal sovereign of the estates of the papal dominion, and at bitter enmity with the king, who wanted Rome to be the capital of United Italy. The bet was this. That I would not dare to appear in the Pope's presence wearing the Order of St. Maurice and St. Lazarus, because if I did he would thus have to bestow a blessing on the king's decoration. I did not let them into the secret that I was going to place the cross between two war medals. Hence, when I entered the Audience Chamber, Monsignor Howard came up to me, and seeing the order, said, "I presume that is a war decoration, and has nothing to do with any political or religious matter whatever." I replied, "Certainly not," that it was for service in the Crimea. "Very good," said he, "then you can have the *entrée*." Pio Nono then entered, and walking down the long corridor, speaking to one, then to another in his well-known, kindly, genial way, came opposite to where I stood, and just glancing at the decorations, said, "Do you think the cholera will travel from Naples to Rome?" "I thought not, if the authorities would look well to the sanitary condition of the city." He then continued on, addressing the company, touching their strings of crucifixes and beads till he reached the further end of the long gallery, when he turned round, raised his hand, and blessed Catholics and Protestants alike. Thus the bet was won! When I arrived at the hotel, the disappointed ones said, "When His Holiness stopped opposite and spoke to you, we certainly thought he was giving you a good wigging for appearing with that order upon your breast, but you have done us thoroughly."

When the war was over in the United States, the Americans, especially the ladies, came over in swarms " to do " Europe, and give their daughters a polish. It was not only the fashion, but a regular craze set in to cross the Atlantic " to see the wonders of the world abroad," notwithstanding that their greenbacks were exchanged at a discount of 40 per cent. They lavishly spent their money broadcast. They secured the best rooms in the hotels; gave the best prices in the shops for articles *de vertu*, completely swamping the English buyers by giving double the usual charges for copies of the old masters. They excited quite a sensation in the coral, cameo, and mosaic stores by the free-and-easy way in which they spent their money. Some of their countrymen pretended " to do " Rome in a couple of days, rushing about like madmen from museum to church, and hence to ruins, hardly giving themselves time for meals, at which they would read their Murray or examine the maps. I was crossing the country one day when two young American girls were of the party, who delayed our starting not a little by two huge trunks which they insisted on having chained up behind, making our conveyance

J. Vaughan-Hughes, Esq., M.D., L.R.C.P., London.
Knight of the Royal Order of St. Maurice and St. Lazarus of Italy.
Surgeon-Major, retired, Crimean War, 1854—5—6.
Author of "Seventy Years of Life in the Victorian Era."

dangerously top-heavy. So I asked them why they travelled about with such monstrous impedimenta. "Oh!" they said, "they were obliged to do so, because if they did not trouble them a bit at the hotels they would be thought nothing of, and be snubbed as 'nobodies.'" I could not help seeing that there was some wise forethought in their plans, and that the usual acuteness of the Yankee was to the fore in this instance, and they could, as they say, "whip the English into fits." Here were two unprotected young girls travelling alone thousands of miles from their own land, perfectly at their ease, yet possessed of a shrewdness and tact quite characteristic of Brother Jonathan's family.

Again I came across an American gentleman in charge of four pretty young ladies travelling about in style. He was the envy of all the bachelors, who regarded him as a most fortunate man, and did not fail to express their sentiments. "Oh! you innocent and simple young fellows: you who don't look beyond the surface," said he. "I only wish any one of you had my place for the next trip, and then I should see how you would like to look after four ladies and nineteen trunks and packages. Just try it at one custom house, and then tell me I am a most fortunate man, if you have the cheek to do so." "But what in the world do they want such a lot of boxes for?" "There you are again, you greenhorns. When you are married you will quickly be installed into such mysteries. Don't you see, if ladies change their dresses four times a day, that the gowns must have plenty of space to themselves to avoid crumpling." They might have ejaculated, "Truly we live and learn," but were lost in surprise, and said nothing.

Mr. Parker, C.B., the eminent archæologist, being a friend of my family, I had an unusual opportunity of seeing and studying the ruins of ancient Rome under his guidance. He had spent quite a little fortune in excavating different portions of the city, and possessed a fine collection of large photos, from which he lectured to his numerous friends. One of the underground prisons he discovered had been utilised and converted into a *depôt*, a sort of refrigerator, for butcher's meat. What dramatic changes hath not time wrought!

There were a great many assassinations in Rome at that time. It was not safe to go out at night except in company, and with lanterns and sticks. The streets were not lighted with lamps. I was at an evening party in a suite of rooms on the third story (the fashionable and healthy one, high above the stench of the streets) when a gentleman was steathily followed up the dark staircase to the top landing, then stabbed in the neck, just missing the jugular vein. We heard the shriek and a rustle down the steps, but before any of us could get outside the assassin was gone. We were much grieved, for this gentleman had been forty years in the city, and had shown many acts of kindness towards the poor. We heard afterwards that he had been mistaken for somebody else. This wanton act of cruelty roused a good deal of indignation in the English colony, and a deputation was formed to call on Antonelli, the foreign minister, stating the case, and asking to be allowed to carry revolvers in self-defence. All the consolation we got was this sarcastic and ominous reply, " Oh, yes! certainly," said he ; " but you must take the consequences," and we knew what that insinuation meant.

The populace hated their French protectors, and many officers on patrol were stabbed, and one died of his wounds while I was there. The Pope would now and again come in his carriage, surrounded by his noble guard, and get out among the promenaders in the Piazza di Spagna, when the ladies would gather round him like a flock of pigeons, and kneeling down on the dirty flags, in their splendid silks, would seize the hands of His Holiness and salute them, or failing that would kiss the hem of his garment. There was no Protestant place of worship allowed within the walls of the city in those days ; we were obliged to attend a most un-church-like building outside the gates. We were not allowed to congregate even in a private room to read and expound the Scriptures, except on the sly! All this bigotry is now dead and buried, and religious liberty prevails. Hence the Americans have erected a splendid church in the very heart of Rome, with a lofty spire pointing heavenwards, and not towards the Vatican, where everything inclines good, bad, and indifferent. We will now stop, and then proceed with Chapter XIV.

CHAPTER XIV.

BEFORE we finally take leave of Rome and its renowned antiquities, we must just climb up into the brazen ball crowning the grand dome of St. Peter's, and get a peep through its bull's eyes of the magnificent panorama of the Campagna, backed by its distant hills, and on the other side the meandering Tiber flowing down to join the Mediterranean Sea. Again, let us take a farewell turn on the Monte Pincio of sunny fame, where do congregate the *élite* in their smart carriages and still smarter dresses, where some American ladies would outshine in splendour those of any other country, and did not fail to attract to the sides of their hired equipages and liveried servants the young impecunious Italian nobles, heirs to large estates mortgaged up to the very hilt for generations past; these handsome, plausible gentry would leave no stone unturned to secure the affections and the money of these rich women, in order to restore the social position of these fallen but proud old families. But—and there is always a nasty but in the fulfilment of these selfish schemes—when the case had advanced so far as to elicit the reply, "Ask papa," the worthy noble finds that dear papa is showing off at the sacrifice of capital, and not living in the usual way on his income at all, and can make no settlement on his beautiful and fascinating daughter. Then the disappointed—one cannot say disinterested—lover slopes away, and is no more seen on Monte Pincio for the remainder of that season. Then you ask a Chicago merchant, rich in pork and credit, how he dare act in such a prodigal way, his answer was, twenty-six years ago, "Well, I can go back to my business and make as good a fortune, and as quickly, again," and so he would, for money was made rapidly in the metropolis of hogs in those days.

We will now pass on to Naples—shining beautifully in a cloudless sky like a white-washed sepulchre without, but inwardly stenchy and offensive. Vesuvius, slightly smoking in the distance, first attracts the visitor's attention, and when we get to it we are told that the feat to accomplish is to take some raw eggs in your pocket, climb unaided up its steep side knee-deep in loose lava and cinders till you reach the crater; then if you have not already fallen and broken your eggs, you descend into its mouth and thrust the eggs into the hot dust to be cooked, which takes about half an hour, then you take them out and eat them. This I performed safely, but at the expense of a pair of boots, the soles of which were burnt off. Of course Pompei and its wonders were duly done and studied à la Murray, then we proceeded viâ Castella Mare to visit lovely Sorento, basking in its orange groves. We made the Tremontana Hotel, on the edge of the cliff overhanging the bay, our headquarters, from whence we rowed over to Capri in order to enter its celebrated "blue cave" in the waters of which reflecting the sky, a man will plunge in and swim about looking like a silver fish, amid ripples of phosphorescent light—a curious dazzling phenomenon, decidedly worth a visit provided the weather is fine. Returning to Sorento we next took a journey inland to Amalfi, and thence by very good road cut out of the cliffs overlooking the seas on one side, and bounded on the other by terrace upon terrace of orange gardens, till we reached Salerno, the whole ride singularly wild and picturesque. Not being safe to visit the ruined temples of Pæstum in consequence of the roads being infested with brigands, we returned to Naples where I gave myself up for a time to the study of the original statues of the heathen gods, unearthed from the temples in Pompei by Government excavators. Some, especially the colossal statue of Hercules, seemed as fresh looking as if they had been sculptured yesterday. The various surgical instruments taken from a doctor's house interested me very much and tended to confirm the old saying, that "There is nothing new under the sun." While the wonderful preservation of the loaves of bread with the baker's stamp, the coffee-berries, currants, and spices were no less attractive from a domestic point of view to the ladies.

It is not my intention to act as a peripatetic guide to the "lions" of the places I happen to stay at, unless I can point a moral now and again. I shall make a return visit to Italy in the course of ten years, and then I shall describe the changes, social, moral, and religious, which shall have taken place in the country's condition when it has become happily united and cemented under the liberal government and free under the auspices of a large-hearted king; and throws off the yoke of the Austrians, who were so hated in Venice when I was there, that when the officers entered a restaurant, the Italian gentlemen would walk out.

To economise my time I took a berth in a coasting steamer and left Naples for Genoa, which we reached in forty-eight hours, touching at Civita Vecchia and Leghorn *en route*—trade poor, and people half asleep in each town. Genoa may be defined as a city of marble palaces of a bygone golden era, when their owners could afford to keep them up, but in modern times tenanted by a poor and squalid lot of people, who tramp their marble halls and staircases with perfect unconcern and contempt as to their former grandeur. Such are the changes which a declining commerce has produced, not only at Leghorn and Genoa, but also all along the Riviera till one reaches the large and prosperous community of Marseilles. I therefore early took my departure from Genoa, chartered a carriage, from which I enjoyed, on a lovely bright day to my utmost fill, the varied beauties of the world-renowned landscapes along the celebrated Corniche road. The day's journey terminated at San Remo, a health resort not thought much of at that time. The town runs up a spur of the Alps at an angle of nearly forty degrees, is well wooded, and is a very pretty sight from the sea, and *vice versâ* from its summit. The streets are narrow and bridged over here and there by solid masonry to give the houses stability against earthquakes. The fruit was very cheap —I bought twelve apples for a penny, and as to oranges they were a glut in the market. How will this be in a dozen years hence, when the railway is completed along the coast and its crowds of English and Americans appear to spoil the primitive simplicity? Leaving San Remo and its cheap hotel at seven francs a day, I continued along the *route à la Corniche*, which, if anything, becomes more bewitching as one nears Bordighera and Ventimiglia, up and down hill on a perfect roadway, passing bold and lofty promontories and well-wooded hills; then skirting the bases of precipitous and frowning cliffs washed by the angry waves of the blue sea, crowned here and there by the ruins of venerable towers of bygone ages to protect the residents from pirates. Again we descend into a richly cultivated plain with its curiously shaped olive trees, luxuriant growth of vines, figs, citrons, oranges, oleanders, myrtles, aloes, and even palms, and though last, not least, the showy mimosa with its feathery blossoms and delightful perfume. Passing by the model estate of Mr. Hanbury, a paradise of beauty, which he kindly allows visitors to see, our road ascends and curves round a spur of a pine-clad mountain, when there suddenly bursts upon the sight a splendid panorama, consisting of the town of Mentone, with its eastern and western divisions lying at one's feet, with Roccabruna, Monaco, and the l'Estérel hills in the distance, and the wide expanse of the sea with its ever-varying shades of blue and green. Such a view in a flood of sunshine is a treat indeed, and not to be forgotten by any tourist, however apathetic. As we descend into Mentone the road is cut out of the solid rock, and a deep gorge is crossed by the Pont St. Louis, a fine specimen of masonry, which forms the boundary between France and Italy, and where I had to submit to my luggage being examined, my Italian privileges having now ceased. I put up at the Hôtel de Londres, a small place, but the cooking was excellent, as I was informed by a Leicester clergyman, who had ministered there for some years. My first visit was to my old friend, Dr. Henry Bennet, at the Hôtel des Anglais. Ill health had compelled him to leave London every winter and take up his residence and practice in Mentone, which became through his influence and that of his book "Eastward Ho and Westward Ho" the most popular resort for invalids with delicate chests along the whole length of the Riviera. The natives regarded him in the light of the founder of its prosperity, and styled him "the King of Mentone," and frequently pressed him to assume the office of mayor, though a foreigner. He was a perfect Frenchman in thought and speech, and he carried in the muncipality great weight as far as sanitary improvements were concerned. He had a fine suite of rooms in his hotel, where he reigned supreme; the landlord and servants obsequiously submissive to all his orders. He filled the hotel with his patients. In the large dining-room there was a T-shaped table at which he presided, and insisted on having the windows open at the cross part, much to the alarm of those delicate ones who thought too much fresh air would kill them. Those, however, who were obedient to his will were privileged to have seats at the cross portion of the table, which was called the "House of Lords," while the tail part was styled the "House of Commons." I had breakfast with him in his elegant apartments full of knick-knacks and presents from grateful visitors, when he offered to drive me in his handsome carriage and pair as far as Monaco to hear the celebrated band of musicians, the pick of all nations, and to witness the play at the gaming tables, which I accepted in anticipation of much pleasure, for the road had lovely scenery all the way, and the Casino had acquired wide-world renown for the numbers of people it had ruined and the constant suicides that had taken place in the first moments of despair and bewilderment at having lost all. A bright sunny afternoon favoured our delightful drive, and we both enjoyed the visit exceedingly, returning in the shades of evening in the glow of a setting sun with keen appetites for dinner. After struggling up the mountains with a party of ladies on mules to see the magnificent prospect from S. Agnese one day, and on another to make an excursion to Castellara, and not forgetting to note the immense commerce in flowers going on per post between Mentone and England, I regretfully took my leave of this beautiful health resort, and made my way to Nice.

The Corniche road continued still to present some splendid bits of scenery *en route* to Nice, especially as one approaches Villafranca Bay, and taking the high road over the promontory which in its descent looks down on the town nestling in the hollow. Nice is said to have three distinct climates according to your position in the city, whether this be in the old town, on the Promenade des Anglais, or in the sheltered situation of the "Strangers' Quarter," lying back some distance from the sea front. Here one meets in the winter season crowds of Russians, Germans, French, and English, who congregate together as much for pleasure as for health; and as money flows freely, living is dearer in comparison with other places on the Riviera. Therefore, after mounting Castle Hill and doing the Public Gardens, there is not much to see; I departed by train for Cannes, instead of travelling by road along the coast which is flat and uninteresting. Cannes may be defined as a city of detached villas, snugly embowered in their own detached grounds, which extend for miles on each side of a splendid wide road, and having a centre made up of fifty fine hotels, the outcome of its well-deserved popularity as a sheltered wintering place for delicate persons with weak chests. A tourist may spend a very pleasant week there. The islands of St. Marguerite and St. Honorat are well worth a day's visit. The quaint old fortress and the fortified monastery are fine specimens of middle-aged strongholds in the days of bows and arrows. It is well also to ascend to see the old parish church and pottery works on Mount Chevalier, from which a fine bird's-eye view of the town at its foot may be had, with the bright sea in front and the Alps in the rear, which afford such a protection from the dreaded mistral wind from the north-west. Cannes is a quiet family place, where home-life predominates over fashionable display, and does not pretend to compete with her more flashy neighbour, where high life reigns supreme, and boasts of its "Battle of Flowers" as not second to that held in Rome.

Leaving Cannes I take rail to Hyéres, another health resort, well worthy of a short visit, because its climate is so mild for invalids. The graceful large palm trees lining its public promenade, bearing fruit which actually ripens, is a truthful testimony to its warm sunny aspect. Being three miles from the station and the same distance from the sea is rather against it; still it is much frequented by families seeking quietness and moderate living expenditure. The natives cultivate largely the violet and the rose, which grow profusely and are exported in large quantities. Passing by Toulon, the great naval harbour of France, I reach by rail Marseilles, its greatest commercial seaport, the counterpart of our Liverpool, boasting 300,000 people all alive and active, and carrying on an immense maritime traffic with Africa, India, and Australia. The thing to do is to mount the rather steep climb of the rock on which the Cathedral of the Notre Dame de la Garde is situated, crowned by the gilt figure of the Virgin, the landmark and object of devotion to the sailors at sea. From the terrace a grand view of the big city at one's feet with its huge shipping docks is beheld. Again a boat should be taken to the Chateau d'If, where Mirabeau was confined, and the scene is laid of Dumas' "Monte Christo." Marseilles is fully exposed to the mistral and is one of the coldest places in winter I ever visited. Before leaving the South of France, the land of lemons and oranges, I may just relate a legend which is superstitiously believed in by the lower orders : it is this. When Eve was expelled from the Garden of Eden she carried away with her a fine lemon, which she carefully nursed for a long time seeking a suitable soil to plant it in. At last arriving at Mentone she fixed upon that charming sunny spot as the best she had come across. So she deposited her lemon there, where it took root kindly, and has ever since thriven so plenteously and luxuriantly that the fruit is held in high esteem in Paris and deemed the finest in the world.

CHAPTER XV.

HAVING bid farewell to Marseilles, the *grand vitesse* landed me safely in Paris in about thirty-six hours, which I found in an awful state of confusion and consternation, in consequence of the unexpected failure of Overend and Gurney's bank, which was universally regarded as safe as the Bank of England. English gentlemen and ladies were vociferating loudly over their losses, and scanning eagerly the last news from London. After having had a good look at the beautiful Eugénie, whom I was lucky enough to see walking arm in arm with the Emperor in the Place de la Concorde, I made the best of my way to London to safeguard my own interests, as I was told that the "Bears" were trying to ruin the other banks by making a run upon them. But my bank was forewarned, and had protected itself against their sudden onslaught by getting into their coffers one and a quarter millions of money, and thus could meet every demand. When the settling-day came round the "Bears" had to repay 3 per cent. on the bank's stock; and thus the biters were bitten, and in some cases even to ruin! Here, again, Providence intervened in my favour, and I was thereby enabled to carry out my longed-for plan of settling in London. Beginning with unfurnished apartments in George Street, Hanover Square, I was lucky enough to secure the whole house after I had been there a few months. From the dining-room window I could see, and was often amused at, the splendid weddings which so often took place in St. George's Church, the steps up to which were carpeted with red cloth, generally indicative of a *mariage à la mode* among the aristocracy, and as these were frequently regarded a *mariage de convenance*, the steps were nicknamed "the steps to ruin," and in many instances it was only too true.

When my first London season came round I thought it would be to my advantage to be presented at Court, and as the then Adjutant-General kindly consented to act as my sponsor, I went and was introduced, not to the Queen, but to the young Prince of Wales, who represented her Majesty at the *levée*. I felt disappointed, and so did an elderly officer who had come all the way from India to see his Queen herself. He told me that he was old enough to be the Prince's father, and remembered his being born. But the fact was, her Majesty had been so cut up by the unexpected death of the Prince Consort—Albert the Good, as he was called—that she had not appeared in public for some time. The next best thing that could happen to me was to get a hospital appointment, which I succeeded in doing the first year of my residence in London, which brought me into personal contact with all sorts and conditions of men, women, and children, from the duchess to the dustman, from the peer to the pauper, especially with that perplexing portion of the people since described as the "submerged tenth." As a hospital physician I came into close communion with the degraded classes, and in one's mission of mercy among them gained their confidence. The fact was very soon and very forcibly revealed to me, that the drinking of rough, *cheap* spirits in their raw and immature character was the cause, as a general rule, of their pitiful downfall, their deplorable debasement of body and mind. I don't think the fact is brought home with sufficient emphasis when the West End talk glibly of the moral degradation of the East End. No one would believe the deleterious, the diseasing effects of these vile concoctions, first upon the body, then upon the mind, except those who have had actual experience of such in our public hospitals, and in the homes—if you can call them such—of those who apply as outsiders. Those who will closely look into this perplexing problem as to what can be done to stem the torrent of evils associated with this engrossing vice, find themselves hedged about with many difficulties, though the glaring truth is apparent to any impartial looker-on, that this spirit-drinking is the prolific mother of many miseries. When the man or the woman is once down, and has lost all self-respect, it seems an impossibility to reason them out of the vicious and uncontrollable cause. They know it, they feel it, they confess it with tears; and it matters not what position in society they may have come from, they are all tarred with the same brush, which marks them as the "devil's own." No blood ties, no social ties, no knowledge, scientific, literary, moral, or religious, in the least degree influences them, and one can only commit them to the gracious intervention of God's good Spirit to move them, come when and where that may.

Under these dire circumstances what can society, what can the nation and its Government do to redeem this pitiable condition of the lower classes and, by self-impoverishment, the very lowest classes? What will the upper middle and aristocratic orders do to ameliorate matters? Go into what is called "good society," and just see and hear for yourself, as one perfectly disinterested and unbiassed. You cannot help observing and feeling that there is some great controlling power at work, obstructing greatly efforts at reform, and encouraging this gigantic evil, this pernicious agency floating freely, without let or hindrance, in every nook and corner of the kingdom. Why is this drink question tabooed? Why is it a forbidden subject in fashionable circles? Why are you treading on delicate ground when you venture to allude to it under your breath? Why are conscientious people put down as fanatics who dare to give their opinion courageously on this momentous subject? The reply to these tangible questions is plain and evident enough to those who are not purposely blind. Vested interests is the answer; interests involving every moneyed class in society; 139 millions of gold invested by thousands of well-to-do people in the higher and middle ranks, who through the medium of huge brewing companies have each and all a direct pecuniary stake in the manufacture and *consumption* of intoxicating spirits. The kings of the liquor trade, counting their millions, who have made their concerns into *limited* companies, have immense power in both houses of Parliament, and exert that influence to protect and increase the traffic, so as to enrich themselves and their legion of subscribers, at the expense of the well-being, moral and physical, of the great mass of the people. That day is greatly to be deplored on religious, mental, and physical grounds, when the spirit-lords of the United Kingdom converted their grand paying properties into limited companies, tempting outsiders by the inducement of heavy dividends to take shares in their respective establishments, thus giving each individual subscriber a direct moneyed interest in the success of their venture, and what is worse, implanting in their minds a strong selfish motive to uphold a wrong and to shut their eyes, or assume a silent attitude, against what is a glaring national injustice, which if they held themselves aloof and impartial they would condemn and endeavour to suppress by supporting the God-blessed Temperance movement throughout the country. There can be no doubt whatever that the strong and increasing wave of this movement alarmed their lordships, and filled them with fear and apprehension that their fine property would be depreciated as time went on, so, worldly-wise, they resorted to the above lamentable expedient of propping up a falling house.

The magistrates, many of whom are owners of public-houses themselves, have not the courage nor

J. VAUGHAN-HUGHES, M.D., L.R.C.P. LOND.

*Knight of the Royal Order of St. Maurice and St. Lazarus of Italy ;
Surgeon-Major, Retired, Crimean War, 1854, 5, 6.*

the incentive to withdraw licences, not even when the publics are admittedly too numerous and their removal is desired by the local inhabitants—yea, not even when the houses have disgraced their rights by harbouring thieves, and become the resort of prostitutes, betting-hells, and the depôt of stolen goods, are they disestablished.

The great majority of the " publics " and gin-palaces are "tied houses" belonging to the wealthy brewers, and these domineering owners and masters can and do exert widespread social and political influence; so that any one, for example, who aspires to the coveted position of a M.P. has to reckon with and conciliate this powerful caste, which so often turns the scale at elections, and always in favour of that party which will shout the loudest for compensation to the publican, and no Sunday closing, &c. Though this pothouse influence is now becoming more or less counteracted by the Temperance party, which is every day gaining more and more strength in every town and village, the centre of hope, as the saviours of the country, are the Bands of Hope. The children —the rising generation—being secured, the parents become more or less interested in their well-being, and thus this valuable movement rouses their paternal instincts and excites their sympathies.

This is a subject of such vital importance to the commonweal, not only to this England of ours, but to the whole world, that I shall stop here and give it the next chapter to itself.

CHAPTER XVI.

WHATEVER I may have said in the previous chapter, I feel it does not devolve upon me as a layman to give moral advice, or thrust my opinions down the throats of others, as to whether they ought, or ought not, to drink strong alcoholic beverages; but what I do feel I may venture to do, and to do it without offending fixed prejudices, is to try to remove from the minds of the great mass of the people the crass and pitiable ignorance with respect to the misconception of the physiological action of alcohol on the living tissues of the human frame, and the tendency of the spirit to engender a variety of well-known diseases which the total abstainer is not subject to. There is a wonderful consensus of scientific opinion "up to date" that alcohol is a compound of carbon, hydrogen, and oxygen in certain fixed, defined proportions, forming a peculiar liquid, unique, stable, and singularly tenacious—a marvellous agent for evil, without a corresponding minimum for good. The greatest enemy in the universe manufactured by man for man, and the most diseasing of all liquids to the healthy organs of the human form divine, towards whose delicate organism and construction it yields not the slightest particle of nourishment, or the smallest modicum for the repair of its structure by labour or exercise. And why not? Because when it is once swallowed, neither the stomach nor any other organ in our constitution has the power of digesting it, decomposing, or separating and re-arranging its ingredients for the process of assimilation; but we have to submit in childlike helplessness to its irritating and narcotic and benumbing influences. It is rapidly absorbed into our circulation, and carried into every nook and corner of the entire fabric, depositing itself unchanged and unchangeable in the delicate and sensitive tissue of every vital organ, notably the cells of the brain, producing drowsiness, stupidity, and paralysis, interfering with a healthy train of sound thought and reflection, and muddling the logical capacity of the mind, rendering unstable also the spinal movements.

It disturbs and ruffles the quiet, natural and harmonious function of every organ with its temporary artificial stimulation, setting up organic mischief in its sound structure, slowly or rapidly it may be, but with deadly certainty, in exact ratio to the quantity collected and stagnating within us, and the inability of the lungs, skin, and kidneys to expel the burden in a given time, and the varying strength of individuals to resist its morbific action. In a word, the frame is in a state of artificiality in contradistinction to its condition in a state of nature. It is beside the question here to comment upon alcohol and its uses as a medicinal drug; that must be left to the wisdom, courage, and discretion of medical men, upon whom must rest the sole responsibility of prescribing it, not as a luxury, but as a curative agent. Again, there is another characteristic peculiarity connected with the introduction of alcohol into our frames, namely, its singular tendency to accumulate by degrees, and fix itself in every part of our structure with an irresistible affinity—humanity bends beneath its despotic sway with absolute submission.

This fact leads us on to ask ourselves the very pertinent question — What are the effects of the gradual accumulation of this narcotic irritant and diseasing agent upon our healthy bodies? Well, the following are some of its disastrous results:— After our patients—it matters not what section of society they belong to—have continuously, daily, and habitually drunk wine, spirits, or beer in what some would deem moderate quantities (an indefinable standard) for a period of time, varying with constitutional differences, they are compelled to pull up, and put aside their alcoholic beverage—be that what it may—and why? because the whole system from head to foot has become gradually overcharged, soaked, we might say, like a sponge, with the continuous influx of alcohol, and the poor body, thus groaning under its intolerable burden, rebels against any further drinking, and a forced abstinence is imperatively demanded, till the bilious or gouty attack, headaches, fever, or other storms of serious sickness have subsided, and the alcohol is more or less washed out of the system by the physician's prescription.

Well, we will suppose the attack is safely over, and

they have narrowly escaped a fatal result in the form of paralysis or "Bright's disease," what do the convalescents do? Do they take a lesson of warning from their oft-repeated attacks? In the majority of cases, not they! No, in vain does the conscientious and patriotic physician reason with his patients, some of whom, perhaps, are blessed with the possession of even the most eminent and intellectual attainments, and disinterestedly reveals to them the real source of their ailment and the danger of its repetition. Some will exclaim in heated language, "What is the use of my splendid cellar of choice and valuable wines, mellowed with age and laid down with anxious care and great expense, if I am not allowed to enjoy them? Am I to abandon my boon companions (friends?), and throw into a state of confusion my recognised position in society?" I heard one man of considerable talent say, "I will die first," and die he did, in the course of time, a raving madman. You may argue till you are black in the face with such thoughtless beings, and others even in their most serious moods only pay passing heed to your remonstrance. Irresolute man, with childish efforts, resolves and re-resolves to be wiser and more circumspect for the future, but generally ends in falling back to his old habits. Now I would ask any practitioner engaged in a large practice in London, whether the above is not a true type of myriads of cases which come before him every year. Is it not very humiliating to a man of any moral or religious feeling to have to record the fact that such cases as above described constitute at least two-thirds of the labours of every active medical man in our huge metropolis, and also in all our large centres of population throughout our country? There is not a section of society which does not come under this ban!

Such a mode of passing through this life must be condemned as a farcical drama unworthy of a man of common sense and sound reasoning, even taken from a worldly, social, or national standpoint, but how much more less becoming in the professing Christian, who, with his eyes open to its bitter fruits, obstinately refuses to give up his daily luxury (or even its occasional use), which prevents him from keeping the body in subjection to his rational mind and thought, and which clouds over every refined feeling of our nature. Let us look the above facts fearlessly in the face of truth and science, and may we not justly say that they constitute a key-note to the argument against the *continuous* use of alcoholic drinking, and, further, form the basis of our indictment against them as *daily* human beverages. It is to be hoped some good will eventuate to the reader when he reflects that we cannot alter by one iota the peculiar characteristics of alcohol when it is once within us; and, secondly, let him be thoroughly convinced and warned this evil spirit has an irresistible tendency to accumulate within us, and set up disease in our vital organs, notably the heart, brain, and lungs.

Let all those struggling young members who are desirous of getting on and succeeding in either of the professions, or in any of our competitive commercial pursuits, remember and take to heart that nothing tends so much to obstruct their progress as alcoholic drinking, leaving alone excessive smoking. Let them record deeply the stubborn facts which have been laid down for their guidance in the log-book of their memories, so that they will serve them as an unshakable rock upon which they can rest their faith and practice, and also base their replies when asked for their reasons for total abstinence, or, if not total abstainers, for ceasing to be daily and habitual drinkers of an alcoholic beverage.

There are four hundred honest, courageous, and patriotic medical men in London who have associated together to give up alcohol, and not to prescribe it for their patients if possible, and then only as a drug. And I shall be excused if I agree with them, for after fifty years of my life spent amid the sufferings of my fellow beings, and witnessing the fearful evils arising from drink in active warfare and in peace time, also in my hospital and private practice in London, embracing every rank in society, graduating down from the peer to the pauper—the evils involving in their destruction and ruin the high and the low, the rich and the poor, men, women, and children indiscriminately—my large and sad experience will not allow me to sit passively down and do nothing to reclaim and reform them. Before I quit this important subject, I would like to have just a little say in respect to the indulgence in drink, even to a moderate extent, upon the prospects of a professional man in London. This will be endorsed by many a poor talented fellow who has taken early warning by the forelock, but this I shall leave for the next chapter.

CHAPTER XVII.

My last chapter concluded with an expression that I had something further to say in relation to the habit of drinking intoxicants of the stronger sort among the young aspirants to fame in the three learned professions, and among those who intended to gain their bread by brain work. Well, those who have come to the front in their respective professions—some of them, whose names need not be mentioned as they stand out indelibly as household stars, illuminating the unthinking and ignorant masses by their speeches and their lives—these big minds tell us that it is physically and mentally impossible to retain their position of eminence if they did not make a point of being ever on the watch against any indulgence in excess. Nay, further, that they shunned any approach to a quantity that would lead to a state bordering on narcosis, headache, a flushed face, or confusion of ideas, such as would prevent them from rising in the morning with brain refreshed, or induce a feeling of languor and seediness, ill-prepared to fight the day's battle with a cloud of anxious, expectant, and argumentative people, perhaps sickly ones, impatiently clamouring for immediate relief, and watching every expression on one's face with a lynx-eyed scrutiny and earnestness. These wise heads have arrived by personal experience at the unshakable resolution that an unalcoholised brain —a brain free from the tainting presence of spirit in its delicate tissues—is in the most favoured and active condition for the mind to work upon. And if this be a logical conclusion on their part with respect to their prosperity and success in a worldly point of view, how about the higher classes of thought and order of things? As the action of the mind involves the reasoning soul, is not the whole mental being placed in a more susceptible position for the presence and active operation and indwelling of the Divine Spirit, when it receives deeper and more efficient and sensitive impressions from a material organism that is not more or less benumbed, narcotised, and handicapped by the presence of alcohol circulating through its delicate cells? I would appeal to all Temperance workers and ministers of the Gospel, and all those who would efface themselves by doing rescue work among the "submerged tenth," to reflect upon this burning question in this light, as it constitutes the strongest argument in favour of total abstinence.

But let us come down once more to consider our subject from a worldly standpoint, as connected with our every-day life. What facts do we glean from comparing individuals? What encouragement do we get from watching those who take strong drink and those who do not? Do we not find that those who will make the self-sacrifice and curb their desires are more to the fore in their work, whether we regard this as the labour of the mind or of the body, or of both combined. Are they not more precise, more decided, more ready, more enduring at their work, and do we not extract out of them the fullest extent of their natural powers? Let us take, for example, the artisan, the watchmaker, the engraver on stone or metal, the electrician, &c., do we not find that delicacy and refinement of touch which is the very essence of perfect skill, the eye guiding the hand with unerring rectitude? If the surgeon, for instance, is called upon for immediate action in time of war, or in a mining district, with its oft-recurring accidents, we see that he maintains that power of instant decision and self-command which is the first quality for the emergency. Then, again, our much-respected nursing sisters, now faithfully to the front, will be seen to possess great endurance night and day, which strikes with wonder and envy those less careful of their own powers and abilities. Thus, then, these grand and cardinal virtues—precision, decision, presence of mind, and physical endurance—are the outcome of total abstinence from intoxicating strong drinks to the very fullest extent that the Creator has implanted them in our mental and physical condition; hence we enjoy the sweets and the delightful fruits of those talents with which we are entrusted by Heaven in their most valuable bearing upon ourselves and upon our fellow-creatures.

This being so, ought not the authorities regulating our free education in the Board Schools to insist, as a very important item in their programme, that the teachers, male and female, should instruct the little children—the fathers and mothers of a future generation—in the knowledge that alcoholic beverages, beginning in moderate quantities, but leading up inevitably to larger quantities, if *daily and continuously* taken, create in our frames a score of diseases which would not exist in us but for the presence and stagnation of the spirit in our vital organs — besides reducing to a lower standard of ability our natural gifts of mind and of body?

Let these facts be plainly instilled into our little ones of every grade and station by parents and instructors, public and private, so that when they grow up they will not go astray from sheer ignorance.

I will conclude this chapter by affirming that alcohol is such a fixed body, and has such a strong affinity or liking for our tissues, that, as a rule, we cannot shake it off as quickly as we drink it, hence its evil effects ; and, to aggravate matters, the raw, immature spirits drunk by the lower classes have a strong narcotic, irritating and maddening, and diseasing action on the mind ; and following in the wake of disease comes the loss of manly strength, of time and money ; and linked to this sad triplet of troubles are weak resolves, idleness, and worthlessness.

"And they all began with one consent to make excuse." This well-known rebuff and refusal to an invitation to meet others to celebrate a memorial feast—a feast of reason, is not inapplicable to the position in which the physician is posed when he endeavours to call the attention of his patients and friends to the drink question. It is a lamentable fact that with one accord they begin to apologise for the daily habit of drinking alcoholic stimulants, and this with an unusual amount of disturbed equanimity and warmth of expression. Evidencing a disposition to shut up the mind and reason against any argument, and a disinclination to be logically convinced upon the subject—they will have none of it. We find little of the openness, candour, and willingness to hear the truth and facts of the case which is usually evinced when conversing on any other matter of daily interest.

An answer which is first and foremost on the tip of the tongue of the great majority is this, "My doctor has ordered me to take some stimulant." One of the most fashionable of these in the present day is whisky in some effervescing alkaline water. Heaven help the poor kidneys which are daily flushed with this and such-like irritating depletants. Well, we will grant that the doctor has done so at a time, perhaps, when extreme weakness and a flabby heart have supervened on a long illness, and he wished to bridge them over the temporary exhaustion. Now, is it not very unfair and unjust to make the poor doctor the scapegoat for the subsequent troubles when the occasion for stimulating has passed away, and they still continue to take alcohol habitually? They would be acting more honourably and generously towards the faculty if they confessed the truth that they went on with the luxury because they liked it, and took all the blame and responsibility on their own shoulders, and thus exonerated the doctors, who at first only prescribed it medicinally.

Again, there is a small community of weakly beings in this wealthy country of ours, degenerate offsprings of decaying families, to whom a small quantity of alcohol appears a necessity of life, without which they feel, they assert, that they would melt away, and would be incapable of meeting the small demands upon their strength—a strength which will not carry them through half a day's work, or no work at all, or it may be that they are rusting out their lives in a state of *dolce far niente*—a condition often seen among the idly rich, who often bore one with their *maladie imaginaire*. Such-like beings of both sexes affirm with no little warmth that they would faint, swoon, or die away if they did not have their daily reviver—a "pick-me-up" to tide over the despondency arising from congenital infirmity or the sinking sensation at the pit of the stomach. Here the doctor is placed in a difficult position—he has to choose the lesser of two evils: either he must yield with a good grace and submit to expediency, or lose his moral hold upon his patients as a gentle persuader and admonisher should he decline to visit and watch over them.

I have a word more to say in reference to this particular sinking and die-away feeling at the pit of the stomach, which is almost invariably experienced, now and again, by those from whom the alcoholic stimulant—the artificial prop—is withdrawn, and which is temporarily removed by the drinker resorting to another quantum of his paralysing narcotic. I believe the sinking sensation, more intolerable in some than in others, is the cause of more pledges being broken than anything else. Then comes the question, how is it to be overcome, and finally disposed of, stamped out, in fact, by those who have made up their minds to abstain. I generally observe that it continues with more or less of severity from two to six months, and then disappears altogether. In those of a very nervous temperament it requires no little patience, perseverance, and moral courage to resist the temptation, the inward crave to fall back on the old pain killer, which is in reality the veritable cause of the sensation and distress.

If the upper ranks of society would sink their pride, and resort to what has been found so beneficial among the working classes, namely, the homely oatmeal porridge well cooked with milk or good beef tea, they would get not only certain relief from their passing distress, but an acquisition of strength truly remarkable.

Again, when common tea is taken as a beverage, the infusion should not allow to brew more than three minutes before it is drawn off, inasmuch as sodden tea in most persons gives rise to a very serious form of depressing dyspepsia; so depressing and painful is it among the poor seamstresses of London, who take it three or four times a day, that it is impossible to relieve them till it be abandoned. It is, therefore, no wonder that they add rum to their cup when they can afford it—thus adding mischief to mischief. "Tea Dyspepsia" was the name I gave to these very numerous cases among my hospital patients. I will conclude this article by expressing a hope that I may live to see the day when the upper crust of society will wave their exclusiveness, and make the self-sacrifice for the sake of the healthy and happy wellbeing of those below them by drinking stimulants occasionally instead of daily as a necessary adjunct to every meal.

If they would but set the fashion afloat, for strong is the force of fashion, those in the lower social grade would, from sheer love of imitation, follow the good example, which would react again on those of a still lower type, and blessed would be the change all along the line.

Some of my readers will think that I have been rather long-winded over this, to not a few, unpalatable subject; and yet it comprehends the most burning question of the day in the social economy of our race, not only in England, but in the Greater Britain. Notwithstanding all our grand reforms and boasted civilisation, our scientific progress, our increase of wealth and luxuries, refinement and knowledge, Britain is still left under the ban of its proverbial drunkenness and debauchery, the very scorn of nations. If we look at the horrid sequences of this dreadful system—its curses, its calamities, its huge difficulties, it may well arouse the attention and devotion and earnestness of all our young people, upon whom devolves in a great measure its cure and suppression. Viewing the vastness of the subject from a vital and patriotic standpoint, I don't see that I have said one word too much for the reasoning mind to reflect upon.

CHAPTER XVIII.

HAVING visited nearly every country in Europe, and having time and means at my disposal, I thought it would be advantageous and profitable to go further a-field and "see the wonders of the world abroad," as revealed to us in a tour round the globe. Hence, accompanied by my wife, we took a cabin in that most delightful of the P. and O. steamers, the *Victoria*, and left our shores in November, 1889, when winter was beginning to stare us in the face. Nothing very sensational occurred to us between England and the Mediterranean. Even the Bay of Biscay was in a kind mood and comparatively calm, and did not churn up either sex as is its wont. We had a lively lot of passengers on board, and leaving behind all the icyness characteristic of the British nature, a general thaw took place, and figuratively shaking hands all round, we one and all made up our minds to enjoy ourselves. Every berth was taken up in this favourite ship, the helm of which was under the experienced guidance of the commodore of the P. and O. Company's fleet. We had therefore a large first-class company, which had to be dined at two separate hours—namely, the House of Commons at 6 p.m., and the House of Lords at 8, the captain presiding at the latter more aristocratic hour, when evening dress was the rule and not the exception.

A good deal of card-playing went on, not unmixed with some gambling—an evil sequence not to be surprised at among a lot of idle rich young men; but the highest stake played was by a bewitching young damsel, chaperoned by an elderly lady, who threw down before an admiring group a most telling trump card, which consisted of an assertion, made through her well-tutored duenna, to the effect that her piquant and fascinating *protégée* had declined sixteen offers of marriage already, but the siren kept back the secret fact that she had speculated in a return ticket to Malta in hopes that she might be fortunate enough in securing a seventeenth which would be to her taste and liking. Now there were many well-gilded and good-looking eligibles on board, but somehow or other none of them came up to the winning post, and Malta was reached without anything of an engagement having been made. It was most amusing to the looker-on to witness the clever way in which she handled the ribbons of her team of admirers—coaxing and wheedling some, and gently rebuffing others. But she was determined to finish her game pluckily by inviting six of her most promising devotees to a champagne dinner ashore, with all the delicacies of the season, and so liberally did the bottle go round, that at midnight, on coming to terms with a cabman to bring them back to the ship, they quarrelled and knocked him down, the issue of which was that our diners-out were taken to the police station, where they were kept in durance vile for three hours till the superintendent was roused out of his bed, who kindly released them just in time to catch the steamer before she left the harbour! Thus ended an escapade, and an unusual spice of self-centred vanity, which served as a subject for a nine days' talk among the young people, and varied the monotony between Malta and Brindisi.

I introduced myself to the Rev. G. M——, going out to Sydney to join the Incumbent of St. Philip's Church. He was a fine specimen of what is defined as Muscular Christianity, and an eloquent extempore preacher. When I asked the captain to allow him to perform the services on Sunday in the first-class saloon, he surprised me by objecting rather brusquely, and stating that he should officiate himself, being, as he said, bishop of his own ship! So our only Episcopalian clergyman on board was forced to be content with holding a service in the second saloon, where I read the lessons for him, and we secured an excellent choir and mustered a good congregation, the waiters crowding the doorways, and others listening through the open skylights to catch the words of a most heart-stirring address.

Brindisi, 2,640 miles from London, was reached on a most brilliant Sunday. There is nothing worth noting except an old Roman gateway and the remains of an ancient fort. No service was held; all seemed busy in the shipping of fresh passengers and luggage, haling from the overland route, and the whole surroundings betokened a working week-day appearance.

After a delightful voyage of two and a half days in a perfect calm we reached Port Said, where I landed just to say that I had trod on African ground. It is a low, dirty place, with equally dirty Arabs, but the rapid way in which this unwashed crew coaled the steamer was a wonder to every one, and at nightfall, when it is carried on under the electric light, their black, greasy, nearly naked bodies frisking rapidly about, passing and re-passing along their to-and-fro gangways, they are more like so many unearthly demons than anything else one can compare them to. Our distance from London is here 3,570 miles.

We passed through the Suez Canal at night under the guidance of the electric light radiating from our foremast, which illumined the water for a considerable distance ahead, and doing away with any difficulty in passing other vessels at the various sidings *en route*. As we neared the pretty French town of Ismalia, quite an oasis in the desert, we witnessed a very interesting sight to the eyes of Westerns. About 500 camels were employed in carrying off in box panniers the sand from a heap forty feet high, which was a source of trouble and expense to the Canal Company, because it kept drifting into the cutting and necessitated dredging out. The sagacious animals quietly lay down to be loaded, and then struggled up to mount the hill in their usually sluggish fashion, in order to deposit their burden at a safe distance from the bank. After passing in review Mount Sinai with its three points, there was little worth recording in steaming down the Red Sea, except that it was not quite so like a Turkish bath at

120 as usual. When we were in it midway, and no land visible on either side, we were startled by ladies shrieking on deck, and running hither and thither shaking their skirts; the alarm being occasioned by several large locusts settling down on the vessel and hiding themselves away in any nook and cranny they could find, even to the crawling up the ladies' legs or ascending inside the gentlemen's trousers. Some, two and a half inches long, were secured as specimens, and were furnished with pretty green wings. We could well understand how a cloud of such formidable insects would soon make a clean sweep of anything green, and lay bare in a very short time thousands of acres of agricultural produce. It must have been a fearful curse on Pharaoh and his people when the plague of locusts was sent, for it is said that they filled all the houses without distinction, and ate up every herb of the land, all that the hailstorm had left. "Very grievous were they," covering the face of the whole earth, and consuming every green thing through all the land of Egypt. The God of Israel and of Moses must have been sorely tried and angry in those days. Having demolished our insect pest, which for a time created so much alarm among our fair ones, we reached Aden in peace the following morning. This town, with its fortress, was formerly remarkable for its huge tanks for the conservation of rain-water to supply the natives and the shipping, but these are now obsolete, other means of supply being substituted. The boys diving into the sea after some silver coins thrown into it by the passengers were most expert, for it mattered not how far down

the shining piece had got, they never failed to reach it and bring it up to the surface triumphantly between their teeth. Imposition is the order of the day here with Arab purveyors of fancy goods. One very ordinary article for sale is the long boa made of ostrich feathers. They began by asking £3, and kept aloof from any deduction, gesticulating that they were giving them away at that figure, and that it was simply ruin to take less, looking as innocent as they do at a mock auction in London, till the vessel showed signs of leaving, and just as we were about to haul up the gangway ladder an Australian gentleman went down to their bumboat, and, displaying two glittering sovereigns (an irresistible sight to an Oriental), brought back four of the boas—which was a bargain certainly, and out of which he could make a good profit when he reached Sydney. At Aden we were 4,965 miles away from home.

Crossing the Indian Ocean we hardly encountered a single sail. Having had a glimpse of the Socotrine Islands, where much of our medicinal aloes is obtained, we entered the fine deep harbour of Colombo, where steamers of any size are safely anchored behind a grand solid stone breakwater of about a mile in length, and a fine promenade for the townspeople. As the Indian mail had not arrived we had the whole day before us, so we went ashore to visit this picturesque town, so prettily embosomed in its evergreen trees, yielding abundance of fruit of many kinds. Declining a ride in the quaint two-wheel vehicles drawn by a man between the shafts, we chartered a waggonette and paid the museum a visit, which contains a fine collection of Singalese objects of natural history, notably the turtles, which I should say are the largest in the universe, and snakes of a prodigious size. Being Sunday, we attended Divine service in the cathedral, a small church of no pretensions to beauty, and while we were inside a violent tropical rain came down, which passed through the wooden roof, warped into cracks by heat, down the walls, and out at the doors, a wonderful sight for English eyes; but the deluge of water did not distract the attention of the congregation or upset the placid native mind, who entered heartily into the responses and the singing with a correctness of pronunciation which we at home are strangers to. The native portion of the town was very smelly and dirty, with a surface drainage, and appears built on marshy ground, hardened by added soil and regularly dyked and drained, but in the new part the buildings are good and solid—even fine, such as the barracks. All the streets are made to radiate in a straight line towards the park as to a common centre. The public roads are beautifully kept, and as smooth as those made with asphalt. A large body of Lascars left our vessel at Colombo, their three years of contract service being over with the P. and O. Company, and when they left the ship they gave three good hearty English cheers from the barge, showing how well they had been treated by the Company's officers and crews. I was much pleased with the natives, who conduct themselves in a very orderly, quiet manner, and seem well contented under their English rulers, under whom they thrive and have implicit faith. The free-and-easy way in which the local jewellers trust our people is something astonishing, putting a wonderful trust in an Englishman's word. In one case I heard of a city man who was entrusted with £15 worth of jewels on approval, and when he got to London had the stones tested and valued, and the tradesman, being an expert, offered him £50 for his bargain, which he declined, whereupon the owner sent off at once his cheque to Colombo. On his return to Melbourne he invested a much larger amount on the same condition, the precious stones being principally sapphires in settings of cheap gold, the usual custom with the Singalese makers, and the same good faith was observed by both parties. It is not an easy matter to distinguish the sexes; the male has a very scanty beard, and both he and his mate wear their coal-black wavy hair long behind, and wind it up into a knot on the head. The cut of the man's features is decidedly feminine. They are both very cheery and amiable, and dearly love money-making. The very lowest are so industrious and thrifty that they get on and become rich. We had no time to take a trip by train to Candy, a town in the mountains 8,000 feet above the sea-level, which is cool and beautiful, and where tea plantations are numerous. That man deserves well of his country, and indeed of Europe too, and his name ought to be perpetuated by a splendid monument, who first thought of substituting the tea for the coffee plant in Ceylon, when the latter had by repeated cropping exhausted the soil! I must not forget to mention that there is in the public gardens a tree called "the Traveller's Palm," from which, when nicked, fresh water flows out. We need to reside in a hot and thirsty land to appreciate fully this God-sent provision to His people. Our distance here from England is 7,058 miles.

Leaving Colombo at 1 p.m., and steaming down its beautifully wooded coast, green to its water edge with palms and cocoanut trees, we cross the Line at midnight of the next day, and the following morning we are 170 miles south of it, traversing a dead-calm sea without a sign of life on, or in, the water, not even a flying fish disporting itself to vary our monotony. We had not proceeded much further southward before we encountered the South-East Trade Wind, which slightly headed us all the way to Western Australia, and more or less disturbed the equanimity of some of our fair passengers, especially when the deck chairs broke away from their moorings, often causing a ludicrous upset. We had shipped at Colombo a very pleasant and intelligent traveller, Mr. Theo. Davis, our British Vice-Consul at Honolulu, who had been touring through India with his son, a gentleman who took a deep and active part in mission work, especially among the young men and children in the Haiwaia Islands, where he was the proprietor of some very extensive sugar plantations. His cheery conversation, interspersed with most amusing anecdotes, kept our saloon table quite lively; and what with concerts, dancing, and theatricals, we passed away many hours that would otherwise have been very dull and wearisome, and tended to shorten the ten days' steaming required before we could be landed at St. George's Sound, the first point the mail steamers touch at on the Australian continent. It is very remarkable that between Colombo and this point we never sighted a single vessel, nor had we a glimpse of any land nor the sight of any living thing, fish, flesh, or fowl—which is very astonishing considering the immense expanse of ocean we had traversed, 3,390 miles. We are here 10,448 miles from our dear old home, and as this chapter has been rather a prolonged yarn, I shall rest upon my oars awhile before I begin another which will be descriptive of scenes and people so widely different to those we have left behind at the Antipodes.

CHAPTER XIX.

ALBANY is the name of the town and port in King George's Sound where the mails are left for Western Australia. It possesses a fine long pier, supporting a railway, cranes, &c., but the water is too shallow to allow large vessels to come up alongside of it, hence we had to land from a steam-tug. We found the town a progressive one, with several good buildings, especially those for public worship. Overlooking the town and harbour is a steep hill, up which we ascended, and from the top were rewarded with a magnificent view inland of forty miles, and with the sea and shipping at our feet. The ground was covered with a variety of wild flowers, notably with the white-blossomed myrtle. Our party returned to the ship laden with a large quantity of these flowers, which made the saloon quite gay-looking.

We took on board here an immense quantity of bananas, which is a regular article of commerce, and the huge spikes of fruit were suspended by their strong stalks over the deck-houses to ripen. Albany is the terminus of the railway to Perth, which is the capital city of Western Australia. Considering that we were now, December 19th, in midsummer at the Antipodes, the air was so cool that we required our winter wraps, and this, with a roughish sea, continued all the way to Adelaide, which we reached on Sunday morning, December 22nd. This city is situated about six miles from the landing-stage—a stage from which is exported the finest wheat in the world—where we deposited several of our passengers, whose acquaintance had ripened into pleasant friendship during our voyage, and from whom we had pressing invitations to go and stay, with characteristic Australian hospitality; but the heat is intense to a fresh European, the town being located in a sort of well-like hollow, backed by hills to the north and east, which seem to concentrate the rays of the sun into a sort of focus below. These hills are a very pretty object from the deck of our vessel, being thickly wooded, and dotted here and there with white villas peeping out of the green—residences of the well-to-do merchants who reside there during the hot months. The railway to Melbourne zig-zags over them also, and the views, they say, from this line are very grand. Many persons leave the ships at this port of call in order to enjoy the splendid prospects, and get to Melbourne much quicker than we can steam it. Here we revelled in the luxurious Adelaide grape, and we took on board a large quantity of eight different kinds of delicious fruits to add enjoyment to our Christmas dinner, and also piles of evergreens and flowers to decorate our saloons and drawing-rooms. It was at Adelaide that we received our first Antipodean telegram, hailing from Sydney, giving us a hearty welcome to the Australian Colonies, warning us that we had touched the fringe of civilisation again, though we were now 11,455 miles from home.

Continuing our course northward, we arrived on Monday night in sight of Melbourne, having been piloted up the tortuous channel of Port Philip for forty miles, and reached the harbour of Williamstown, to which we were securely lashed at 10 p.m. Here we were in deep water, and there is a terminus of a short line to the city. As we were to remain there all Tuesday, we took our seats in the train and went off to pay a visit to this wonderful upshot of a mushroom town which shows what heaps of gold can do in a short space of time. It would be simply futile to try to describe the magnificence of some of its public buildings. They are on such a gigantic scale that I do not believe there is a town in Europe which can boast of so many in so small a space. The Houses of Parliament, isolated in their splendid public gardens, and the Town Hall are superb in size and architecture, and strike the visitor with wonder; and no less so do also the extraordinary height of the stores and offices in Collins Street and Elizabeth Street, some running up to an elevation of thirteen stories, so valuable has become the ground for building purposes. In Burke and Owenson Streets we met the fashionables promenading in their Sunday best, it being Christmas week; and though an Englishman would say that the get-up was, upon the whole, rather loud and vulgar, still one could see that the crowds were well-off, and no signs of poverty were visible whatever. Melbourne is a very extensive city, spreading over a large area, with outlying suburbs of considerable size and population—some as much as 10,000—made up of four-roomed shanties in plots of ground, the occupier being the owner; and when a man has by industry and thrift acquired one of these freeholds, he has a vote and a stake in the welfare of the city, and he becomes a true Conservative in feeling and principle, and you hear no more of socialism or rowdyism, divide and divide again, &c.; and though they listen attentively to what Mr. George has to say, they end in laughing at him. Mr. R., a well-known and extensive merchant in Melbourne, asked us to stay with him. He was brimful of information respecting the social, political, and religious aspect of the city, and he told me that, provided the wants and needs of the Church were clearly made manifest to the people, money to any amount was always forthcoming both for the clergy and the buildings.

Taking our seats in a cable tram, we came down Collins Street with a fearful rush to Spencer Station, where we got into the train for Williamstown, and on the road down we passed close to the race-ground, most peculiarly and conveniently situated in a hollow, with an amphitheatre of hilly slopes around it, so that men, women, and children can look down, in their thousands, and enjoy the races at their feet in comfort and safety. This natural formation of the land would have been singularly well adapted for the Olympic games, and only required a canvas covering to make it a Coloseum on a gigantic scale.

We passed Christmas Day at sea, between Melbourne and Sydney, and at luncheon we had a most luxurious display of viands, comprising a large boar's head stuffed with minced meat; a game pie decorated with a pheasant's head and tail feathers; and in the centre a huge cake three feet high, replete with ornaments on its three stories, and crowned by Old Father Christmas in his own proper costume, backed by dishes of prawns in jelly, crayfish, &c. The big saloon, itself beautiful in white and gold, was rendered still more so by a most elaborate arrangement of evergreens and flowers, the work of our fifty waiters. At 7 p.m. we sat down to a dinner of several courses of delicacies in season and out of season, such as the richest nobleman in England could not have got together for love or money. We had, of course, to thank our refrigerator for yielding, as from a huge ice-house, such things as green peas and ducks, fresh salmon, game of all sorts, brought from home to supply us the whole voyage out—and to top all we had a dessert set before us consisting of eight different kinds of fresh fruits, such as would gladden the eye and moisten the palate of the most exacting epicure.

I got up at 5 a.m. to see the sun rise over the Pacific, and to enjoy one of the most lovely sights in the world, namely, the entrance into Sydney Harbour by the "Heads," a narrow passage between two sharp rocky projections, and a glorious trip up the port for seven miles to Sydney itself. *En route* the scenery is unique, consisting of pretty creeks, and suburban villas on the slopes of well-wooded hills, always green to the water edge, and piebalded with white villas, all protected by verandahs, and some more pretentious with towers or turrets. The harbour was dotted here

SYDNEY.

and there with many yachts of all sorts and sizes (every Sydneyite being a born yachtsman), interspersed with a large sprinkling of huge steamers and sailing vessels hailing from every clime, and as we neared the " circular quay "—the well-known landing place—we passed six men-of-war sleepily at anchor, keeping guard over this, one of the wealthiest and most bustling of ports. Within so small a water area I should opine that there is not in the whole commercial world so much energy and exchange of commodity going on as at this, only one of the quays of the city. The number of landing stages, the repeated going to and fro of the local steamers to the different points of this port, consisting of a multiplication of inlets, each with its stage and adjoining gigantic warehouses, a collection of busy centres most perplexing and confusing to a stranger at first. Not one-half of the extent of these active shipping points can be seen from any one spot on the opposite, or what is called the " North Shore," nor can the harbour be photo'ed as a whole, though what one can take in is a wonderful sight under a brilliant clear sky. Perhaps the grandest view of all is obtained from the top of the lighthouse built near the south " Head." The electric light radiated from this tower is so powerful that it quite dazzled my vision as I was sitting in a drawing-room window four miles away, and from the top of it I saw one day upwards of thirty yachts racing up and down the harbour—a very pretty panorama as they each turned round the light-ship with their white sails glistening in the sun. I will not attempt a description of the public buildings

TOWN HALL, SYDNEY.

in Sydney—they are so many; but the Post Office, Cathedral, and especially the Town Hall, stand out pre-eminently beautiful, notably the latter, which the Sydneyites may well be proud of, as containing the largest organ in the largest hall in the world.

The people of this city are a picnic-loving community, and to carry this pleasure into practice make a holiday whenever they can devise an excuse. Wishing to see how a party of excursionists would conduct themselves, I early one morning joined a train going to the Hawksbury River with about four hundred men, women, and children, surprisingly got up in their holiday attire of silks, muslins, and feathered hats, with their brown arms and hands encased in long gloves to hide their workaday look. When we arrived at Peat's Ferry on this river, called the Rhine of Australia, we boarded a steamer, which took us up a remarkable serpentine stream, having this singular peculiarity, that after turning one promontory we get into a sort of lake-like reach which appears completely land-locked, and when one gets to the end, and you fancy the steamer is going headlong into the rock, it suddenly turns round and gets into another reach of the same appearance. The banks are very picturesque, and would yield many a good landscape, the red sandstone rock standing out from thick foliage and the eucalyptus issuing from the crevices interspersed with many flowering shrubs—notably the red Christmas bush—and dotted here and there with wooden villas for summer residences, which are shut up during the winter. On our return we had an opportunity of examining the fine railway suspension bridge consisting of seven spans, each of 480 feet long. It produces quite an ocular delusion, for the further span when viewed from either end appears so small-looking that one cannot believe that it is the same width and height. The engineers have been much complimented on this fine piece of iron trellis-work.—Now with respect to the behaviour of this company of pleasure-seekers. I have never in any country witnessed anything so well conducted and orderly. The characteristic "billy tea tin" accompanied each family, and I did not see any one drink any intoxicating beverage whatever; hence there was no rowdyism, or practical joking, or vulgar brawling, and when they entered the train for the homeward journey of a hundred miles it was done as quietly as if they had been so many lords and ladies, instead of the representatives of every working class in the city—for all are expected to join the fraternity of working men and women, if they mean to hold their own in busy Sydney. Before we left the Hawksbury, I should have mentioned that I saw a catfish caught which has a nail-like spear projecting from its head, and a stab from which is so much dreaded by the fishermen as it is very dangerous, and also what they call the stinging fish, which strikes with its tail and hurts one considerably. It being a hot day many would have enjoyed a good bathe, but they feared the sharks, which ascend this river from the sea. Before proceeding to descant upon the Sydney races and the caves in the Blue Mountains, I shall rest awhile.

CHAPTER XX.

On Saturday, January 4th, I paid the racecourse at Ranwick a visit of inspection. It is situated on a flat with rising ground on one side, so that the whole circle can be clearly seen without going on the grand stand. Racing is quite an institution among the Sydney people, they are a regular horsey class. Every colonist is born, as it were, in the saddle. The races occur about once a fortnight, the prizes are of small amount. I saw both flat and hurdle races. The bulk of the horses differ from ours about the rump, which slopes downwards like a barb, and tends to bring the hocks closer together; but they have the advantage over English horses in having deeper chests with very muscular forelegs and well-developed large joints, with the head small and stag-like. I saw twenty run in one race and eighteen in another, and they were all so fleet that they ran throughout in such close quarters that one might have covered them with a sheet; no one horse beat his opponent by a length or two, as one sees so often in England. The two-year-old stands up in as good a form as our three-year-old does, thanks to the climate and the grass. In one race I saw twenty horses jump the hurdles almost simultaneously, and came to the post in a ruck together like a flock of pigeons, and coloured like a bed of pansies—one of the prettiest sights I ever beheld. I cannot say much for the betting ring; it was about as noisy as Epsom, differing, however, in this, that many ladies came down from the grand-stand and joined the groups of gentlemen in the gambling ground, and it is to be hoped acted as checks to bets of extravagant amount. The crowd outside were very orderly and good-tempered, and the book-keepers, being all publicly registered, confined the stakes to the small sums of one shilling or half-a-crown. I saw no drunkenness on the course, nor any strong drink taken in the booths, but there was a large demand for fruit, which was excellent and cheap, and the "billy tea tin" was not forgotten. There was none of that "rough" element present which is so prevalent on English race-grounds; and as I walked back with the crowd to the city I saw no disorderly horseplay whatever. The women and children were quite safe from insult or molestation of any kind. I could not help asking myself, are all these people, the outcome of every class, really the offspring of English people? Well, all I can say is, I wish their relatives at home would behave as well. I can bring in a word here about Sunday closing; in Sydney they have it, and one Sunday night I was returning from the north shore, and passed along the streets in the principal thoroughfares, and I found all so quiet and peaceful that it might be well compared to a city of the dead! I was told that if a man is seen zig-zagging along in a state of drunkenness in the public streets, he is immediately "run in" by the police, when we, in our large towns, would let them alone to find their way home, provided they were not disorderly; but in Sydney, whether disorderly or not, the authorities are down upon them sharp, and will not look on with indifferentism upon such a reproach to social morality.

No visitor should fail to take a tram-ride of six miles to see the pretty little bay of Coogee, a sweet nook nestling in shrubs, and rapidly becoming a popular sea-bathing resort for the citizens. It would be well also, in order to judge of the wide extent of the other outlying suburbs, all in touch with one another as far as the large town of Paramatta—a distance of sixteen miles from the mother city, and forms a very interesting ride by railway, which gives also a good idea of the huge area upon which this widespread city is built, each suburban villa or mansion being surrounded by its own well-wooded grounds. Balmain, so well seen from the Observatory Gardens in Sydney, is situated on a spur of land running into the port, and is now a large municipal town of itself; there one can see how the thrifty artisans are building houses for themselves, and very near may be seen a new grand dock, which is excavated out of the solid sandstone rock on one side of Cockatoo Island, which will take in the largest steamers afloat. Having obtained an introduction to Major ——, the manager of the Mint, he kindly showed and explained to me the whole process, from the assaying to the blocking out of each sovereign, which, if it were two-tenths of a grain too light was cast aside by the working of a very singular automatic piece of machinery, the amount of alloy being 11 per cent., as in England. I was asked to take a seat on the platform and give an address to an audience of several hundred men at the Young Men's Christian Association Hall, which the working-men put up at a cost of £40,000. It contains a library and reading-room, a gymnasium, and a coffee-room, &c. I was told that I should have to face a large body of sceptics, who would not attend any ordinary place of public worship, but would slip into this hall and listen to its bright and cheerful music, and tolerate without a sneer or interruption the short addresses from different *laymen* on the subject of morals and religion.

Rising up early one morning, I took the train to the Blue Mountains, at the foot of which we crossed the Nepean River, that supplies Sydney with water—a distance of forty miles—irrigating also the Emu plain, noted for its extensive orange and peach plantations. Our train begins the ascent by zigzagging, being drawn up one incline, and pushed up the next by the engine and carriages going into a siding at each angle, thus reversing the order of going at every gradient, till we reached the plateau, or dividing ridge, when we went along a slight rise till we got to Mount Victoria. Finding that I had time to spare, I continued on, to see a grand engineering feat—the "Great Zig-zag," which terminates the mountain railway and brings one down to the town of Lithgow, in a valley boasting of four valuable colleries and a large pottery manufactory, the manager of which was kind enough to show me the whole pro-

ZIG-ZAG RAILWAY, BLUE MOUNTAINS, LITHGOW VALLEY, N.S.W.

cess. He complained of the competition and other difficulties the company had to contend with, by the old country deluging the Sydney market with its condemned goods, the imperfections of which the squatter could not detect.

On my return journey, the scenery from the Zigzag was even grander, and I had plenty of time to dwell upon it, as the ascent is a slow affair, and done on the same system as I have already described. Mount Victoria was my resting-spot for the night, in a fairly good hotel, but the bed was very hard. This mount is covered with villas and a few restaurants, and is the resort of residents from the hot towns during the summer month. Here the climate puts one in mind of Scotland.

The next morning we were up to an early breakfast, and took our seats in a coach, which carried its eight passengers to the "Half Way" house, as it is called, where we lunched, and having changed horses, continued our journey, through dense forests of eucalyptus, till we reached the Caves, now named "Janelon," at six o'clock, in time for dinner; the constant jolting over the ruts having made us desperately hungry. The one hotel here, occupying, with a road and a small brook, the whole of a pretty little creak, is styled "The Accommodation House," but was not very accommodating, it being crowded with tourists, twenty-nine of whom had to make the most of twenty-four beds. Professor L——, of the Sydney University—a most learned and agreeable companion—and myself were fortunate in getting a small bedroom, with two beds in it. Mr. Jeremiah Wilson, the proprietor and discoverer of the caverns, gave us most excellent meals, considering the distance we were from any stores. The next morning I made one of a party of ladies and gentlemen, overflowing with life and good-humour, to pay the right-half of the Imperial Cave a visit, which is lightened up by Government with electricity, and our guide illuminated the more beautiful parts with the addition of the combustion from the magnesian wire, each person having to pay five shillings towards this item of expense, otherwise everything else is free. I will not attempt to describe minutely the splendid dazzling beauties of this huge underground cavern. The white and red colouring in distinct divisions of what is called " The Shawl and Curtain Drapery " is most peculiar, and as transparent as hanging sheets of porcelain. Again, another remarkable feature is the singular shape of the stalactites in the Mystery Cave, where they assume most fantastic forms—some like twigs of trees pointing sideways, and some even upwards, which is quite inexplicable considering that the accretion from the carbonate of lime in solution is from above, and the natural gravitation downwards. The bones of wallambi and other animals are found here encrusted in the deposit, and when the crust is broken the bone within is found intact. A good specimen was shown to me of a small vertebra and a jaw-bone, with alveolar process complete, and these in a cavern six hundred feet below the surface. Another wonderful sight is the " Broken Column," the upper part not being in line with the lower, which can only be explained by an earthquake breaking and diverting the column from its original position, how many thousands of years ago I will leave geologists to determine! The cavern called "Lucinda," after the wife of the discoverer, is sweetly pretty, and it boasts of a fine specimen of the ~~shute~~ formation. After a good deal of stooping and corkscrew ascents and descents, we regained the iron gate which bars the entrance, and returned to the hotel to luncheon, after which refreshment we started again to explore the left half of the Imperial Cave. This is very much a repetition of the right half, with this very important exception, we had to visit the Underground River, which was to be reached by descending a dark shaft of 50 feet by means of a wire-rope ladder of thirty-two rungs, which vibrated most alarmingly. The first round had to be seized in a doubled-up position, and in this cramped attitude we made the first step downward and feel our way from rung to rung till we got into a pit of Egyptian darkness, for we could not carry lights. When once at the bottom, we found ourselves at the side of a quiet, flowing stream of pure limpid water, cool and refreshing to the taste, down which the visitors amused themselves by sailing on its surface wooden floats, on which were fixed lighted pieces of candle, which gave to the sides and roof of the tunnel a weird, unearthly aspect, and only wanted a blue sulphur flame to make it look like Dante's Inferno! Now one would suppose that this feat would be difficult enough for men to do, but four ladies of the party had sufficient strength of nerve to accomplish it, and seeing this, though many years their senior, I made up my mind not to be beaten by women, colonial or otherwise. Hence I summoned up courage to face the peril, and descended safely, amid applause. I need hardly say that our ladies did not hail from Belgravia. These afternoon explorations were rather fatiguing, and we emerged again to the light of day with intense appetites that made a deep impression on Mrs. Taylor's dinner, the cloud of flies notwithstanding. In the evening we entertained ourselves with music and singing, and I recited some anecdotes connected with my Crimean war experiences, which amused the colonists not a little—the Baby Incident exciting much sympathy in the minds of the fair sex. The next morning we paid a visit to the Lucas Cave, which is remarkable for the huge dimensions of its cavities. The Exhibition Cavern, as it is called, being two hundred yards in circumference, and required two hours to see it properly. The winding zig-zag descent to it is weird looking in the extreme, when you look back and upwards and see the visitors coming down in single file, each with a candle in hand, stumbling and falling now and again with a horrid, ghost-like screech, and enveloped in pitch-like darkness, they resembled so many shapeless demons going down into the bottomless pit. The swaling of the candles over the dresses of the ladies and the coats of the gentlemen, gave rise to much laughter, as the spots of grease on each person gave them the appearance of a spotted hyena, but they all took it in good humour, as it was impossible to hold the candlestick straight when one's attention was directed to all sorts of curious sights. The bespattering of your neighbour went on in perfect innocence, while you in your turn were served exactly alike, because we were all on different levels. In the afternoon we visited the "Devil's Coachhouse," an immense cavern, 200 feet high, open to enter at both ends, and lighted by a large opening in the centre of the roof. I could not throw a stone with all my force one-third of the way to its ceiling, and a wooden gallery made round its roof for visitors to see the interior the better, looked very queer—their bodies resembled midgets in size and their voices sounded as if they came from the skies, and calling out to me, said that I looked like a small fly seated on a rock at the bottom. There were other caves to explore, but I had had enough; and I left the next morning at 5 a.m., having had a high time of it; though it did rain a good deal I was sorry to leave such a pleasant company. I drove back alone in a buggy and pair, and passed through the Hartley Valley, where the hares are so numerous that an English sportsman is asked as a favour by the farmers to shoot them. And the wallambi, a sort of small kangaroo, is met with frequently, for whose scalp fivepence is given and for the skin sevenpence. They boast also some pretty feathered pigeons and parrots, but no rabbits trouble them in the mountains. The grass is so rich and nourishing that the oxen are as sleek and fat as those stall-fed at home. When we arrived at the ridge of the hills I was shown two small rivulets, one going west and originating the River Murray, and the other passing eastward and forming the Nepean River, which supplies Sydney with water. I could not help remonstrating with my coachman for driving his horses so fast, and never slackening rein on hill or dale. They are nearly thoroughbred, and they are strained most unmercifully, for they only last about four years, and then turned over to the cart or the plough. They are replaced by fresh young horses which are cheap, costing £4 or £5 a head. This plan the coach proprietors find pays better than feeding the poor animals on corn to keep them up to their work; fortunately for the poor beasts the grass is very nutritious. The wind and endurance of the colonial horse strikes an Englishman with wonder—a British horse in harness could not stand such work for a week—and their surefootedness is astonishing down or uphill, along rough roads full of ruts, sludge, and loosened stones they keep on their legs, which are as fine as racehorses'; their great strength lies in the shoulder and in a very muscular forearm. On returning to Victoria Mount I had an opportunity of admiring the celebrated Victoria Pass, which consists of a gulf between two precipitous cliffs, bridged over by a wonderful piece of masonry of great ingenuity. It was constructed by the convicts in days gone by, one of whom cut his name on the rock. The gorges visible on each side the bridge are 1,000 feet deep, and looking down from the stone causeway the big fir trees at the bottom look like so many blades of grass. I was shown the building in which the chain gang were confined during the night, and also the court-house where they were tried for misbehaviour. These places are now used for better purposes. In the valleys coal is found, and at the pit's mouth is sold at four shillings a ton. Shale is also present, from which they distil kerosene. Some of the trees are very large, and of great age, the rings in some indicating a thousand years. When the squatter wishes to clear the ground for grazing, he kills the trees by removing a ring of the bark, then it dies and stands up denuded of leaves, and the grass grows up at the foot. The old trees often rot in the centre, and in the cavity thus made the people make a fire to cook their food, and take shelter from snow and rain. Before I take leave of this land of caves I must just parody what the Book of books says with regard "to those who go down to the sea in ships, and see the works of the Lord and His wonders in the deep," by stating that they who go down into the bowels of the earth at the Janelon Caves see also the wonders of the Lord hidden from sight in the midst of the rocks! for these mighty hollows ought and should be seen by every visitor to New South Wales, for it is impossible for any one to exaggerate their superb grandeur.

CHAPTER XXI.

BEFORE leaving Sydney, I must not fail to state that the best mode of seeing this beautiful port, with its numerous harbours, is to charter a steam launch, and begin at Manley Beach and the middle harbour, then cross to Watson's Bay, and so work upwards, crossing and recrossing till every inlet is seen and admired, finishing up with a trip along the Paramatta river, whose banks are picturesquely dotted with the villas of the rich and their woody inclosures. Having left my card and address at Government House, his lordship being away in the mountains during the summer, I left this charming city with great reluctance, and took my passage for the Island of Tasmania, which is a two days' voyage due south from Australia. This colony rejoices in two large prosperous towns, one at the north end, and the other at the south, 130 miles apart. Launceston, at the north end, is prettily situated on rising ground, sloping down to the Tamar, a tidal river, and a brisk trade is carried on in tin and wool and apples. Here I resided for some time at the house of an old magistrate, who was well up in the history and commerce of the island. On Sunday we attended

FERN TREE VALLEY, SCOTSDALE, TASMANIA.

Divine service at St. John's Church, built of stone by the convicts in days gone by. The sermon and service were decidedly sluggish, the temperature in the shade being 97°, so it was excusable. On Tuesday we took our places in a train which went zigzagging through the mountain wilds to a township called Scotsdale, passing *en route* some exquisitely beautiful creeks and water-gullies, with lots of tree ferns in them. Here we had an opportunity of walking into the primeval forest, and examining the huge trees, some upright and some fallen, centuries ago. Avenues of dead trees most weird in appearance, produced by "bush fires," and bounded on each side by the green eucalyptus, extend to a great distance. These dead monsters are called skeletons —looked ghostlike—and when the interior, which is like tinder is ignited, it goes on burning to the very top, then falls from its own weight. I should say that these monster trees, from their origin to their fall, would be at least 2,000 years old. In this locality grows the wattle tree, the bark of which yields three times as much tannin as our bark, and is largely exported to the tanyards of England and America. At Waverley, a short drive from Launceston, there is a woollen factory in a pretty creek among the hills, where an enterprising Scotchman, with the aid of a well-directed water-power, and supplemented by a Government subsidy, has succeeded in erecting some modern machinery, which will turn out all kinds of cloth, good enough for volunteer uniforms, trouserings, shawls, and blankets. I was surprised to see that the proprietor had got the electric light laid on for the works, and also to hear that he could not put up with the free-and-easy way of the local colonials, and found it paid better to import his employés direct from Scotland. The great sight which the Launcestonians are so proud of showing the visitor is the wild-looking Gorge. A tortuous path leads up the hill commanding the Gorge, through which gushes the turbulent river Esk, and when a similar pathway is completed on the opposite side, and the two rocky banks are united by a suspension bridge, a view will be obtained of rock, wood, and rushing frothy waters, as can hardly be surpassed in any part of the world, enhanced as the prospect is by the pretty upstanding town and shipping harbour at one's feet. The tourist should not fail to pay a visit to the tin-smelting works close at hand, and see the ingots of metal moulded, and which are shipped in large quantities to Europe. The heat from the furnaces is intense, and the fine body of men were streaming down with perspiration; and on my inquiring whether they quenched their thirst with beer or any alcoholic liquor, they all replied unreservedly that they had tried it over and over again, but found from experience that they could not do with it at all; and that oatmeal and water was the only thing that could support them under the fearful strain of such physical pressure. Finally, I must mention that in the Museum will be seen, a fine, clever picture by Dowling, a native artist, representing a group of the aborigines—very repulsive, but life-like; also some good specimens of one from the Bischoff tin mines, which should be visited if any one is desirous of seeing for himself the richness of this colony in minerals. It would be ungrateful not to mention how I enjoyed the delicious apricots, peaches, and plums, from standard trees, so refreshing in the hot weather, and which adorn the tables at every meal, accompanied, as in Australia, with tea, coffee, and cocoa, but no stronger drinks whatever. Receiving a pressing invitation to a friend's house in the centre of the island, we left the hospitable roof of the old magistrate, and made our way by the main line to Ross, where we were met by our host, and driven in a carriage a few miles into the country, where a new experience awaited me. This gentleman lived on his own estate of 5,000 acres, which fed 3,000 Merino sheep—400 of which were a stud stock, several having taken valuable prizes at the agricultural show. One ewe especially had distinguished itself, having taken a silver cup twice over, and yielded a fleece weighing $22\frac{1}{2}$lbs., a fact difficult to believe in England, where we get only 7 or 8 lbs. of wool from a sheep; but thanks to the climate and the nutritious nature of the grass, these heavy fleeces are not uncommon in Tasmania. A large river runs through the property about 500 yards from the house, and an American windmill pump sends the water up to the house and gardens, which, by irrigation, yields an abundance of the usual fruits with the addition of cherries, strawberries, and grapes. The rabbits were the great plague on this station; it might be defined the irrepressible rodent, as its fecundity and multiplication is so rapid that our friend had to keep going two men throughout the year, who were paid £1 each per week, to suppress the nuisance. It was but small pay for that colony as they had to find their own ammunition, but they liked the sport and stuck to it. I believe they get some small capitation fee for each scalp from the Government. I only saw one live kangaroo on the estate; they are gradually being exterminated, as they eat up the grass, and, besides, their skins are valuable. A great domestic inconvenience in the home life of the island is the difficulty of obtaining female servants, and when you have got them to retain them, for if they are at all nice looking and capable, they are sure to be snatched up by the men and married. And in a country place this family trouble is still more felt with regard to men servants, since nothing, love or money, will induce them to work indoors, their whole heart is bent on an out-of-door life. One day we drove off to pay a call at Mona Vale, one of the grandest mansions in the colony, where the Duke of Edinburgh was entertained. There I fully expected to see a butler and two footmen at least; no, nothing of the kind, only a quiet-looking young woman answered the door, but in the gardens, which were beautifully kept up, I observed three gardeners at work. We then paid the Principal of Horton College a visit, where young men are educated, and there also female domestics waited upon us. Though our host was a member of the Legislative Assembly, a magistrate and warden of his township, and the owner of a flourishing estate, such was this difficulty and worry in connection with indoor servants experienced by him and his household, that his wife and daughters, ladies in every sense of the word, were obliged to give an active hand in many little domestic arrangements—in fact, while one moment they would be helping to clear the dining table, the next they would be amusing us with some excellent classical music in the drawing-room, for parents as a rule in Tasmania, as in Australasia generally, make it a sacrifice and care to give their children the best education money can command. Though in the estimation of many self-made colonials money makes the man, knowledge, notwithstanding, is held in great respect, and stands forth as a dominating power. The neighbourhood of Ross is well adapted as a residence for sportsmen, there being fishing and shooting in abundance, and the horses are very fine and swift; and as each man and lady is brought up as it were in the saddle, riding exercise is very much to the fore as an every-day pleasure. Picnic parties into the mountains amid lake scenery is a common source of bringing young and old together—social gatherings which are carried on without stiffness or formality, thus knitting together in one sympathetic bond all the families for a circuit of many miles. We were loath to leave our host and his happy and cheerful surroundings of wife and children, but we had to move on, and our next stay was at Hobart, the capital of Tasmania; but we were not allowed to enter as strangers, our friend accompanied us, and he being a M.P. knew everybody and everything, hence we had a most useful and instructive cicerone. We were shown the Houses of Parliament, Government offices, the Museum rich in curios connected with the natural history of the island and its minerals, the quay where much active commerce was going on with all parts of the world, and the very extensive and beautifully situated public gardens on rising grounds overlooking the harbour and Government House. I called upon the Dean of St. David's Cathedral, and read the lessons for him on Sunday. This building is not yet completed, though the foundation stone was laid by the Duke of Edinburgh twenty years ago—in fact, the Nonconformists are much more in advance of the Church of England as to their buildings, especially the Congregationalists, who have a very fine freestone Gothic building with a high spire in Elizabeth Street. Hobart is in a lovely situation, at the foot of Mount Wellington, which is often capped with snow even in the summer time, and which should by all means be ascended, especially as half way the coaches land you at Ferntree Arbour, a charming spot shaded with large tree ferns. Now having explored the city, I will just relate as shortly as possible what the traveller ought to see. Let him go down to the pier and take the excursion steamer to what is called the "Eagle Hawk's Neck," a narrow strip of land which joins the Tasman peninsula to the mainland. This point was guarded formerly by dogs and soldier sentries, to prevent the convicts from escaping into the open country; their penal settlement being on the peninsula, located at a place called Port Arthur, now falling into ruins. The courageous and daring attempts to pass the dogs and sentries by the convicts were quite romantic, but they invariably ended in disaster by a well-directed shot, or if they escaped the bullet starvation stared them in the Bush, where food was scarce and difficult to get without firearms. Those who would wish to read these harrowing accounts, so sensational and blood curdling, should get a book entitled "For the Term of his Natural Life," written by a convict, a gentleman who had been transported for a crime for which he was quite innocent. In those days many persons were exiled for very slight offences. It is rather a stiff walk from the "Neck" to the "Blowhole," a natural curiosity in the shape of a tunnel through a rock through which the sea rushes with a deafening roar!

Another trip worth taking is to go by steamer to the viaduct which crosses the Derwent river some miles above Hobart, and then take the train to Plenty Station, then get out and walk to the artificial ponds, where salmon and trout are hatched, and when matured turned out into the Derwent, where they afford capital sport to the angler, who uses a live grasshopper on a bare hook, and soon fills his basket. The curator kindly supplied our party with tea at the side of the pools, where we amused ourselves watching and feeding the young fish which were quite tame, and the keeper could whip out any of the larger ones with an artificial fly for our inspection, and then throw them back again. In this valley we had a good view of some luxuriant hop plantations, and thousands of acres of apple orchards, bearing some most tempting fruit grown to a great size in a well-irrigated loam soil. The jam factories in Hobart are quite an institution, and are supplied to any extent by fruit from these prolific valleys.

yielding peaches, apricots, and plums, from *standard* trees, pruned down to about 12 feet. There is now a large export trade of apples to London, since they have learnt how to pack them properly. Thousands of cases of this fruit in the green state are shipped off to England in chartered steamers, where they fetch a high price, as they arrive in our country in the winter time. I doubt not it will not be long before a plan is discovered of exporting the fresh apricots and peaches as well.

Before we part company with Hobart and our dear kind-hearted friend, I must make a remark upon the young women. They are well formed and strong, tall, and walk uprightly, with complexions and good looks which will bear favourable comparison with those we meet with in any of our own large towns. The men are tall and well set up, and it is not an uncommon thing to see men on the streets who stand 6 feet 2 inches or 6 feet 3 inches in height. We bade adieu to Hobart on a Friday, taking our passage to New Zealand in the well-equipped steamer *Mararoa*, in rather gusty weather which sent the ladies to their berths. This continued all Saturday, and more or less on Sunday, in consequence of which we had no religious service, though there were three clergymen on board. On Monday night we neared the coast, and as it was not safe to enter the Bluff Harbour at night, we kept outside till morning dawned, then steamed on and reached the pier at breakfast time, after which we ascended a steep hill of 600 feet, flying the signalling flag, and from thence we had a magnificent view over sea and land. On Wednesday we had reached Port Chalmers, where our steamer was put into a dry dock, so we had plenty of leisure to make our way to Dunedin, eight miles off by train, where an international exhibition was being held of colonial produce and manufactures. If we wished to see evidences of the astounding progress our colonies have made, we could not have had a better opportunity than the fine display at Dunedin, a Scotchified town, where the people of any other nationality were boycotted till a few years ago, so jealous and selfish were its founders. They may well be proud of their grand stone buildings, especially their churches; one in particular, standing out pre-eminently so, the Presbyterian, which is like a noble Gothic cathedral, with a splendid tapering spire. The town is prettily situated on steep hills and well-wooded dales, up and down which rush cable-trams at a furious rate, which the residents state were the first ever started in the world. The views from these various suburban eminences are simply charming, grasping in a bird's-eye prospect the long port and island opposite, the public park, the University college, and other large prominent buildings which the industrious, thrifty, and canny Scotchman has erected. And, though last not least, the sight of its wide streets, lined with large shops and high plate-glass windows, displaying their elegant wares from every country; its banks and hotels, to compare with which there is nothing so English-like in any other town in New Zealand.

CHAPTER XXII.

No one should leave Port Chalmers without ascending to the cemetery, which is well laid out as a flower garden and public recreation ground, situated on a rocky plateau overlooking the harbour and pier, and dominating also the peninsula on which the town is built, and around which a good drive has been made yielding pleasant views in every direction. There is also a striking object in the form of a very fine stone-built Presbyterian church, in the Gothic style, with high-tapering spire, perched on a pinnacle of rock, such as one sees in some Roman Catholic towns in Europe. We are here 1,034 miles from Hobart, and continuing our course along the eastern coast we arrive after a passage of 200 miles at Lyttleton Harbour, the port of supply and export for the city of Christchurch, which is eight miles inland. This short distance was difficult to traverse, leading as the winding road did over a high mountain, and was a great impediment to commerce till it was tunnelled by an enterprising and popular superintendent of the province, Mr. Sefton Moorhouse, and a railway made to connect the port with the city. Christchurch is the centre of life in the magnificent and fertile Canterbury Plains, a fine and extensive view of which may be had from the Lyttleton hills and from the spire of the cathedral which I ascended, though the ladders are rather rickety. The plains overflow with fruitfulness irrigated as they are from the watershed from the hills which bound it on all sides, and are 100 miles apart, all the tributary streams centring in the beautiful silvery Avon, in which trout do abound, and takes a pretty serpentine course through this rich land, yielding an immense quantity of corn, wool, flax, and fruits, but especially horses, which are bred here in great numbers and then exported to India, where they produce a valuable stock for the cavalry and artillery by interbreeding with the native stud. I met a gentleman who, with his partners, owned 17,000 acres of fine pasture land; he told me nothing paid so well as the breeding of horses —cheap on the spot, but fetched a good price when they reached Calcutta. No immigrant need imagine that he can purchase land in these plains at a low figure, and unless he has a long purse he had better stay at home. The visitor should not fail to pay a visit to the splendid Museum with its large and unique collection of objects of art and of natural history; the lovely Public Gardens, through which meanders a river teeming with trout; the noble Cathedral; the old Provincial Council Chamber, the most perfect of its kind in New Zealand; the Government domain and the Botanic Gardens. As a tourist I can only summarise by saying Christchurch abounds in public institutions of every kind and need, and especially places of public worship of every known sect, even down to the Salvation Army. A very pleasant time may be spent here and in its eight extensive suburbs, some of them with 10,000 people. If the traveller desires to go further a-field, let him take the coach to Nelson through the Buller Gorge, or to the west coast by way of the Otira Gorge, or he can diverge and visit the Gold Fields at Hokitika if money fascinates him. Cook and Son help one well for boating and fishing and local excursions. Returning to Lyttleton, I may just mention that the men occupied at the shipping business don't do amiss, provided there is no loafing and shuffling. They get one shilling and threepence an hour, and with thrift and sobriety can occupy a cottage of their own in three years. The union men pay four shillings and sixpence a month to their club, and for this get during illness or incapacity for labour £1 a week for six months, then ten shillings a week for a month, and finally five shillings till they are well. The climate is delicious, like our English summer, and barring the apprehension of a coming earthquake would be a charming place to settle in and be content. A tourist fond of enjoying a picturesque sight of unusual beauty could not do better than mount one of the low hills above the town which is so prettily built on the slopes of the gullies leading down to the harbour—the streets being in terraces one above another—every square yard being utilised.

Taking a steamer, and continuing our passage along the east coast for 175 miles further north, we reach Wellington, since 1864, the capital of New Zealand, in which we land on a fine, but dusty and windy day, characteristically windy, hence its nickname, "Windy Wellington." The large Government buildings, the Houses of Assembly, and even the Governor's palace, are so many shams. In the distance you exclaim what splendid freestone structures, and when you go up to them and tap them with a finger you find that they are nothing but wooden erections, painted and rough cast with sand to represent stone; but they are very handsome, being ornamented with pillars having Corinthian capitals well carved, and elaborate cornices, and surmounted by towers or high spires. They are regarded by the citizens with great pride, and a wonder of the world as the largest buildings of wood in the universe. A Roman Catholic church perched on a pinnacle of rock high above the town was enough to deceive any one, but on going up to it was found to be wood also, but sculptured with figures at great expense. It has been discovered that it is safer to live in a wooden dwelling than a stone one in case an earthquake should pay them a visit. Their grand harbour is land-locked and has deep water to its very edge, capable of floating the largest iron-clad war vessel. The town is confined to the space between the hills and the port, of a horse-shoe shape, so that the people have been obliged to build their houses up the steep hills, and in the gullies, and on any flat available space, natural or artificial, that they could stick a building on, hence the quaint aspect of the city from any high point is picturesque in the extreme. This being so hemmed in by the guardian hills has prevented the city from spreading

landwards, and it boasts of being the most compact
town in New Zealand, the Empire City as they
love to call it. To see its extent the visitor should
take a train ride from one end of it to the other, a distance of three miles for a penny—the cheapest ride
in the world—then he will be able to judge what
a bustling, busy place is Wellington. A very good
bird's-eye view of the town and the beach where the
fashionable promenade and bathing goes on may be
obtained by ascending a winding road which leads up
to Mrs. Rhodes' house, built on a spur of the mountain at the east end of Wellington. Then again
there are other "lions" to see, such as the Botanical
Gardens situated in a creek, dotted on each side its
little streamlet with high tree-ferns, and crossed now
and again by rustic wooden bridges. English trees
have been planted here between the native, reminding
us of home. The walks are so tortuous and inter-
lacing that the garden may be compared to a Rosa-
mond's Bower, in which we might lose ourselves.
On our return through a singular looking suburb, we
noticed how curiously the villas appeared perched one
above another on plateaus of rock blasted to get a
flat basis to rest upon, and behind them the bare
mountains denuded of trees. Again an outlying
district called the "Lower Hut" is the centre of
amusement for pleasure parties; there being a racecourse, and tea gardens for picnics, &c. Before I
leave this delightful town I must not forget to say
that it is lighted with electricity; that the "publics"
are closed on Sunday; that I did not see any
drunkenness on that day, or rowdyism or brawling;

that there were no signs of pauperism nor any pawn-shops visible. General contentment seemed to prevail. Earthquakes had not visited this locality for so long a period that the speculators had taken courage and built some very grand stone and brick stores, while the authorities had erected a very fine post office and customs house on the quay. These with the huge meat-freezing factories gave the town an aspect of great commercial importance, which it merited. As at Christchurch so here, the places of public worship and schools are so numerous that every phase of religious sentiment is represented, and though the citizens may be called worshippers of Mammon the sabbath is well observed and orderly. Thus I have given a very short summary of this pleasant resting-place, which in my opinion is sufficient for the passing tourist. And now we leave Wellington and proceed not by steamer to Napier—oh! no, certainly not—the right thing to do is to take a railway ride of a hundred miles over the most interesting part of the colony, namely, over the Rimutaka Mountains to Palmerston, on the west coast. It cannot be compared to a trip over the Rocky Mountains, nevertheless, the wild scenery we meet with and the Fell engine with its central rail working up the steep gradients is a sight worth some trouble to inspect, and implies great engineering skill. At Palmerston, situated in a well-wooded and fertile district, there is a break at present in the Wellington Manawatu railway, and we had to take a coach and four, which was a pleasant change, through a well-cultured valley till we reached the Manawatu

Gorge, a fearfully dangerous pass of three mile in extent, up which we were coached with a perpendicular rock overhead, and the same below, and traversing a roadway made by blasting the face of the rock, so that if a wheel came off or our horses shied we should have been sent down into the abyss below, in which roared a perfect "hell of waters." There was no railing on the side, and the wheels would go as near as eighteen inches to the edge, the look-out was fearful, and shook the nerves of even the old hands present! We were, therefore, very much relieved to find ourselves out of it. On the other side of this gorge they are making a single line of railway by blasting the rock for a road, and tunnelling through the projections here and there, a very slow, expensive piece of cutting. A few miles further on, our coach stopped at the flourishing town of Woodville; here we had a refreshing lunch, and then proceeded by train to Napier, 95 miles off, through a fine well-watered country pasturing thousands of sheep and cattle. This was a hard day's travelling, and we were glad to find ourselves at the Masonic Hotel at Napier, where our Scotch host gave us very excellent rooms. Napier is the chief city in the Hawke's Bay Province, one of the best agricultural districts in New Zealand. It is a diocesan city and the residence of the Bishop of Waiupu, who, when he attended the synod of bishops at Lambeth Palace, was greeted with the pun, "Here comes the representative of church free sittings, *Why a pew?*" The town rests on a lovely site, which neither the pencil of the artist nor the photographer can do justice to. The houses of the well-to-do stand brightly forward on a succession of rounded hills and their intervening valleys, embosomed in evergreens and flowering shrubs, a very paradise of beauty and serenity. The glorious peninsula of villas ends in what is called the "Spit," where there is a fine basin for ordinary sized vessels; but the spirited authorities are making, at great cost, a splendid breakwater to accommodate the largest steamers. I should advise a tourist to walk or drive round this peninsula, a distance of five miles, as he would be well rewarded. The roads and pathways in and around Napier are excellent. Again the thing to do is to drive to Taradale, a native village seven miles off, in the midst of English civilised dwellings and cultivated fields. We entered the chief's principal lodging—a large room, on the floor of which matting was laid down for men, women, and children; here his family and retainers slept, each having a proper allotment. We were warned not to go too far into it by our guide because the "live stock," as he called them, were too numerous, and would be unpleasant mementos to take away with us. The centre props to the room were ornamented with idols, carved in wood, hideous looking monsters. This dwelling was surrounded by less pretentious ones made of wattle, reeds, and clay like wigwams. Outside these were seen the Maoris squatting and cooking their meals, and who took very little notice of us. They are a very fine athletic race with an intelligent aspect, and some of the young women were quite good-looking with olive complexions, oval faces, and coal-black eyes, with long wavy dark coarse hair.

On our return journey we passed the racecourse, an institution so characteristic of this horsey people, and is here located in the midst of thousands of acres of garden-like land, yielding abundance of every produce. Horses, cows, and sheep, looking sleek and fat, amidst a people thriving and smiling, a veritable land of "milk and honey." Hovering above we saw several hawks, hence the name given to this district!

On Sunday we went to the Cathedral, a fine brick and stone building, which is strengthened in the inside by heavy buttresses in case of an earthquake coming. While we were examining the interior, the dean came up to us in a most affable manner, and gave us a very excellent account of the church from its beginning, and the difficulties he had to encounter to get it erected, and the danger and risk of a possible earthquake that he had to provide against. The dean has a very pleasing, expressive face, very like that of the Saviour, especially the one painted by Count d'Orsay. Although a spare-looking man, he has a powerful voice and an excellent extempore delivery, just suited to the place and its people, hence he is very popular. He asked me if I would read the evening lessons for him which I did, and afterwards invited us to the deanery to tea with Mrs. Hovell, his son, and two daughters, with whose amiability and courtesy we were much pleased. Dean Hovell is cousin to Mr. Mark Hovell, the specialist who attended the Emperor Frederick with Sir Morel Mackenzie. There is Sunday closing in Napier, and the streets are remarkably quiet; and on Saturday night the promenades were crowded with well-dressed people, English and native converts alike; and the Salvation Army were busy at the corner of our hotel doing their level best to induce their listeners to think of the higher life.

CHAPTER XXIII.

On Monday we left Napier at six in the morning to commence the wonderful inland coach journey of about two hundred miles to Oxford, *viâ* Taupo. We carried the mail, and each passenger was only allowed one portmanteau. I don't think the ladies had the least idea what they were going to encounter in the way of roughing it. For the first twenty-five miles we drove up and down hills, and through about forty creeks, having 2 feet or 3 feet of water in them, with a shingly bottom. Down into these the five horses dashed with as much impetus as they could muster in order to get up the opposite slope, urged thereto with much shouting and whip-cracking by the driver, conveying a most unpleasant jolt to our bodies. Then we would slowly ascend some high mountain, we men getting out to walk; but when once on the summit we were rewarded by some really very grand views — notably from the tops of Mounts Tauranga, Kuma, and Titiokura. Then we would have to descend some fearful ziz-zag road cut out of the side of a hill, with a precipice on the other hand looking down gorges 400 feet to 1,000 feet deep, with rushing torrents. At the sharp turns in these awful

roads our Jehu would amuse himself with shouts and
flicking of his whip, which sent the nerves of the
strongest of us into a most unpleasant state of
tremor. To watch our dismayed looks was, I dare
say, fun to him, but it was decidedly painful to his
living freight. Hence we were very glad to find
ourselves at the half-way house, and get a little
respite from the continued jolting of our heads
against the roof of the coach, and the thuds to our
nether ends by bumping down on the hard cushions.
In the short space of four hours I never, in the whole
course of my life, heard so many exclamations of
oh! and no wonder, our very spines felt like a mass
of jelly. Having had a refreshing lunch and changed
our horses we all got into a good humour again,
especially as we were told that the track would now
become less perilous and distressing, with less
screeching from our fair companions. We passed
a most interesting sight *en route*, and that was the
collecting together on the side of a hill by stockmen
and their collies 10,000 sheep, an immense flock,
reminding one of what Israel had in patriarchal days.
Again we met a party of Maoris filing along on
horseback, the ladies riding cross-legged, like their
lords. We dropped some letters into an old box
stuck on a post close to the road-side, and this was
the primitive depository for the correspondence of a
township some distance off, not a habitation of any
kind being visible anywhere, and there could have
been no thieves, certainly.

The evening of the first day found us at Taravera,
having traversed a distance of fifty miles. There we

had an excellent dinner and spent the night; the daughters of the host waited on the guests, and then amused them with some music, and in no way felt it *infra dig.*, in New Zealand. The next morning we started afresh to traverse another fifty miles, principally over a desert-like plateau, without a vestige of life on it, and for twelve miles no water for birds or animals to drink. Hence we passed carcases of dead bullocks and sheep, which had succumbed in their journey across this waterless track. The plateau, as far as the eye could reach, was wearisome in its perpetual sameness: a barren wild of fern and small shrubs of the Tei tree growing in loose soil of powdered pumice-stone, the only relief being in front of us a high volcanic mountain of 8,000 feet in full activity, and the snow-capped Ruapehu. At the half-way house there was another luncheon and a change of horses. A wide stream passed through the grounds, and on this we threw large flat pieces of pumice-stone, which floated away on its surface—contradicting the usual saying, that a stone sinks in water. Starting once more, we descended by a tortuous dusty road, from which we enjoyed splendid views of the grand inland Lake Taupo, and the valley beneath us, from which issued here and there from the green bush white clouds of steam, indicating the spots where the hot springs were located. Having run along the shore of the lake for some distance, we arrived finally at Joshua's Spa, in the midst of this valley of geysers. This is the most extraordinary situation for a sanatorium I ever saw or heard of. This spa, called Joshua, after the name of the proprietor, consists of a number of separate wooden buildings erected in a land-locked hollow, naturally excavated in a valley of pumice rock and soil, through which passes a small stream of hot sulphurous water from a neighbouring spring, supplemented by hot ebullitions in the grounds, which are diverted into baths for the use of invalids. Of course we did the singular sights of the locality. A short walk leads you down to the celebrated Waikato River, which takes its origin in the lake. Near its banks we look with amusement at the geyser called the "Crow's Nest," with its peculiar border of sticks encrusted with white silicate of lime. These sticks were said originally to have been placed round the edge to prevent the Maoris' children from falling in, and become fossiled in time. Next came the "Witches' Caldron," belching up its steamy contents at a temperature of 180° F. Further on we came across the "Paddle-wheel Ben," in which the sulphur gas issues forth from a rocky cavern with a gushing, hissing sound—a blow-hole I called it. On returning we started a brace of red-legged partridges. As to our meats, the mutton, our only flesh meat, was very stringy, because the weather was so hot, or the gas did not agree with its keeping, for what we had to eat at dinner was killed in the early morning of the same day. The sweets were excellent, and we had an *entrée* of wild ducks brought in by the Maoris, who shot them by self-made shot. We passed two days very pleasantly with our friend Joshua, a most obliging and gentlemanly host, at whose expense I made an innocent pun. How came it about that

Joshua had no father ? because Joshua was the son of *Nun!* The Lake Taupo is the largest in New Zealand, being twenty-four miles long by fifteen broad, but we did not take our excursion on it in the steam launch, as we could admire its broad expanse and its smoking volcano at the further end from the hills, which the next day we had to ascend on our coach. We were told that there was some very good gratuitous shooting here of wild duck, pheasant, and partridges during the winter months, which it was not our pleasure to wait for. Early in the morning we took our leave of the Spa and our seats on a coach and five horses, and continued a jolting journey northwards through a most uninteresting wilderness of fern and bush, till we reached Rotorua, a distance of fifty-six miles, where we were refreshed by a really good dinner, followed by sound sleep till five in the morning, when I went out and had a delightful swim in a bath, in the grounds of the Palace Hotel, which was only slightly impregnated with sulphur. Subsequently we walked a short mile to the regular baths connected with this world-famed health-resort. These are on an extensive scale, under Government control, with a regular doctor engaged, and in every other way the organisation is perfect. The use of the "Rachel" bath softens and smooths the skin, while the larger amount of silicate of lime in the celebrated "Priest's" bath excites the surface, producing strongly a prickly feeling and intense perspiration, and being at a temperature of 103° F. the patients do not remain in it more than fifteen minutes as a rule. They say these two baths have cured some most obstinate cases of chronic rheumatism and inveterate skin diseases. Knowing that I was a physician from London, the authorities took good care to give me every information, and praised the sanatorium as the best in the world, and statistics would show that its reputation was well sustained by Australasia, at any rate as the sick flocked from all the colonies for relief when all medicines had failed. There is a good Maori settlement adjoining the colonial town, possessing an English church. There is an excellent understanding between the natives and the English, the former highly appreciating the education their children get in the colonial schools, and the clergyman makes many converts to Christianity through the medium of the Church services, where they receive instruction in their own language; but he complained sadly of the obstacles thrown in his way by the English selling the Maoris strong drink. I remarked to a resident who had been there fifty years that I seldom met a Maori with grey hair, and he replied that he had never seen one with a bald head. I asked him if there was any truth in what I had heard, namely, that the English settler would marry a Maori girl, and after living with her for several years and getting lots of children by her, would, when he had prospered and become rich, desert her and his children, though she had materially assisted him in getting the wealth. He replied, "I am sorry to say such is the case in many instances within my own knowledge." To show how very fertile the soil is about the hot springs, Mrs. Macrae, our hostess, told

us that some of the onions in her garden weighed
11lbs., and two pumpkins scaled respectively 103lbs.
and 120lbs. Mrs. Macrae, who kept the hotel in
the vicinity of the pink and white terraces, the pride
and glory of New Zealand, gave me a most graphic
description of the volcanic eruption of mud which
destroyed them and her residence, and from which
so few escaped alive, and left the traveller to mourn
over the loss of the sight of these lovely silica
incrustations.

If one did give up making the usual excursions
from Rotorua, it would be a great mistake not
to pay a visit to the native village close at hand,
and study a little the peculiar customs and habits
of the Maoris. It comprises a collection of native
huts called whares; also rather a fine meeting-house,
well carved and painted outside, with a statue of
our Queen in the interior. There are boiling pools
where the villagers cook their food, and warm pools
where the men and boys do bathe. They manage
very cleverly also to divert the hot stream from
these pools into a variety of holes, which act as
ovens, and thus obviate the necessity of making a
fire. We will ask our readers to follow us, as we
ought to have done before, along this wonderful
inland drive, through the very heart of the North
Island of New Zealand, as indicated on a map. We
were now *en route* again on a mail coach, drawn by
five horses, as usual, and our destination is Oxford;
the drive proved to be the most dusty I ever experienced. Talk of swallowing a peck of dirt in a
lifetime, I should say that a month would be quite

long enough to inhale that quantity if we had to traverse this road daily. First of all we had to zigzag up a series of hills and dales till we reached a mountain ridge, along which we travelled for some miles, with precipices on each side, and in the gorges below a depth of hundreds of feet could be seen the trees of a primeval forest, and though huge in size when looked at from above, appeared like so many saplings. This was really a superb sight when the clouds of dust would permit us to enjoy it. We came across many bush fires, where the trees are cleared by burning, and English grass seed is sown and covered with the charcoal dust, and a fine crop arises in a few weeks, to the great joy of the settler and the success of his sheep run. Our journey was only one of thirty-five miles in extent, and yet till this space is covered by a railway the excellent health resort at Rotorua will not be patronised as it deserves to be. We arrived at Oxford in good time for a thorough brush down, and our clothes to have the thick layer of dust brushed out of them. My long brown coat was as white as a miller's. It was quite refreshing to see a railway again, and to find one's self in the vicinity of ordinary civilisation, while the surrounding farms and homesteads looked like dear Old England, barring its characteristic hedgerows. We were up betimes the next morning, and after breakfasting at 6.15 took our places in a train which landed us at Auckland by 2 p.m. There, indeed, we did meet with a welcome change from the rough life we had been comparatively leading for some time past. We put up at the Star Hotel, where we were accommodated with some fine lofty rooms, while the table was luxuriously supplied, conjoined with an efficient staff of men waiters; the essential bath-room on every floor, and the whole house conducted in as good a manner as a first-class hotel in London; a few minutes' walk from the port, and other centres of life and amusement, but I will leave a further description of beautiful Auckland for another chapter.

CHAPTER XXIV.

A DESCRIPTION of beautiful Auckland painted in the most vivid word-colouring would fail to give the reader a fair idea of its varied loveliness. It is situated on an isthmus with a sea view nearly all round, and unique in its bright grandeur, surpassing anything of the kind I have ever seen. The sight of Naples and its bay, with Capri and Vesuvius in the distance from the Mount St. Elmo is not to be compared to it, and any one of the views that the eye can grasp of the separate harbours of Sydney does not match it, and if one's mind is recalled to the sight of the entry into the Bosphorus at Constantinople, or the passages up to New York and San Francisco with the morning sun glowing on those splendid cities, still Auckland bears the palm, and stands out preeminent in a situation of beauty so extensive and comprehensive that nothing in my opinion can come near it. I would ask the visitor to go with me to the top of Mount Eden—a rise of 650 feet above the town, and only three miles off, with a winding road to its summit. From this historic old crater and Maori fort, in excellent shape and preservation, a panorama unique in extent and sublimity is to be seen which the citizens may well be proud of. From its base to the sea we have the lovely city with magnificent buildings of halls, churches, museum, hospital, and huge warehouses, with harbour crowded with shipping from all nations, and further out numerous yachts with their white sails like so many butterflies flitting about, backed by the opposite shore, with Mount Victoria clothed in verdure, dotted with suburbs of elegant villas. Right and left of Mount Eden there are extensive suburbs also nestling in pretty nooks, clothed in evergreens, reachable by a tramway. Now let us turn round, and an extraordinary sight faces us. No less than twenty-four volcanic cones on as many round hills dot the landscape, extinct for ages past. Again, between these hills are located large mansions in parklike grounds, interspersed by homesteads and even hedgerows, putting one forcibly in mind of old England, and the simile is enhanced by a railway winding its way through the dales. Before we descend let us face the city again and admire the well-kept central Public Gardens, the big building to the left being the Provincial Hospital on a high site dominating the public domain. The Museum, Law Courts, and Government House are nearly obscured by trees. It is very difficult to get a good photo from Mount Eden of the city and its surroundings. We will now take the steamer constantly going to and fro to the north shore on the opposite side of the harbour, and take a ramble in Davenport, the fashionable summer resort, much prized by the Auckland people. Rising from the centre of this suburb is Victoria Mount, about 200 feet high, with a well-shaded wooded walk to its flagstaff top, from which a view of the city opposite is afforded of the most splendid nature, far surpassing that from the north shore at Sydney, especially in the afternoon, when the sun's rays are in full play upon it. Having now admired this exquisite bit of scenery, we can take a cab or the coach and enjoy a most agreeable drive of four miles to the Lake Takapuna, another favourite resort, along the road to which and on its banks are springing up numerous dwellings in their snug grounds, rejoicing also in a large popular hotel, with boats on the lake. This lake is very deep, and has no outlet, contains fresh water, though only a narrow strip of ground separates it from the salt water of the ocean. If we continue along the north shore we come to Northcote, another very pretty suburb, and near to this a popular settlement called Birkenhead, in which there is the Colonial Sugar Company's Works, an extensive refinery. On the side of the hill, one above another, are the rows of cottages belonging to the work-people, exceedingly picturesque. Auckland and its western suburb is a thing to be seen and not forgotten from this elevated quarter, and no visitor or tourist has done himself or the lovely city due justice who has not rambled at his ease along the north shore, and taken in his fill of such a delightful prospect. We will now return to our hotel, and tomorrow charter a hansom cab and pay St. John's College a visit, so interestingly associated with Bishops Patterson and Selwyn. There we shall find an extremely pretty, but quaint-looking, old wooden church, with memorial brasses and windows to those good self-denying men. On the road back I called on Dr. Cowie, one of the handsomest of bishops, to whom I handed my letter of introduction, and was heartily received. I was shown over the large Selwyn Library, and over his most singular wooden palace, fixed to the side of a steep ravine, with the bedrooms below and the reception rooms on a level with the ground above, but all the windows overlooking the harbour and north shore; a grand picture, truly—nestling in peace and quietude—a soul-inspiring spot for an ecclesiastical student. The bishop had one feeling at any rate in common with myself, we had both been in active warfare; he as chaplain to the forces in India, where he had been actually engaged in carrying shot to our men in the midst of the din and danger of a fight. What a contrast to his present position! Now that I am on the subject of Colonial Bishops, I will here introduce a rather weird story told by Sir George Bowen when he was Governor of New Zealand. A very good heading to it would be this, "A New Zealand Chief's Preparation for the Higher Life."

Among the loyal Maori chiefs invited to meet the Duke of Edinburgh was one of the original signers of the treaty of Waitangi in 1840, and who had ever since been a firm friend of the English. One of the Anglican Bishops afterwards said to the Governor, "Do you know, Sir, the antecedents of that old heathen?" "No my dear Bishop," was the reply, "but I do know that he brought five hundred of his clansmen into the field to fight for the Queen, so I invited him to meet the Queen's son." "Well," continued the Bishop, "when I first arrived in New Zealand that chief came to me and said that he wished to be baptized. I knew that he had two

NEW ZEALAND CHIEF.

wives, so I told him that he must first persuade one of them to return to her family. He said he feared that would be difficult, but that he would see what could be done, and came back to me in two months. When he returned he exclaimed, "Now, missionary, you may baptize me, for I have only one wife."

I asked, "What have you done with our dear sister, your first wife?" He replied, smacking his lips, "I have eaten her!"

The Maori priests were the scholars of the tribes, and to them were entrusted the important business of tattooing. This was considered a very grave undertaking by the chiefs, each of whom indulged in special patterns, which distinguished them from one another in the same manner as our coats of arms do our aristocratic families. I give a sketch of an old chief who gloried in a kind of shawl devise which marked his particular rank, and the little kingdom he reigned over. This disfigurement is supposed to overawe his enemies with fear, and to hide the wrinkled traces of old age. Girls before they marry are not honoured by a tattoo, and the married very slightly so on the lips, chin, and eyebrows, but all this custom is fast passing away from those who join the English community. The Maoris as a people merit a few further remarks, but I shall make them as brief as possible, just of sufficient interest to instruct the coming tourist. They are not supposed to be the original natives of New Zealand, but immigrants from the South Sea Islands. Captain Cook when he visited the country reckoned them at 90,000 double what they are now. They could weave coarse cloth from the native flax; work and polish their sacred green stone, and very hard work it is; make canoes and ornament them with rude carving; make battle axes and spears and fishing nets, and grotesque personal decorations.

Some of the best specimens of this handiwork

may be seen in the Auckland Museum, and the Dunedin Exhibition, where a fine chieftain's tomb was on view. The white spots are bunches of feathers from rare birds. The carving is really wonderfully skilful, considering the simple tools employed. Primogeniture is a recognised law. The spell called "Tapu," acts as their principal mode of government, and the cast of the spell over anything was sufficient to make it sacred—not to be touched, and hardly to be looked at except with veneration and awe. The influence of "Tapu" strengthened the hands of both chiefs and priests in their dealings with the people. The Maoris believe in a future state, though it required the aid of Christian missionaries to convince them that God was omnipotent. They love pleasure, and have many sports, the principal being horse-racing. They erect their storehouses on piles to keep away the rats. They are naturally a war-like race, and when the Anglo-Saxon first invaded their country he found them no mean enemy to contend with. Their fortresses, called "Pahs," were most ingeniously contrived to keep our soldiers at bay; protected as they were with rifle-pits, ditches, and stockades in front, we were often defeated in our attacks upon them. As to the sale of land or other property which is common to the individuals composing the different tribes, this cannot be effected without the consent of all concerned, hence a good deal of trouble has arisen to Europeans buying their lands in consequence of some individual objecting to join the majority, somewhat like one juryman not falling in with the other eleven in our country. Then angry feelings and contention arose, and force has been used to settle the conveyance. The Maori of to-day has not much to thank the English for, since he has learnt all the evils of civilisation without acquiring its virtues. The only wise thing they have learnt in coming into contact with us has been the giving up of the hideous tattooing; but against this we must set their artful cunning in over-reaching us in their bargains, and we have taught them to be ardent smokers and heavy drinkers, whenever they can purchase the "fire water," hence they become lazy, given to cheating, and mulish in obstinacy.

Can we be surprised, then, at the population decreasing and the whites increasing? Can we feel otherwise than that the Maoris are doomed? though it is a crying pity that we don't influence them for good, for they are a fine manly race, and deserve better things than being made bad imitations of ourselves. Why are not our missionaries and temperance workers to the fore? The Episcopalians did, single-handed, much good work among the natives for several years, then crept in the Roman Catholics and Wesleyans, introducing their creeds, with the result that they quite bothered the Maori's intellect, which is fairly shrewd and quick, and they were unable to understand the religious divisions of the three churches, and remarked very sensibly and pointedly, "If these learned priests cannot agree among themselves which is the straight road to Heaven, and the correct religion to follow, how can we poor unenlightened Maoris be expected to know how to choose?" Can we be surprised, then, that between these three stools the puzzled native falls to the ground and relapses into paganism? The Bible was translated as far back as 1837 into the Maori language, and it may be asked how many converts has it made? The Maoris struggled against us for eighteen years, and stopped all progress, but in the year 1840 the chieftains agreed to the following treaty, namely, "The Maori chiefs ceded to Queen Victoria the right of government over the whole of their country." The Queen, on her part, gave the chiefs full right over their property, but ceded to Her Majesty the right to purchase the land if they were willing to sell. And, thirdly, "the Queen agreed to protect all her Maori subjects, and granted to them the same rights and privileges as if they were Englishmen." Notwithstanding this treaty, quarrels and angry passions were roused in connection with land purchases, and fighting went on between the natives and our red-coats, which seemed to excite them like the red cloth does at bull-baiting; and matters did not mend till our soldiers were withdrawn and the colonists were left to settle their own affairs with the Maoris.

We will now take leave of the Maoris, and hark back to Auckland, and for an hour or so seat ourselves on its large pier and landing stages, which I reckon could not have cost less than half a million of money. Let us just dwell on its busy scenes, with Mount Eden in the background. What is the occasion of this lively sight? Why, in the first place, one sees huge ocean steamers taking their cargoes of thousands of carcases of sheep, frozen in an immense factory adjoining the pier, which communicates with the shipping by a railway, so that there is no time lost for the meat to thaw before it gets into the refrigerator of the vessel. Again you will see hundreds of bales of fine flax, which the colony yields in immense profusion, and with it sacks of hops and bundles of merino wool, all of which are exported to England. As to the cereals, the oats are grand, weighing 45 lbs. to the bushel, and much appreciated in our country. Then come packages of Kauri gum from the Kauri trees, very precious, while the wood is plentiful and valuable, taken from the Thames Valley, down whose beautiful river the logs are floated during a "freshet," and caught by booms.

Of all the precious minerals which New Zealand yields—gold, silver, copper, antimony, manganese, and coal—gold is the only one I shall allude to, as it is that which is most interesting to those already there, and to those about to go. £45,000,000 of gold was the amount of the find from 1853 to 1889. A splendid outcome, and it is no marvel, therefore, that the colony has flourished so well since it was first constituted in 1840. Personally, I feel an unusual interest in this matter, because a friend of mine, Mr. Charles Ring, of Ringcote, Auckland, was with his brother the original discoverer of gold in New Zealand. In prospecting for the precious metal he first came across it at Coromandel in 1852. The Government had offered a reward of £5,000 for the first discovery of "available" gold, and when

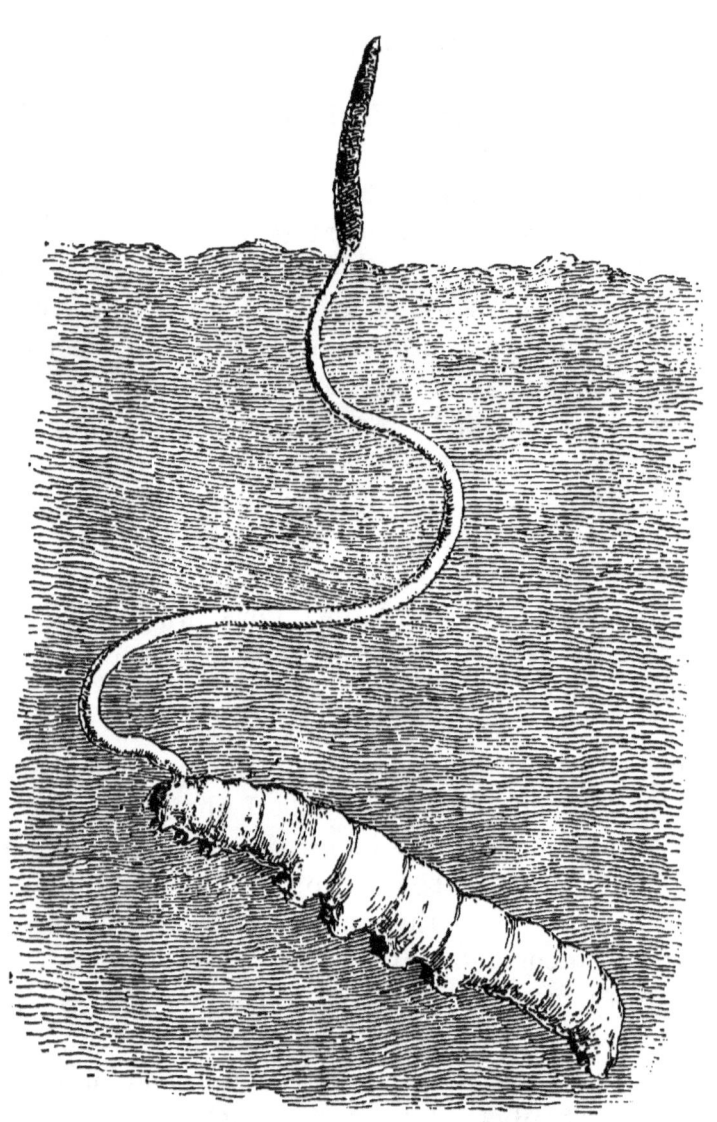

NEW ZEALAND VEGETABLE CATERPILLAR.

Messrs. Ring applied for the reward, it was refused on the ground that the Maoris objected to the spot being worked, hence it was not "available." Notwithstanding, the Government instigated these gentlemen to go on prospecting in order to ascertain to what extent the auriferous deposit existed in the colony, and they did so at their own expense, and they continued to make discoveries, and because they were not "available" through the obstinacy of the natives, they still kept back the reward. A mean and shabby thing to do—thus utilising the time, talents, and money of these public-spirited men for the public welfare without a just recompence.

I now come to speak of the most extraordinary thing I met with during my tour round the globe, namely, the New Zealand Vegetable Caterpillar. Our old scientific teachings are completely upset when we insist that a vegetable production must of necessity take its origin and extract its nourishment from the soil: that it is through the medium of gases dissolved in water, constituting what is called "sap," which ascends the plant till it reaches the leaves, where circulating through the cells, it becomes subjected to the influences of light and heat, and deoxidation is effected, oxygen being set free to purify the air, while the carbon descends, constituting woody fibre and vegetable growth. This physiological explanation is of no avail to us in our efforts to explain the nourishment and growth of the Vegetable Caterpillar—a most startling phenomenon—a singular freak of nature! Remarkable to relate, this plant fulfils its destiny by possessing the power of reproducing itself by means of minute seeds, which are massed like so much red sand on the ends of the twigs. They are clearly seen by an inch magnifier, packed together firmly somewhat like the maize in the cob. These small seedlings find their way into the interior of the caterpillar through the pores of the animal's breathing apparatus, represented in the drawing by the round marks. Once inside its body hair-like roots are sent out, which ramify into every nook and corner of its soft tissue, absorbing no gases in the usual way of soil-growing plants, but directly taking up the albuminous fluid from the body of the grub, which, as the plant bursts outside and develops itself, gradually sucks dry its very existence, starves out in fact its very life, and the caterpillar shrivels up by degrees and dies of inanition. In this condition they both fall down to the root of the tree, when it is said the Maories collect them into bundles, boil, and eat them—quite as palatable perhaps as fat snails consumed as a relish by the natives of other countries. This very peculiar and interesting specimen of creative genius is indeed unique, and like many other created things, at present beyond our comprehension. We must be content to await patiently the greater developments of scientific research. We must remain students all our days, and keep our scientific eye open to the reception of new laws, and the rejection of old conclusions. This perpetual going to school, this attitude of honest and humble study, will tend doubtless to keep the mind fresh. Thinkers must all admit that God works in a mysterious way, and because we cannot at once understand and explain His wondrous marvels, let us not shut ourselves up

in our own vain conceits, and say that there is no
Creator. " We are fearfully and wonderfully made,"
so says the Psalmist; but he goes on to say, " and
that my soul knoweth right well." Do we know it
right well? Do we really and practically feel it? Do
we humble ourselves at the sight of God's grand and
indescribable developments? Do we confess our intellects very small, very midgy-like, veritable pigmies,
when compared with His magnificent intelligence. If
we do, then we may venture to say and to feel that
our faith and hope is based upon a solid rock which
cannot be shaken by the attacks of sceptics, be they
ever so sharp, delusive, fascinating, and plausible.
Sometimes I give a lecture on this singular phenomenon so inexplicable to the scientist of the day,
and end by drawing some useful moral reflections
from it, such as the following:—

The introduction of these seedlings into the caterpillar, and the gradual destruction of its body and the
extinction of its very life, may be very aptly taken to
illustrate the effects of the smaller sins into the hearts
of men and women. In a thoughtless and unguarded
moment we permit these little evils to penetrate into
our minds, where they take deep root—a tenacious
lodgement—till they gradually expand into some besetting sin, monopolising the whole soul, which we
cannot of ourselves shake off. And if we do not apply
earnestly and vigorously for the power of the Holy
Spirit to come to our aid and help us to weed it out,
it will take as firm a grip of us as this plant does of
the grub which it cruelly kills, and hinders from per-
fecting itself for the higher life of a splendid insect, a

beautifully coloured moth, soaring upwards to the skies in self-delight and the admiration of all beholders. It shows also very forcibly how necessary it is for us in going through this world, replete with temptations and traps to catch the unwary, that we should be steady and unswerving sentinels, wide awake and ever on the watch against the insinuating arts and wiles of the Evil One, going about seeking where he can drop his seedlings of sin and mischief, and also knows so well our salient points of weakness. Whether these be the outcome of our various positions, high or low, rich or poor, old or young, or not, none are exempt from attacks. As we pity this unfortunate caterpillar which is shrivelled up into a mere shell, and even as a grub looses its comely aspect and its chances of a higher development, so must we pity the human being whose soul is so perverted and disfigured by continuous sinning that it is not fit to mix with the company of the angels in heaven. We lament over the being who is so careless and slumbering that a little evilly-disposed wish is allowed to enter a corner of the heart, where it finds congenial soil till it expands into a masterful giant! To get this wish gratified all the cardinal virtues are sacrificed and ignored, such as truth, temperance, self-respect, honour, justice, humility, and faith, and all the helps to the acquisition of these virtues are set at nought, even voted a bore, or tolerated only for social appearance sake, such are prayer, bible reading, public divine worship, and all that belongs to the formation of the Christian character. As men and women in the image of our God we rob ourselves of our higher life and dignity, and become not unlike this caterpillar and its parasite, which thinks only of sensual gratification. We may well take this warning lesson from the New Zealand caterpillar. Let us strive to safeguard ourselves against the first insidious entrance of the small seedlings sown by the Evil One in our minds, which grow so big and formidable, and create in us such a cruel injury. But should we in an unguarded moment have allowed one to penetrate our hearts, let us quickly search and weed it out before it has time to take deep root within us, and thus hinder our spirits from soaring heavenwards, and mounting from strength to strength, and from glory to glory, till we have reached that spiritual peace which passeth understanding. Finally, let us bethink ourselves how such a depraved mind prevents our shining here as lights and helpers to others, and checks our ascent to God's glorious home, clothed in our beautiful resurrection bodies, which He has promised to those who love and serve Him steadfastly and faithfully.

I cannot take my leave of beautiful Auckland without a word with respect to the social aspect of the upper classes. They are so thoroughly English in their ways and feelings that it is difficult to imagine oneself out of England. They are very fond of music, and though their assembly room was burnt down twice by an incendiary, they have now erected a third one of stone and brick, which has 1,800 sittings. All the concerts are by amateurs, who invite their friends, and most agreeable evenings are spent. There is a great deal of quiet sociability going on among the families, without any pretence at anything grand or expensive. The

AUCKLAND YOUNG LADY.

excellent tramways running in every direction tend to bring friends cheaply and conveniently together. The churches are large and well attended, mostly evangelical. At one of these where I read the lessons for a popular preacher, who was giving his farewell sermon before leaving for England, every seat was taken, and in the vestry afterwards I was surprised to see that there were in the collection of £8 17s. 10d., 256 threepenny pieces, and only four coppers; so I asked for an explanation, and was told that the working classes look with contempt on copper coins, and consequently give the lowest silver one. So well understood is this at all church collections, that when the clergyman's daughter wanted small change from John Chinaman, who is the greengrocer in every colony, he drew out a handful of copper. "Oh, no, I don't want that," said she; he immediately replied with, "Ah, I sees what missy wants, churchy money," and handed over a quantity of threepenny bits. The young ladies' complexions are singularly fair and smooth for so sunny a climate, and their growth is precocious, a girl of fourteen being equal to one of eighteen in England. The young people are naturally fond of picnic gatherings, the lovely climate and picturesque neighbourhood being well adapted for such pleasures. We will now close this chapter, as we are leaving the land and betaking ourselves to sea again, with the following remarks on strong drink in its bearings on the workpeople. This splendid seaport, one of the most bustling in the colony, boasts of very extensive suburbs of wooden cottages, each containing four rooms, with necessary outbuildings for animals, all enclosed in a quarter or half an acre of land. I inquired who they belonged to, and I was told that they were freeholds, and were owned by the occupants. Now, a good, steady, hard-working man will get his shilling an hour for eight hours a day, which would amount to £2 8s. per week, and I was informed such a man would, in about three years, become the owner of one of these cottages. Then I inquired, how about the drink? The reply was very suggestive. "It can't be done, it is quite impossible." The man who drinks stagnates or is lost, and, if they are not up to time at the shipping business, they are turned off without the least compunction by a lynx-eyed foreman. Hence if a working man is to get on in the colonies it is by sheer hard, sober efforts, and no drink. No one need emigrate and expect to succeed who cannot make up his mind to follow these rules; abide by them, and prosperity and independence is the result, without failure. No one, be he a temperance advocate or otherwise, can be blind to the fact that this colony's welfare and progress is intimately bound up with the Englishman's resistance to alcoholic liquor, while he has the constant warning before him that the Maoris are gradually being exterminated by it.

CHAPTER XXV.

HAVING already secured our passage in a deck cabin while in Sydney, and had our heavy luggage placed therein, for a voyage to San Francisco by the mail steamer *Mariposa*, we had nothing to do when she arrived at Auckland but say farewell to our numerous friends, and to enter comfortably into our berths and possessions. The vessel being altogether under American management, and manned throughout by Yankee officers and crew, was not nearly so agreeable and luxurious as an English ocean steamer would be; in fact, the food was atrocious, the flour had turned sour, the meat very tough, and even ship's biscuits were tainted. I pitied the poor children who were deprived of good bread and milk. And the waiters were a scratch lot. However, we had to put up with it, as there was no competition on this line; but there was one consolation, the *Mariposa* was a good sea-boat of 3,000 tons and 3,000 h.p. It was rather monotonous steaming for 1,700 miles, only varied by some good concerts of an evening, when we sighted Tutuila, one of the Samoa Islands. There a schooner came out to us with letters in exchange for some we gave, but no passengers landed. Accompanying the schooner was a swarm of canoes, very cleverly paddled by both female and male natives; some of the girls were quite pretty looking, and the men with straight, well-knit, athletic frames, with reddish skins and expressive features, good teeth, and wavy black or brown hair—nothing of the negro type about them, but decidedly of the Malay stamp, and I can well believe that the Maoris descended from them. Both sexes were quite at home in the water, reminding one of the Arabs at Aden, swimming and diving like amphibious animals. They brought carved sticks and bludgeons and fans on board for sale, and seemed quite *au fait* in striking a bargain. These islands have a nominal king, but are really under the protection of America, England, and Germany, which gives them a code of laws. Hence the inhabitants are rapidly becoming civilised and christianised by missionaries. We saw on one of the group a church with a tower to it, and some school buildings. A passenger, presumably Irish, wanted to know how long we should be before we reached Halleluja, meaning Honolulu. Before we could get there we had to encounter some rough wind and rain, which disturbed the peace of some of our party. Such changes are very sudden in the Pacific, which at such times much belies its name. After leaving Samoa there was little to record till we reached Honolulu, where we arrived at two in the afternoon, and were greeted and welcomed by an applauding multitude and the music of the royal band, which played us into the harbour. Honolulu is the capital of the Hawaiian Islands, and though governed by a native king and a representative constitution, is virtually under the protectorate of the United States of America, which keeps a watchful eye over its doings. On landing we called on Mr. Theo. Davis, recently our Vice Consul, and were advised to take a buggy and drive up the winding road to the top of the hill called the "Punch Bowl," which dominates the city. From this old extinct crater a very splendid and extensive view is to be had of the town, harbour, and pretty suburbs, embellished with flowering shrubs, and on the left, rice fields, now waving with corn. In the valley between the foot of the hill and the town are situated the Chinese vegetable and fruit gardens, irrigated in a marvellous manner, by diverting the mountain stream into rills. The cleanliness of the white-robed Chinamen, together with their thrift and industry, is most praiseworthy, and, as shopkeepers, most successful. They constitute, with the Japanese, a large and important section of the population, about 20,000—the whole of the Islands numbering not much more than 80,000. From the "Punch Bowl" hill one cannot see well the line of the streets, they are so shrouded in leaves, but the king's palace, the Government buildings, and the two spires of the Cathedral stand out in strong relief. The natives proper put me very much in mind of the Maoris in face and form, but they are sadly decreasing in numbers, while the Americans and English are increasing, and no wonder, for the babies fade away and die early, because the parents on both sides smoke and drink heavily, the late king setting the example; but it is said the reigning queen is a great temperance advocate, and will not allow any intoxicating drinks in the palace. On Sunday we went to hear the bishop preach in the Cathedral, and in the same grounds we found the old pro-cathedral now given up to the Chinese converts to Christianity. As a service was going on, we entered, and heard an English sermon being interpreted, sentence after sentence, to the Chinamen. Though the clergyman could read the Bible and say the prayers in their language, he would not trust himself to preach, for fear, he said, of being misunderstood. They sang their hymns to our tunes in good time and voice. There is a good attendance of women in the morning, but not at night, as it is not the custom for Chinese women to go out at night into the streets. Being desirous of seeing the limits of the city, we took our seats in the tramway, which bisects the town in every direction. On the tram we entered into conversation with a very intelligent lady, who spoke English perfectly, yet she had never been out of Honolulu. Her vocation was that of mistress at the Chinese school, where she had to teach English to the boys in the morning and the girls in the evening. She told us that there was not much difference in the capacity for learning between the two sexes. As a rule they were quite as quick as the English children. Education was free to all classes; but the daughters of the upper ranks attended school with their feet contracted, the small toes being bandaged under the great toe, so as to bring the foot to a point. This is the outward sign of the fashionable Chinese lady of rank. The girls from the working classes do not thus disfigure their feet; they do not presume to be *à la* mode. Besides, the poor are apt to despise their daughters, especially with regard to education, and to favour their sons only. There are extensive sugar plantations in the other neighbouring islands, the value of the several estates being worth a million of money. The lines of railway intersecting the plantations are thirty miles in extent. America is the principal market for the sale of this commodity. Mr. Theo. Davis, our upright, honourable, and intelligent Vice-Consul, has been the life centre of this great industry for a number of years, and the public fêtes which have been held in his honour when he left for England, speak eloquently of the great good he has been to the Hawaiian community; and well he merited all the applause, for he has thrown himself most actively into all philanthropic and Christian works, and is one of the most popular men in Honolulu. Before leaving Honolulu and its delightful climate, the tourist should take a trip in a local steamer, and visit one of the group of islands where there is a very fierce volcanic eruption going on, called the Kilanea, one of the craters passing under the name of the "House of Fire," which the title gives one a fair idea of.

On leaving the Honolulu Pier we were again entertained with music from the royal band to "speed the parting guests," but the quiet, serene life we had been enjoying was soon to be interrupted by a dreadful storm at sea, and that sea the Pacific; Heaven forgive those who gave it that name! For two days and nights we did not have our clothes off, for the rolling and the rocking was so violent and jerky that we could not keep in our berths. Those poor ladies who had cabins on deck could not get out, and no stewardess was allowed to go to them, as it was not safe to walk the decks, which were being swept fore and aft by huge waves, and the wind was so high that the cabin doors could not be opened. The officers of the ship had never been in such a hurricane before, and it was a question for forty-eight hours whether the good ship could weather it out or not. No meals could be had because the cooks could not keep the pots on the range, and no end of crockery and glass was broken in the saloon racks. However, there is an end to all troubles, even to those at sea; hence, after a stormy passage of six days, we all most gratefully hailed the sight of land with a thankfulness, the sincerity of which was depicted on every face, pale and haggard indeed, but expressive of a deep feeling of gratitude to the Giver of all goodness, and to that Mighty Power which could still the waves of the troubled deep, and command it, as of yore, to be calm!

After passing through that narrow passage called the "Golden Gate," we were soon warped to the side of the quay at San Francisco. After some little delay at the customs house in connection with the examination of our luggage (which I must say, to the credit of Cook and Son's agency, we were helped not a little), we took a carriage, and drove off to the Palace Hotel. Oh! the difference between this exquisite sort of luxury, comfort, and enjoyment, and that of the vessel which we had just left was something to calm the most ruffled feelings, and to soothe the most sickly and woebegone passenger after such a sea voyage. We were soon revelling in rooms most exquisitely furnished, in which every possible convenience was present which talent could devise and money accomplish. Arranged on a dial in the sitting-room were a series of knobs to press, which by electricity would indicate to the porters whether you wanted ice-water, a fire, refreshments, an out-door porter, or a laundress. Hot and cold water was laid on into the marble baths and wash-stands. It is a monster building of eight or nine storeys, containing 1,800 rooms from basement to attic. It has a central court covered with a glass roof, in which several carriages can wait at a time, and visitors can sit in easy-chairs, smoke, and converse. There is a balcony round each flight, ornamented with hanging creepers and flowers; from each of these you can look down on the court below and listen to the band playing. There are double corridors on each storey, and these are so wide and high that they are called streets; ours was called Market Street, after the main street in the city. There were velvet-seated lounges at the side for the visitors, and plenty of room in the centre for a carriage and pair to drive along if need be. The vista was such a length that you could not distinguish a person at the further end. Imagine, therefore, six of these double thoroughfares one above the other, and communicating with each other by "lifts," or "elevators," as they call them, smoothly running up a party of twenty or more at a time, and stopping without a thud at each stage to let them out in squads to their several apartments; and this up and down work went on from early dawn to midnight. Of course, there were many staircases with marble steps covered with soft carpeting, independent of the elevators, for those who liked this mode of taking exercise. There could not have been less than 4,000 people under the roof of this little town when we were there, all well fed and housed in the lap of luxury and ease, without confusion or worry; every one thing and every one person had its place, and in that place they were always to be found, like well-disciplined sentinels. San Francisco is said to be built on a hundred hills; anyhow the visitor must see for himself that the streets are all up and down, and yet cable and horse-trams bisect it in every possible direction, and most convenient they are, at 2½d. a ride, running to and fro every few minutes, varying in colour according to the district they go to; they pay well, as they are the common conveyance of the masses, who foot up to the number of 300,000. Though this city of gold is said to be the most abandoned on the face of the earth, religious liberty is in evidence to a remarkable degree, for there are no less than 113 denominations, including the Chinese, who form a very important part of the population, counting up 30,000, and occupying a square half mile, which they monopolise in the very heart of the city. They are very closely packed, the lower orders sleeping in bunks one above the other, as on board ship, with a narrow alley between of about two feet in width. So the visitor to Chinatown must be prepared to find it not a little smelly, and swarming with "live stock," some of which he might carry away on his person. Domestically speaking, Johnny is a very important personage; 6,000 Chinese are domestic servants to the Yankees, and very honest and reliable they are. Three thousand are laundresses, 15,000 are common labourers, and the rest are shopkeepers and well-to-do merchants, some of whom may be seen driving in their carriages and pair, and reputed to be wealthy. In every living room, large and small, high and low, good and bad, may be seen altars and idols, candles and incense, and much praying goes on. All their food is brought in a dried state from China—mushrooms, ducks' eggs wrapt up in clay, pork, fish, potatoes, &c. When the tourist visits the Chinese quarter he had better take a policeman as an escort. Fortunately we had a friend who had been a citizen of San Francisco for many years, and he was very kind, not only in taking us about to many places of note, but in supplying us with much interesting local information. For instance, he took us to Nob Hill, where all the rich merchants live, hence its nickname. It must be understood that there are thirty millionaires in the city, whose possessions vary from three to twenty millions each ; hence they have erected mansions on Nob Hill at a fabulous cost, marble and polished granite entering largely into their structure. From this spot we passed on to a cemetery occupying a singular but picturesque position on a sand-hill, from whence there is a good view of the people's pleasure park and public gardens, with the racecourse adjoining, where our friend's son was killed by a race-horse bolting and jumping the boundary rails, falling upon him and crushing him to death, leaving a young wife and baby to mourn his loss. From his monument in the cemetery could be seen the exact spot where he was killed, the sight always acting as a reminder to the father of the uncertainty of human life. Our friend was the composer of the "Grand Entrée March" for the Knights Templars when they congregated at San Francisco in 1883 from all the States of America. It was performed by thirty performers of the Native Hawaiian band, which had taken the first competitive prize against all American bands. It was played every evening in the court of the Palace Hotel, where thousands of ladies and gentlemen came to listen to its lively strains, and also to give a hearty welcome to this pilgrimage of Knights Templars, who monopolised every room in the spacious building. Every official grade of masonry was represented from every State of the Union. It was at this celebrated congress of noble and benevolent men that the Rev. Dr. Clinton Locke, of Chicago, said in his address to them, "You read of French gallantry, Italian refinement, and English breeding; but it will not for a moment compare, as far as the sacrifice of one's comfort is concerned for the sake of others, with the unvarying respect American men ever show towards a woman or a child. . . . To the woman unprotected and of good character, is passport sufficient, even in the wildest West, to ensure to her the devotion and the loyal devotional service of every man she meets." As a rider to this gallantry I may just add that when the ladies and gentlemen entered the "lift" at the Palace Hotel, the ladies took their seats in these elegant miniature drawing-rooms, while the gentlemen stood up and invariably took their hats off out of respect to the fair sex. But to continue our sightseeing we will charter a carriage, and drive off to The Cliff, where we can see a colony of sea-lions disporting themselves on the rocks, and from

SEALS ON THE ROCKS AT SAN FRANCISCO.

thence to Telegraph Hill, from which is obtained the best view of the city, its bay, and surrounding country, and finish up our outing at Golden Gate Park, where there is a beautiful conservatory to admire. There is no Sunday closing in San Francisco. It is sad to see all the theatres and shops open as on a week day. Amusements of every kind are the order of the day. When persons are migrating from other parts of America to this city, it is a common saying, "that they are going to leave God behind them." Divorces there are quite common, even among those *recently* married, and easily arranged. The shamefacedness with which young girls talk of the matter, even to their elderly lady friends, is simply astounding to an Englishman, and would make him blush in his own country. We went with our friend and his family to spend an evening at the house of a millionaire—a self-made man, originally haling from Ireland. Among other precious and valuable elegancies which his large mansion contained, was an onyx marble mantelpiece, the upper slab of which was truly splendid, and was said to be cheap at £10,000. Of course our host was very proud of showing off this unique piece of rarity, and turning round to me, said, "I guess that beats anything you Britishers can show in your country." Then we ascended to the flat roof of the house, from whence there is at night-time a grand panorama of the city at one's feet, with its wide thoroughfares illumined with gas and electric lights quite dazzling like a pyrotechnic show. Yet with all these glorious surroundings, and with a handsome queen-like wife to boot, he did not strike me as a happy man, and that peace did not reign in his dwelling.

We attended one Sunday evening a service at Trinity Church, and heard Mr. Reed give an eloquent extempore discourse to a crowd of working men, on the subject of capital and labour, and the inequalities between man and man, and his struggles to get the necessities of life. He also pleaded for temperance workers on the dual basis, stating the remarkable fact that fifty-six bishops of the American Episcopalian Church had decided to be total abstainers, in order by force of example to advance and support this grand work among their countrymen.

CHAPTER XXVI.

HAVING already secured our railway tickets and sent on our heavy luggage to New York, by that admirable system so slow on our own lines to adopt, we drove down to the ferry, where a huge transfer steamer was ready to convey us across the bay to Oakland, a very beautiful suburban town. On arriving at the pier we enter a most imposing wooden structure which serves the purpose of a ferry-house and a railway station. Here we find the great overland train with its long line of sleeping cars awaiting us. We enter it without confusion or fuss, and every one settles down in its sumptuous saloons with its soft velvet-covered seats and convenient tables. We travel along the valley for twenty-eight miles, and then we arrive at Port Costa, where there is something to surprise us. Our long train of eleven carriages, each 84 feet long, has to be carried bodily across the Carquinez Strait to the town of Benicia opposite. This transfer boat, called the *Solano*, is said to be the largest in the world, and is so constructed that it will hold on its immense deck forty-eight cars and two engines divided into parallel portions. Let us descend from our saloon for a moment, and see for ourselves the easy and remarkable way in which the train leaves the rails on the land to meet those on the boat on a perfect level. Then the whole ponderous mass moves off so smoothly that those inside the carriages do not feel the movement. When we reached the other side, both sets of rails again approximated to a nicety, and we trained off again as if nothing very important had happened. To say that this is a grand piece of engineering skill is to say little. Only in America would one see such gigantic works carried out, and yet we are only at the commencement of that wonder of wonders—the passage of the Rockies. Night coming on, we undressed and settled down for a sleep in our berths and sofas. Early the next morning we were greeted by the sun shining on the snowy top of the Nevada range of mountains, which we had reached by our train zig-zagging to a height of 7,000 feet above the valley we had left behind the evening before. These snow-clad hills are covered here and there with fir-trees, and in order to protect the railway from avalanches of snow long timber sheds have been erected at the most exposed situations. Some of these are so long that they resemble long wooden tunnels, lighted at the side by portholes, through which we get a pretty glimpse now and again. It is said that the measurement of the covered ways, when put end to end, would reach one hundred miles, a prodigious work in such an inhospitable region. Sometimes they catch fire from the engines, which leads to much expense to the company; but they are indispensable, as they support sometimes eighteen feet of snow on their roofs. Now the scene completely changes. We descend the eastern slopes of the Nevada range, so different to its western side, which is so full of gold that two hundred and fifty millions have been extracted from it in forty years, and which has enriched California far above any other State of America, till at last we reach the great American desert, and its arid plains yielding only sage-brush and grease-wood. Hour after hour passes by in wearisome monotony, till the eyesight tires over the desolate waste, destitute of the lowest forms of vegetation—and all this from want of water, for it is found if it be irrigated it will produce almost anything, but at present it is all sand, varied with here and there a surface of alkali, which shines in the distance like water, simulating lakes with its deceitful mirage. In this Great Basin, surrounded by mountains, a natural curiosity exists, namely, the river Humbolt runs for 380 miles, and, failing to find an outlet, buries its water in the arid sand, within view of the passing train. Having traversed a run of 460 miles, we leave the State of Nevada behind, and enter the territory of the Mormons, and we soon are looking down upon the Great Salt Lake, which we keep in view for the next one hundred miles. This mysterious inland sea, called also the "Dead Sea" of America, has no outlet. When its shores get dry in the summer, a large quantity of crystallised alkali is collected. At last we reach Ogden, 894 miles from San Francisco, and the journey was accomplished in thirty-six hours, continuous travelling—rather slow, especially for America. A Baptist minister, hailing from the Golden City, told me in the train that the old

Friscoites, who boasted of their being the "Pioneers" and founders of the city in 1849, considered themselves so pre-eminently good and moral on that account that they never need trouble themselves on the score of religion, its duties and needs; and some even replied, when asked what denomination they belonged to, would say that they were "forty-niners."

At Ogden we drop our passengers who desire to visit the Yellowstone National Park, and we put our watches on one hour, it having been found by the Government more convenient to make three changes only in the time between Frisco and New York of one hour each. Continuing our journey for another thirty-six miles, we reach Salt Lake City, and take up our quarters at Cullen's Hotel, where we luxuriated in most delightful rooms, sitting, bed, and bath-rooms *en suite*, with electric light, most excellent cuisine, and good service, which was a surprise to us in the "City of the Saints." The next morning we were greeted with a splendid view of the opposite snow-capped hills in a pink halo of sunshine, somewhat like the Pyrennian range from Pau, in France. These glistening peaks of the Wahsatch Mountains run up into the skies from 9,000 to 13,000 feet high above the sea-level. To a casual visitor no difference would appear in its outward aspect between this city and any other. Everything in the streets seemed to be conducted in a most orderly and peaceful way. The first objects which a tourist seeks for are the Mormon Tabernacle—The Temple—and close by the Assembly Hall (*vide* sketch). First, then, we enter the Temple, with its curved roof like the back of a

SALT LAKE CITY.

turtle. It sits at ease 9,000 people, yet it is only 250 feet long, by 150 feet wide, and 100 feet high, contains a huge organ with 57 stops and 2,846 pipes. The acoustic properties are marvellous. One can hear a pin drop or the hands rubbed together across a space of 200 feet. It is an extraordinary building, all of wood, and every visitor should attend the afternoon Sunday service, and look down on its vast congregation, and hear the organ and choir sing the hymns with astonishing enthusiasm, the breaking of bread by the priesthood, the fervid addresses to show with astonishing plausibility the identity of the Latter Day Saints' Church with that of the Zion of prophecy, which, as one writer has said, " must impress every thoughtful visitor more or less powerfully as the instruments of a gigantic imposture, and his moral nature recoil from them as the spiritual cloak of a carnal church—the perfumed drapery of an ecclesiastical seraglio." We now turn to the magnificent Gothic Temple, all built of granite, 200 feet by 100 feet, and 100 feet high. It was commenced in 1853, and has cost millions upon millions of dollars, and it is not yet completed. A stranger will naturally ask, How do they get the money? Well, it is a fixed law with the Mormons that they prove their faith by their works, by giving 10 per cent. of their profits to complete the Temple. Again, the first Thursday in every month is set apart by the shopkeepers, so that their employés may attend a religious service and contribute donations for the relief of the poor and needy. The Assembly Hall is a pleasure resort for all classes—reading, dancing, and concerts.

We will take our seats in the electric tramway along Main Street to the foot of the hill two miles off, and then a short walk brings us to Fort Douglass, where there is a battery and artillery barracks. From thence we get a good bird's-eye view of the city below, containing its 30,000 inhabitants, the streets inshrined in green foliage, obscuring the line of roads, as in Honolulu, but all the grand buildings, including the Holy Cross Hospital, stand out in bold relief, backed by the Salt Lake and the mountains beyond. We will now return and take a carriage drive through the wide thoroughfares shaded by poplar and acacia trees, and visit the late Brigham Young's house, called the "Amelia Palace," after his favourite wife, who lived there with him, while the other wives resided in a large house named the "Bee Hive;" but we were told by the daughter of one of Brigham Young's servants that his other wives had each a separate house and a separate establishment quite distinct from one another. I got a capital photograph of Brigham Young, who died in 1877. He was President of the 142 hardy "Pioneers" who entered the valley in 1847, who suffered many privations, but who, with extraordinary religious zeal and pluck, have succeeded in founding a beautiful city, making what was once deemed for ages a barren waste into a most fertile country, where every luxury can be obtained, and where useful factories abound.

Brigham Young's tomb should be seen. Our previous informant told us that many of his devotees still believe that he is not dead, and that others were so superstitious that they placed sentinels over his grave for some time; and recently they affirm that his gravestone has shifted; therefore, to make things more secure, they have placed a more weighty slab over the original, and one can see the stone ready for fixing. The visitor should not fail to pay a visit by train to Lake Park bathing resort, a sort of Brighton to the citizens, situated on the shores of the Salt Lake, about twenty miles off, and by all means try a bath in the buoyant water, which contains 22 per cent. of pure salt, in which it is impossible to sink. Care should be taken that none of the water gets into the mouth or nostrils, otherwise there would be danger of suffocation. To the porter who busied himself in getting our luggage into the train I put the question, with as little offensiveness as I could muster, "How many wives have you got?" He replied, very readily, "Only one, and I find some difficulty in maintaining her. It is only the rich nobs and higher classes who can afford to have a lot of wives." This answer recalled me to the social condition of Turkey, where the rich pashas only can indulge in a harem. We will now resume our journey eastward, and before we reach the mountains we pass through a grand valley some miles in extent, full of Mormon settlements smiling with fertile fields and orchards in the highest state of cultivation, brought about by the persevering industry of the people, who, through hard work and irrigation, have turned this valley from a wilderness into a garden that blossoms like the rose. Just look at the bright-eyed and healthy children who meet you with baskets of fruits, strawberries, raspberries, currants, apples, &c., and you will be convinced that you are in the land of milk and honey. A very pleasant little town on this route, and a summer resort for the well-to-do, is Provo, where you can get an excellent dinner at the station.

A short distance to one's right we see the beautiful Lake of Utah, a large body of fresh water, which the Mormons call the Lake of Tiberias, and from this lake runs a fertilising stream they name the River Jordan, flowing into the Salt Lake, styled by them the "Dead Sea"; hence the Latter Day Saints desire to draw an analogy between this disposition of nature and that in Palestine, and that it is in accordance with the Divine plan and purpose that this beautiful valley should be blessed as the abode of the Mormonites!

Now we will commence the romantic story of the route from west to east of the Rio Grande and Denver Railway, 700 miles in extent. Passing through these gigantic barriers, necessitating the ascent of our train to elevations of 7,465 feet, 10,852 feet, and 7,238 feet. These have to be surmounted, and then we have to penetrate through awful gorges, or cañons, as they are called, which are such remarkable features in the Rocky Mountain railway system. Soon after leaving Provo we begin the ascent of the first of these tremendous bulwarks, and by all sorts of twistings and zig-zagging gain what is termed the "Soldier's Divide," the summit of the Wahsatch Range, which sends up its tall spires of rock high up into the skies. After traversing a certain amount of plateau we begin to descend, and get some scenery which, though picturesquely fine, is but a faint foreshadowing of that which is soon to be our delight to gaze upon. The first and foremost object to astonish and fascinate our attention is the Castle Gate entrance to Price River Cañon, one of the grandest single objects in the entire mountain world. It consists of two immense projections from the sides of the gorge of solid rock, dyed with a rich colouring of red, while the pine trees growing about them reach only a short way up, but serve to intensify the varied hues of rock and shrubs. These two huge pillars are respectively 500 feet and 800 feet high, and guard, like sentinels, this narrow passage through the heart of which the railroad runs side by side with the river, one pressing closely upon the other in fearful proximity. The train is brought to a stand here that we may all admire and take away such a recollection as never can be forgotten. After passing through the winding cañon with its lofty and precipitous walls varying in colour at every turn, showing a strife with the elements over thousands of years of time, we debouch at last upon the broad valley of Green River, a stream of good size, which fifty miles further on joins the Grande, to make up the far-famed Colorado. The valleys between these two rivers are rich agricultural lands, extending over a hundred miles. After this our train has to traverse a weird piece of country, reminding one of the Nevada desert, the dreariness relieved only by the sight of a remarkable formation called the Book Cliffs, resembling piles of books on a shelf, and in the distance the glistening mountains of Serra da Sal and San

THE ROYAL GORGE, PASSAGE OF THE ROCKIES.

Rafael. Soon after passing Montrose, we arrive at the Black Cañon of the Gunnison river, considered one of the most stupendous and awe-inspiring scenes in the world, penetrating a gorge of several miles in extent, with perpendicular walls of solid granite on each side, rising from 1,000 feet to 2,000 feet, between which tears along an impetuous torrent, splashing and foaming over its rocky bed; and by the side of this gushing stream has been blasted from its granite side a sufficient platform to lay down a single line of rails. Upon these our train passes through numerous windings and projecting rocks, adding an overpowering impressiveness to the scene. On the bottom of this deep gulf the sun never shines. One of the special features of this magnificent cañon is the Currecanti Needle, a huge granite monolith that rises from the gorge with all the grace and symmetry of an Egyptian obelisk, which is red from base to summit, and stands like a grim guardian in watchful solitude.

As we emerge from this weird chasm we welcome the sunny quiet of the Gunnison valley, which affords a happy relief to one's over-wrought feelings, for our hearts have been standing still for some time with the awful grandeur of this wondrous pass. Leaving Gunnison behind, we now begin the ascent of all ascents—the most exhilarating and surprising railway ride in the world. We first of all have our long train divided into two portions, each to be drawn by two powerful ten-wheeled engines, and we begin our climb to the "Continental Divide," called so because it separates the eastern from the western side of America. As our rise becomes steeper the engines puff out a sullen roar, indicating the tremendous strain upon them; and then, as we get higher we begin to wind round the mountains, and, after struggling by steep gradients for four miles, we find that we have only got upwards about half a mile above the railroad we see below us, on which, comes, following in our wake, the other portion of our train, apparently going in an opposite direction. We wave our handkerchiefs one to another as a passing

RAILWAY OVER THE ROCKIES.

salute. On and upward we go into the skies, with its rarefied and exciting air, along narrow ledges of rock, through cuttings in the solid stone, and passing banks of snow and stunted pines. The track frequently doubles upon itself, and slow is the progress till we begin to think that we shall never reach the top; but everything comes to him who can be patient, and so we reach at last the Marshall Pass, which is covered with a long wooden shed. Here we come to a stand after a gradual climb of 10,852 feet above the sea-level, and yet we are at the base of Mount Ouvry, which is 4,000 feet still higher. On each side of the ridge arises, on the eastern, the River Arkansas, which goes to join the Mississippi, and on the western, the River Gunnison, which flows into the Colorado. We are not kept long on this, the backbone of the Rockies. A cry of "All aboard!" is shouted, and we have to resume our seats, and, having detached one of our engines, we go down very slowly and cautiously; but this gives us more time to gaze upon the magnificent scenery of the eastern slope. The grand Sangre de Cristo range stands boldly out against the skies right in front of us, and below us are the peaks of hills with green valleys and sparkling brooks between them, till we reach the Arkansas plains. At every turn we must admire and laud the great engineering skill which could devise this railroad and overcome its varied difficulties, and yet one never hears his name mentioned. Our descent is by grades of one foot in twenty-four. We soon reach a dining-station, and for a moment our thoughts do not go back to the glories of the Marshall Pass. After this refreshment we were better able to enjoy a trip through the Royal Gorge, the Grand Cañon of the Rockies, whose wonders and superlative magnificence surpass anything we have yet seen, and that is saying a great deal. To make a passage through this gorge the engineer's hand has surpassed itself in ingenuity. No photographer, or writer, or painter, can convey to the eye of man a tithe of its awful and fascinating grandeur. The skill and dogged perseverance of the Anglo-Saxon is here very apparent. With the dashing, foaming River Arkansas rushing through this chasm, the engineer has carved his way by its side through the living rock, and constructed a roadway for a single line of rails. There was scarcely room for the river alone to get through it, and granite projections blocked the way with their mighty bulk. When one reflects that this gorge extends fourteen miles, the very thought was enough to make any man's heart sink within him; but he faced the difficulties with superhuman efforts, and the numerous obstructions were gradually blasted out of the way, and, following the contour of the rocks, a thoroughfare was at last pierced, and its hidden glories revealed, which, once seen, can never be effaced from the mind of the fortunate tourist who is permitted to behold these mighty works of the great Creator and His inspired creature—man.

We come to a stand at the entrance, and our conductor goes through the train, informing the several passengers that the Denver and Rio Grande Company have, in order that they may see the gorge to greater advantage, placed at the rear of the train an "observation car," into which about a hundred and fifty persons pack themselves; it is all open top and side, like a long truck with seats in it. From this point of vantage we can see at our ease the extraordinary wonders of this rocky cleft. We pass down very slowly with the Arkansas river, a very "hell of waters" by our side. The deeper we go, higher and higher become the perpendicular walls of granite, without a shrub to mar their smooth surface, towering to a height of 1,000 feet to 1,500 feet, between which we see an arch of blue sky, but no sun ever penetrates to the bottom of this abyss. No sign of a bird or any other living thing, and the noise of the rushing torrent only breaks the awful stillness.

Overhanging crags overshadow the track here and there, and threaten to fall down and crush us. If we could but mount up to one of these and look down, what a veritable pigmy our train would appear amid such overmastering surroundings! With this fancied picture on our minds, we will now emerge from this grand undertaking of which the Americans may well be proud of as their country's *chef d'œuvre*. As we are now re-entering civilised life again, we will defer its description for another chapter.

CHAPTER XXVII.

EMERGING from the Royal Gorge we next come to the Cañon city, where may be seen a monster building, like two or three of our workhouses rolled into one, with a well-armed guard pacing up and down its grim walls. On inquiry we are told that this stronghold is the Colorado State Penitentiary. After a further run of forty miles we reach Puebla, an old Spanish town, full of life and activity. Continuing our journey northward for 120 miles, we arrive at Denver, our road having run along the base of the Rocky Mountains. On our left, from which may be seen issuing peaks, 12,000 feet to 15,000 feet high, while on our right we behold an interminable plain or prairie, which is like an ocean with nothing but the horizon in the distance, unbroken by hedges or trees, but whose fertility by irrigation from the watershed of the Rockies is unbounded. Those who have money to spare and well-lined pockets should strike off at Puebla for Maniton, described as the Saratoga of the West. There they will find large, sumptuous hotels, with every elegance and luxury for wealthy summer visitors who are in search of health or pleasure. The beauty of the surrounding scenery cannot be surpassed in America. The ascent of Pike's Peak is easy for ladies or gentlemen, though it does run up 14,000 feet into the heavens. From thence they better can see the boundless plains, giving a grand sweep of vision towards the east; and though this peak is so high the American Government have erected an observatory on its summit. It might indeed be justly said that no trip to the Rockies can be considered complete which omits a stay at Maniton. Again, another chief attraction is a carriage drive to the "Garden of the Gods" and Glen Eyrie, where one will be fascinated by a series of coloured rocks of fantastic, unearthly shape, which impart to the scenery a weird aspect in the midst of the most peaceful surroundings.

We will now hark back to Denver, one of the magic wonders as a city on the American continent. Many another has sprung up in mushroom fashion, but none have come up to Denver in the rapidity of its rise; the population having increased from 5,000 to 125,000 in eighteen years. It is the commercial centre for the mining district of Colorado, and here are situated the great smelting and reduction works, and some good mineralogical specimens can be purchased. The hotels are excellent, and the trams run in every direction. We attended divine service at the cathedral, which has been erected through the untiring zeal of Dean Hart, formerly of Blackheath, near London, who came here for the benefit of his health, and is now well and robust, and very popular as an extempore preacher, the only kind of preaching that goes down in the States. The suburbs of Denver are very pretty and neat, and easily reachable by train. The houses are most comfortably built, and very picturesque in the Queen Anne style, each in their own separate grounds. Such satisfaction and contentment do these residences give the people that Denver has been called "the city of homes." The citizens are a rich and go-ahead race. We passed the huge town-hall and state offices with its central dome, and which is to cost when finished one and a half millions sterling. The station buildings are immense, and it is quite a sight to see the grand baggage depôt for passengers' trunks, &c. We now take our places in the train starting for Chicago, shortly called "Sheego," by the people. This is a run of 1,025 miles, and to get there we have to pass the three great States of Nebraska, Iowa, and Illinois. In Iowa they are prohibited from brewing or selling spirits, consequently there is not such a demand for maize (corn) for the purpose of distillation, hence they say the corn trade is depressed in that state, yet to the tourist it seems as flourishing as any of the others. We traverse for miles and miles a more or less undulating prairie with an everlasting sameness of aspect, the chief features of which are its rapid agricultural development, varied with towns and villages cropping up in every direction, shaded by woods and plantations. The farming produce is truly remarkable; for instance, it is said that the maize crop, or corn, as it is called, alone in these fertile plains would fill a goods train 2,000 miles in length, or if we placed the corn on our English waggons it would constitute a procession of trains that would reach round the world. In Iowa the maize is so plentiful, such a veritable glut in the market, that they use it for fuel to heat their ovens. The eye wearies over this never-ceasing land of plenty, "this grand republican valley, watered and drained by its huge republican rivers," the mighty Missouri, and its still mightier brother, the majestic Mississippi, the "father of waters," as the Americans so proudly call it; and we are glad to reach Omaha, the most populous city we have seen since we left Frisco. It has an immense wholesale trade, large smelting works, extensive stock-yards and packing houses, and the visitor might do worse than break his journey here, after his wearisome passage over the prairies, where his patience has been not a little tried. Buy a photo of a settler's family on the plains entitled, "Getting a Start." Mounting our train again we soon reach the bridge which crosses the Missouri, a splendid structure of 3,000 feet in length. It is a grand piece of engineering skill, and as graceful as it is substantial. It may be seen to great advantage from the left-hand windows, supposing that you are approaching it from the western side. The volume of water which is calculated to flow under this bridge in the winter-time is immense; viz., 750,000 gallons per second; but it decreases so rapidly in June that it shrinks into comparatively small dimensions, hence at that season one would little imagine that large steamers navigate the river for 2,300 miles above this point. At Burlington,

which is a picturesque city on the banks of the
Mississippi, we cross that river which never becomes
as shallow as the Missouri, and has a finer appearance because its sides are more richly wooded. The
bridge which spans the river is also a very magnificent one of 2,237 feet long, the draw span being itself
362 feet in extent. Between Burlington and Chicago,
which are separated by 200 miles, we get into a most
prosperous and highly-cultivated country, and as
interesting as it is beautiful, more like England,
being better wooded, and with clean, white homesteads standing in cozy nooks surrounded by green
shrubs and trees. The huge red barns indicate the
prosperity of the farmers, who ought to be well content living in the midst of such Arcadian loveliness.
Thus we pass onward through the granary of the
world until at last we come to a very pretty suburban-
like series of villas, through the centre of which our
train runs, and on inquiring as to our whereabouts
were told that we had entered the outskirts of
Chicago, and that we had yet twenty-four miles to
travel before we reached the heart of the city. This
will give the tourist a fair notion of the extent of
this famous metropolis. It is the most wonderful
of modern cities in its rapid strides, as a great centre
of population, combined with its world-wide commerce
as a meat-producing community. Its growth since
it was burnt down about fifteen years ago is quite
phenomenal. To give an instance of the rapid
way in which they can build, I may mention the
"Auditorium." This remarkable building was begun
and *completed in the short space of two years*. Its

frontage is 710 feet, is 270 feet high to the lantern, it has eleven storeys, contains a theatre, opera house, hotel, library, museum, and an observatory on the top, &c., and up to which one goes in a "lift." The weight of this monster is 110,000 tons, and, wonderful to relate, fifty million pieces of ornamental marble were put down by the human hand. As there will be an immense gathering of people from all parts of the globe to visit the "World's Fair," to be opened in May, 1893, at Chicago, I must be excused if I enter a little more into detail respecting the greatness of this wonderful mart. I will begin by saying that when the Queen ascended the throne the population of Chicago was only 3,000, now it contains one million and a half of the most energetic and enterprising people on the face of the earth. The length of the city is $24\frac{1}{2}$ miles long by $14\frac{1}{2}$ miles wide, and stands on an area of 175 square miles. With the advent of railways it soon became one grand centre for railroads from all parts to focus in, which are kept very busy in transmitting to every corner of the civilised globe its live and dead stock, and its unlimited stores of grain. A visit to its stockyards, many acres in extent, into which thousands of hogs and bullocks are carried by rail every day, is a wonder worth going thousands of miles to see. The day we went there, and there is no difficulty in getting a ticket of admission, there were nearly 8,000 pigs to be slaughtered and packed away. During the twenty minutes that I was on the platform of observation, I saw sixty hogs killed, the carcase dropped into a tank of scalding water, where all the bristles were shaved off by the fans of a water-wheel constantly revolving in the trough, and the body passes out over a slide as clean as a new-born babe. One carcase follows another in quick succession into the cooling gallery without the hand hardly touching them, and almost noiseless, so that each pig is killed, cleaned, cooled, cut and quartered and quite ready for the cook in thirty-five seconds! This sounds too ridiculous to be true, but I can vouch for the truth of it. Otherwise I would ask, how could 8,000 hogs be disposed of in one day if this expeditious mode of killing, &c., did not exist? In the packing-houses 6,000 men are engaged, and what is quite incidental to this business is the small one of 50,000 lbs. of sausages made daily. Now I will take the visitor back through the busy streets, as thronged as London Cheapside, to the immense pile of buildings of ten storeys high, with polished granite pillars, which they call the Board of Trade Buildings, in which is held the Bourse, as noisy as that in Paris, a veritable Babel of tongues. Here we saw on the notice board as one day's sale—700,000 lbs. of lard, and innumerable barrels of packed pork, ready to go to the ends of the civilised world. There is rather a remarkable sight, and in the very heart of the city too, such as one would not meet with in any town in Europe, but everything must give way to the general good of the many in a republican place of business—every sentiment is swallowed up by the trading deity. This ugly monstrosity is a huge iron revolving bridge, which turns on its axis to allow of large steamers passing along the River Chicago. It is amusing to watch the sudden cessation in the traffic in a wide bustling street while this proceeding went on. Every class of vehicle and every style of person had to submit patiently for about fifteen minutes on both sides, and then ensued a rush as if to catch up so many dollars that had been lost by the delay to the traffic; fancy all this at the bottom of Ludgate Hill in London, then you can imagine the concourse collected at every stoppage. I met a gentlemanly-looking man who was wearing a tricolor decoration in the button-hole of his coat—blue, red, and white, and getting into conversation with him on the subject of the American War, and knowing that Americans looked down with contempt on war medals and other insignia of distinction, I asked him what it signified, and he said it was the Military Order of the Loyal Legion of Americans, instituted by the *officers* who had been engaged in the War of the Rebellion! They have a club, and they meet once a month. If a tram be entered in the centre of the city, where the large hotels are situated, the visitor will have a good opportunity of seeing its long, wide thoroughfares, bristling with grand stores and shops for about eight miles, which will bring him to Lincoln's Park, a most lovely promenade, very prettily laid out with flowers and shrubs, and within which is a good zoological collection of wild animals; the elks, buffaloes, and red foxes being very fine specimens. The young people seemed very happy with their boats and swings, &c., all free and unfettered, apparently without a sign of a keeper to keep guard over its proprieties and protect it from any breach of its privileges. A pleasant restaurant, with simple refreshment and mild, cooling drinks, was there, with plenty of seats and nothing to pay. The want of beauty and grace in the womenkind both in Denver and Chicago is very remarkable. In the latter the men are well-made and tall; but the pallor of the face and the dark rings under the eyes denote that the place and surroundings are not health-giving, and the strongest feel a sense of weariness and have a washed-out look. I heard it said that if a man did not make his fortune in ten years in Chicago, the wear and tear is such that the constitution gives way! It would be unjust and ungrateful to take leave of Chicago without a word in favour of that splendid hotel called "Sherman House," with its four hundred rooms, and its pretty central hall with its promenade gallery looking down on its bustling floor, and from which issues of an evening some delightful music and singing. The dining-room is on a large scale, the cuisine is first-rate, and the waiting unexceptionable; the variety of dishes to choose from quite puzzles an Englishman. Of course, being in the very heart of business life and places of public amusement, it is not a dead calm at any time of the day, and what it will be when the Exhibition is on it is not easy to imagine. We therefore leave these nice luxurious quarters with regret, and proceed on our journey to the Niagara Falls. *En route* we pass through a grand fertile country again, with numerous ranches of wide extent, in which we saw large herds of cattle, and the proprietor was said to be fortunate if he could boast of having a thousand head or more, the lot being defined as a "fine bunch" of cattle, in the same manner as

NIAGARA FALLS.

they would say in Australia when a lucky squatter rejoiced in a large "mob" of cattle, where the wives of the aborigines, called "Gins," are such adepts not only in collecting the animals, but as drovers also. We rattle along in a most superbly appointed train, in which we are regaled with most sumptuous fare, cooked "on board" in a wonderfully small space, and waited on by obsequious black attendants in white caps and jackets, with soft voices and noiseless tread, with luscious dessert of strawberries and cream, and especially of peaches, which are indeed the boast of the State of Michigan, where they grow to such perfection; and not only its fruits, but it is proud of its splendid crops of corn, its output of copper, and the production of a large quantity of salt. Traversing this state to its northern end, we reach its handsome commercial capital containing 250,000 inhabitants, Detroit by name, and there we cross the river, and on the other side enter the province of Ontario, where we find ourselves once more under the British flag; but now nothing more of interest worth recording takes place till we get to the "Welland Canal," which has been constructed to unite the Lakes of Erie and Ontario together, a union rendered necessary in consequence of the Falls of Niagara and its whirlpool making the stream unnavigable. We are soon startled by the conductor, warning us that we are approaching the greatest of waterfalls, where the train pulls up for about three minutes to give the passengers an opportunity of seeing from the carriage windows this wondrous roaring cascade! After making a slight curve we pass over a cantilever railway bridge, a great height above the Rapids, and on the other side we find ourselves once more on American soil and soon in a large commodious station, where we descend from our car and drive off to the Prospect House Hotel, where we took up our abode for three or four days. This hotel is said to have been patronised by the Prince of Wales, Duke of Connaught, and Prince Leopold, &c. All very well for such high folk; but an ordinary tourist, whose purse has its limits, it would be as well to think twice before entering such expensive quarters. The best thing for a tourist to do is to get a public conveyance with a pair of horses, and, after having settled as to the charge, then to take first the American side and drive off to see respectively the "Goat," "Bath," and "Luna" Islands, then the "Three Sister" Islands. And descending the steps to where the tower stood before it fell down, one gets very near indeed to the edge of the Cataract, and if the visitor has nerve enough he will see a sight which passes far beyond all human description or painter to depict. He will see a volume of water 15 feet thick rush over a rocky precipice 120 feet high, and some hundreds of feet in width, and finally take a bird's-eye view of the whole from a corner of Prospect Park, and then the visitor has something photoed on his brain that will never fade from it. Now we will take to the carriage again, and drive down the right bank till we get to the Inclined Railway, a sort of lift such as one sees at Scarborough, which takes us down easily to the edge of the whirling torrent; thence we can look up at the Falls, and the boiling waters at our feet,

THE BRIDGE OVER NIAGARA RAPIDS.

and on returning to the office on the bank a good large photo can be purchased as a shadowy reminder of the great original. Driving further on we come to the Whirlpool Rapids, where Captain Webb lost his life in his endeavour to swim them; it was supposed that he got stunned by striking his head against a projecting rock. The wire on which Blondin crossed the Niagara may be seen. Now we will cross the fine suspension bridge, 1,268 feet long, and get on to the Canadian side again, from which a still grander view of the Falls may be obtained, and even a waterproof dress hired, with a guide who will pioneer us behind the fall of water, if you feel so inclined. It is quite safe even for ladies, who often do it in perfect safety. On returning over the suspension bridge stop the carriage midway across it, and gaze at your ease on this "hell of waters," *à la* Byron, in front and beneath you, and that from a mid-air standpoint, because the bridge is 190 feet above this raging tumultuous stream. The "publics" are open on the American side, but there was no rowdyism or brawling on the Sunday. We attended St. Peter's Episcopalian Church. The service was of the higher order of ritualism, and in the evening all was choral and no sermon was given. The congregation was a thin one. I have omitted to mention that the huge volume of water which passes over the Falls is the concentrated collection from the Lakes Superior, Huron, Michigan, and Erie. All this rushes down the precipitous sides of the River Niagara and empties itself into the Lake Ontario, which is the head-spring of the great River St. Lawrence. Having now seen and notified everything worth describing at Niagara, we will proceed onward to New York. Our first halt is at the bustling town of Buffalo, where we changed our carriage, and for two dollars extra each we have the privilege of riding in the "vestibuled car," which is without an equal in any country. The superior style in which it is furnished is only comparable by the excellence of its viands, which taste the more delicious amid such elegant and refined surroundings, and the look-out over the charming scenery as we sit at ease and glide smoothly but swiftly along, must be done to give a fair idea of the position. There is, however, "no rose without its thorn," hence now and again our peace was disturbed by the loud clanging of a bell and the bray from the engine before reaching a level crossing, or a run down the centre of the main street of a town, to give out a tremendous vigorous warning to the inhabitants that the traffic must be temporarily stopped. As there are no bridges over the line as we have, the carriages can be built any height. Passing along this run of 462 miles we come to the great cities of Rochester, Syracuse, and Albany, interspersed here and there with pretty towns and country villages of smaller note, but infinite in number. Large manufacturing buildings, like the cotton mills in Lancashire, crop up constantly, with the everlasting steam-engine predominating everywhere and for everything over the handwork of man; but all this is diversified and beautified by the intermixture of some splendid agriculture, which makes the New York State so worthy of its title, "the Empire State." But before we reach that head centre of commercial vitality and incalculable wealth, I have to describe and admire the last but best bit of our journey since we left the Rockies, and that is the delightful run from Albany to New York, a distance of about a hundred and fifty miles, along the left bank of the Hudson River, which may not only be compared to, but stamped as of superior beauty to the Rhine in Germany. The traffic is so immense that it has a double line of rails, and the iron road follows the windings of this grand river, about two miles wide, and bounded on each side with picturesque scenery of the most fascinating character conceivable. After passing down the line for thirty-five miles, the famous Catshills are seen to great advantage, and on reaching the Fishkill Landing, the gorge known as the Highlands is entered, rough and grand, at the northern end of which the "Storm King" commands one's attention. Again, six miles further down on the same side, standing out on a most romantic site, is the United States Military Academy of West Point. Steaming on another twenty-five miles we get a sight of the basaltic columns, known as the "Palisades." Besides these sights we pass the "river cities" at various intervals, some of which have an exceedingly picturesque appearance. We may note Poughkeepsie, with Vassar College in its rear; Tarrytoon, with its quaint old Dutch church, and Yonkers. The Hudson has some sad tales to tell in connection with the Revolutionary War; for instance, Major Andre's trial and execution. We lose sight of the river at Spuyten Duyvil as we turn eastwards, and

Harlem Bridge is the next object of our attention, and then the terminus of the Elevated Railway, and behold we are in the heart of New York before we can realise it! But we have not quite done with the beautiful Hudson, with its shining surface speckled over with large white paddle-steamers, some for pleasure, others towing half-a-dozen long barges in double line like a big duck convoying a brood of small ducklings, interspersed here and there with yachts carrying high white sails, flitting across the water like so many butterflies, a bright, lively sight and no mistake, and "good for sore eyes," as the Scotch would say. Another very striking feature to a tourist is a number of large buildings on the right bank at frequent intervals on the very verge, and even overhanging, the water. These, we were told, were factories or depôts for ice! Enough, one would suppose, to supply the whole world; but no, iced water is such a favourite drink with the residents of New York that it is placed at your side at every meal, and even supplied to every bedroom—no doubt a great luxury when the temperature in the shade is at 100° Fahr.; but it does seem extraordinary to an Englishman this crave for ice. Every bit of vantage ground that a house can find a lodgment on is secured at a fabulous sum to erect a residence for some city millionaire or other; and no wonder, the prospect being lovely in every direction, which a combination of rock, wood, and river can give to the exquisite picture! a view seen at every turn in the river, with a train on the right whisking along round the corner between two projecting rocks and the shipping in the centre of the stream. Just imagine it—picture it to your mind if you can.

My last chapter I shall devote to my recollections of New York.

CHAPTER XXVIII.

LANDING at the Central Station, well known as the grand central depôt in 42nd Street, it is difficult to give any foreigner an adequate idea of the scene. Supposing we rolled the Euston, Midland, and Charing Cross stations into one, it would be no exaggeration to say that its two façades of 1,000 feet each would be equal to those three combined, and I don't think then that those stations stand on so large an area of ground as this gigantic building. I must here premise this description as only a start, because as we go on we shall find that everything in the building line is on a tremendously exaggerated scale in the city of New York. The rooms for the reception alone for the trans-continental luggage are immense, and here we found our baggage quite safe and uninjured, which had been forwarded from "Frisco," and which they will, for a small fee, keep in hand and transmit to your steamer when you have made up your mind to take your passage home. Just as we were getting our wraps together a respectably dressed lady-passenger asked us if we were going across the city to join our Atlantic steamer that night, and on replying in the negative we were

NEW YORK.

surprised to hear her say that she knew we were *foreigners!* As both parties were speaking good plain grammatical English we were rather startled, I must say, at being called foreigners! But the fact is the people feel a certain pride in being Americans, and do not look upon it as any compliment to be regarded as English. The native born views his country as the first and most go-a-head of any in the whole world. In New York at any rate an Englishman soon feels himself rather "boiled down" from a puffed-up estimation of himself or his country. First of all, then, we must suppose ourselves settled in a good hotel in Broadway, the focus of liveliness, where we can secure a good room and every luxury, barring intoxicants, from 12s. to 14s. a day; but if we desire to put up at a more fashionable one, in the Fifth Avenue for instance, we must expect to pay more, the fare, however, would be no better. The city has so much increased in size and changed in its appearance since my last visit to it thirty-eight years ago, that I was puzzled to know where to start from with a visitor who wanted to see everything and had not much time to do it in. I was told if I wished to ascertain how very much New York had extended itself, that I could not do better than take a seat in the Elevator Railway at Castle Garden and run up the city on one side and then down the other, which we did, and after traversing numerous streets and avenues we reached the terminus at 129th Street: there we descended, and took a horse tram across the city to the terminus of the "Elevator" on the other side and ran back to Castle Garden, a distance

TERMINUS, ELEVATED RAILWAY, NEW YORK.

of twenty-two miles there and back, at the small cost of 7½d. each. A cheap piece of sight-seeing truly! for our vision was simply glutted with the numerous church towers and spires, public halls, monster hotels, and still bigger warehouses, public gardens, and squares, &c. ; but what astonished us not a trifle as we passed along was the singular sight of ladies sitting calmly and unconcerned in their drawing-rooms, into which we could plainly peep as we glided past from the carriage windows, but everybody and every interest must give way where it clashes with the benefit of the masses! Just fancy carrying an "Elevator" along Piccadilly or Pall Mall in London, who would dare to introduce the Bill into the House of Commons! When I inquired whether the "Elevator" had not been the ruin of the owners of the mansions in the fashionable avenues, they replied, "Oh no, no, not at all, just the reverse had happened. They paid better when let for stores or offices than they did as residences, especially those near the stations, which brought the merchants into touch with one another at every quarter of a mile or so." Underneath the "Elevator," which was erected on a delicate-looking iron trellis-work, was a horse tramway, which could deposit one at any intermediate point. This convenient mode of locomotion to commercial men to whom time is gold, is of course everything, for they can time their visits to each other to the half minute.

Having reached Castle Garden again, we descend the stairs and walk about the pretty grounds, which are historically interesting. Here are deposited all the immigrants from Europe, representatives of every nation and speaking a diversity of tongues, it is a curious Babel of sounds. A thousand can be sheltered within the walls, but they do not remain many hours but are sent up-country to their various destinations. They must all show that they have means of support otherwise they are not allowed to land but sent back to their own country; at any rate they are not permitted to loaf about New York as our immigrants do in the East End of London, often adding to our list of pauperism. In Castle Garden was formerly a fort which subsequently became the basis of a concert hall, in which I heard an opera at my last visit to New York. Jenny Lind sang here under Barnum's management and was a great success, very unlike the place as it now appears. As we are now near the lower end of Broadway, we will walk along that renowned commercial highway, with its great variety of architecture, its shops and throngs of people. The first monster building which attracts our attention is the Equitable Life Office, got up in the most expensive style, its marble hall and wide staircase are faced with all kinds of precious stones, notably onyx and yellow marble—very bright and beautiful, nothing like it in London. Next comes the New York Life Office, hardly second to it in beauty and grandeur. The proprietors of these expensive buildings say it is a cheap way of advertising their business. Old Trinity Church must be visited and its many quaint inscriptions in its yard be read; the many shrubs and flowers form a singular oasis in the midst of such a desert of granite, marble, and

BROADWAY, NEW YORK.

sandstone. Opposite the church is Wall Street, so often quoted in money transactions, a busy thoroughfare, and looking back from the bottom of it, the spire of Trinity stands out nobly through the narrow vista of tall houses. Continuing our walk along Broadway we next come to the Post Office, with its fine solid frontage of granite, triangular in form, each of its four stories being ornamented with columns, and near here we see terminating many lines of horse trams, while others are passing to and fro in Broadway, and here we can best study the moil and turmoil of New York Street traffic to the fullest extent—the crossing is actually dangerous. Behind the Post Office we see the Houses of Assembly, now dwarfed into insignificant dimensions by the side of the tallest building in the city, which boasts of fourteen stories of brick and stone, and on the top of these three more stories of iron trellis-work inclosed, and in which the printing and editing of the *New York World* paper is carried on. The proprietor was determined to outdo even Cyrus Field's huge edifice of twelve stories, upon which it looks down and on everything else for miles round. It makes one quite giddy to look up at this pretentious erection, which is a high-standing evidence of the extent advertising is carried on by means of buildings of exaggerated size and outward show; for every one naturally asks, What is that? Taking our places in a tram-car we pass on till we arrive at Grace Church, the most elegant Gothic structure in the city, having a high tapering spire of white marble which glistens in the sun, and is a very prominent feature at the

turn which Broadway makes at this point. Joining
our friend the tram again, for it must be known that
Broadway is five miles long and hard work to walk
its length. We get down in Madison Square, one of
the chief centres of American amusement and
fashion. It abounds in theatres and concert halls,
several first-class hotels and restaurants and half-a-
dozen clubs, all on a grand presumptuous scale.
The gardens of six acres is very prettily laid out with
shrubs and flower-beds, and on summer evenings is
a pleasant resort to smoke a cigar in, while during
the day it is overrun by no end of nursery maids in
charge of well-dressed children—plenty of benches
with backs, and the sexes keep well apart on
separate seats, and don't intrude one upon another
—an instance of gallantry which we might well
copy from. As the ever-convenient tram skirts the
square we mount it again, and continue our journey
now to the end of this extraordinary, crowded,
bustling thoroughfare, replete with its diversified
wondrous sights, a tithe of which cannot be depicted
by the pen of the most gifted ready writer, and we
are dropped at the entrance to the Central Park, a
pleasure ground now justly termed the most beautiful
in the whole world. This I feel is no Yankee boast,
for in all my travels I have never seen anything to
be compared to it in either sphere of the universe.
Twenty years ago it was little more than a swamp
with projecting rocks in it, and it shows what an
energetic, wealthy, and *unfettered* community can do
in so short a time by the aid of skilful engineers and
landscape gardeners. Though the size of this park

is only two and a half miles long and half a mile wide, there are nine miles of carriage drive 60 feet wide, and bridle-paths five miles long, 17 feet wide, while the footpaths varying from 13 feet to 40 feet wide are twenty-eight miles in length. As to the seats, these are for the million, and count up to ten thousand and not a cent to pay: how different to our parks in London! There are some lovely bits of artificial scenery with picturesque peeps here and there from its five hundred covered arbours. The lawns are kept green and smooth like a bowling ground, and no one is allowed to walk on the grass, but rigidly confined to the walks and drives. It is the fashionable promenade for the superbly appointed family equipages and fast-trotting horses. The water area covers forty-three acres, and one lake of twenty acres is divided by a narrow channel crossed by a bridge. On this lake may be seen flitting about in all directions pleasure boats at 5d. a row round its lovely shores. The next thing to see is the menagerie, containing a fair collection of birds and animals. A very fine specimen of a bison and some prairie wolves well rewarded our visit. On leaving the Park we soon enter the renowned Fifth Avenue, in which one can admire some of the handsomest private mansions in America. Foremost is the one belonging to Mr. Vanderbilt, the wealthiest man in the city, said to be worth twenty-five millions of pounds. There is one thing in particular to be noticed in the front of his house, and that is a huge flagstone in one solid perfect piece, 24 feet by 18 feet and 6 inches thick. This remarkable monolith was quarried without a crack, and conveyed on special rails and then on trollies and fixed down as a pavement before the house; and would pass unnoticed, but it is well worth examining, and fills one with surprise that such a large flat piece of brittle freestone could be safely laid down without a flaw—it only shows what money can do. Nearly opposite Vanderbilt's is St. Patrick's Cathedral with its two fine spires of white marble, rather prominent objects in the sunshine. We will now leave New York and go over the East River to quiet, sleepy Brooklyn—a city of families and a city of churches with high spires, which has a million of people. Should one happen to be there on a Sunday morning one can follow a surging crowd which will take us to the late Mr. Beecher's church, a simple building, but containing 2,800 seats. These used to be put up to auction annually, and have realised as much as £12,000. He certainly was a wonderful leader of men. But what takes the visitor more practically over to Brooklyn is to see the splendid and magnificent suspension bridge over the East River. The whole length of this grand structure is a few feet short of 6,000. Between the towers the span is 1,595 feet. It is 85 feet wide; this gives a central space of 13 feet for foot-passengers, underneath a double railway track for passenger cars, worked to and fro by a fixed engine, and on each side of this track is a carriage way. The total length above high water is 272 feet. Its cost was some 15 millions of dollars. It was opened in all its parts in September, 1883, and in the first nine months its railway alone carried $5\frac{1}{2}$ millions of people. The fare is three cents and for pedestrians one cent only. It is of a light airy appearance compared with that of our Forth Bridge, which strikes one as so heavy and cumbersome. The visitor had better walk one way over it and return by the railway.

If the visitor would really enjoy a delicious treat he should not fail to make his way again to Castle Garden, and then take a steamer across to Bedloes Island in the centre of the harbour, on which is erected Bartholdi's statue of "Liberty," the pride of America! Its height is 305 feet from the base to the torch, which represents Liberty enlightening the world. I give some of its dimensions, which will convey a fair idea of its great size. For instance, the head from the chin to the cranium is 17 feet, and in which forty persons can comfortably stand. The length of the right arm is 42 feet, and in the gallery round the torch, which is held in the hand, twelve persons can stand comfortably. The tablet in the left hand is 23 feet long and 13 feet wide. The steps of the ladder up the centre of the body are very slippery, the metal being smooth and polished by constant use; hence it is easier to mount if the shoes are taken off. I need hardly say what a splendid bird's-eye view of New York, Brooklyn, its bridge, and the great length of seventy quays with ships not countable is to be had from the top. Fail not to see this grand national monument. The High Bridge is well worth a visit. First take the Elevated Railroad from Sixth Avenue to 155th Street; then a horse tram will carry you to the bottom of a wooded, sloping hill (Washington Heights), up which there is a path. Along it you walk till you reach the bridge. This bridge was built to convey the Croton Aqueduct across the Harlem river and valley. It is 1,460 feet long, and has thirteen arches resting on granite piers. From the footpath along its side, 116 feet above the river, a very fine prospect is to be had. The fresh water it supplies to New York passes over it in iron pipes 7 feet in diameter, inclosed in a tunnel of brickwork. A short walk further on brings one to a splendid doubled, arched-iron, cantilever bridge spanning the same valley, with a grand carriage roadway 75 feet in width. It well deserves the name of "Washington." On Sundays crowds of excursionists visit these two bridges, near to which are several tea-gardens and convenient hotels. I forgot to mention that the Croton Reservoir, which receives this water—1,000 millions of gallons in quantity—extends the whole length of the Central Park on the left-hand side, that is, two miles at least!

I think I may venture to conclude now by saying that I have written a small illustrated account of all those "lions" of New York such as a visitor *en passant* would care to explore, and which, in my opinion, are worth a voyage across the Atlantic to see, to enjoy, and to admire. And especially so is it worth a week's or ten days' sojourn *en route* to, or from, those tourists going to visit the Chicago Exhibition. If, however, any tourists, men of leisure and of money, are curious to see the seamy side of human nature, they can do some "slumming" by taking a detective, whose charge would be £5 ; then they can imitate the freaks of London society in our East End. Thus safeguarded, evening parties of men can pay a visit to all the miserable dens of iniquity which will occupy the whole night. Passing from water "dives," the home of the "Border Gang," to Sebastopol on the east side, and then on to "Battle Row" and "Hell's Kitchen" on the west side. May it be to their moral edification!

Before I finish, it would not be out of place just to give a few characteristics of the New Yorkites. First, then, comes the cab and its driver, extortionate as our own when they have a chance; hence make your bargain before you enter. As they are painted black and yellow, they are popularly known as "black and tan." The charges are 1s. a mile or 4s. an hour. A trunk outside is charged 1s., and each parcel 5d. — very dear in comparison with London. Now for the mode of living. Americans are exceptionally fond of hotel life, and at all the hotels large numbers are permanently boarded, at a considerable discount to what a passing guest would have to pay. Again, those who cannot afford the hotels go into boarding-houses, which abound in every quarter, and meet the needs of every grade in society, the charges varying from £1 to £2 a week; but the better sort in the avenues go up from £2 to £10 or more, all depending upon the style and position of the room or rooms one occupies, but the meals are alike for all—breakfast and dinner at night. The women-servants, or helps, are not obliging. It would be better for the stranger that he or she should be slow to make acquaintances, and take rooms week by week, for fear of meeting disagreeable neighbours. The "Norman" and the "Earle" hotels are of moderate dimensions in comparison with some. Let us not forget that the charge for cleaning a pair of boots in the hotels is 5d., and not to walk abroad in dirty shoes, otherwise the shoeblacks will bore you at every corner with calls for a "shiner," for which they demand 2½d. I don't know whether my readers have ever been to Petticoat Lane in London, but if they have not they would see a great resemblance to it at the Bowery in New York. It consists of rows of cheap stores, mostly displayed on the sidewalks; numerous low concert and beer saloons; stands with fruits, pea-nuts, and soda-water. You are greeted by the vendors of every article of every variety by the call of "A great bargain!" The rumbling sounds from four tracks of horse-cars below, and the noisy puffing of the Elevator Railway above, produce a sight so unique as not to be seen in any other part of New York, and to the uninitiated is indeed most bewildering. There are four hundred churches of every denomination in New York, which afford a sitting capacity for 250,000 persons out of 2,000,000. Where do the great majority go to on the Sabbath? Strangers are welcome to all the Sunday services, and there is no collection, each church depending on its pew rents and subscribers. The free-school systems give to the children of parents in all grades of society the opportunity to acquire a good education, second to none in general excellence. No separate schools *now* exist for coloured children! There are evening schools for those who are obliged to work during the day. The cost to the city is four millions of dollars, or £800,000 of our money. Beer is fast superseding all other beverages *except water* in the affections of the citizens. The breweries—151 in number—are colossal in size, and yield three millions of barrels in a year. It is sold everywhere at five cents the glass, or ten cents for a larger one called a "schooner." If you ask for foreign beer they will charge at least double for it.

From what I have seen I should say the New Yorkite working-class are abstemious in comparison with the same grade in London, and especially may this be said of their women. The Society for the Suppression of Vice is ever on the alert, and the laws are very rigid in regard to any obscene or immoral publications. The acuteness of the trading community is of such world-wide notoriety that little need be said, other than to remark that they deal in imports to the extent of 500 millions, and of exports to the value of 400 millions of dollars! They must be all wide-awake and to the fore, especially on the Stock Exchange, where the transactions are prodigious. 250,000 to 300,000 shares of stock change hands daily and the value of the railway and other bonds dealt in range from two to three millions of dollars! This Exchange has 1,100 members, and the market value of the seat is worth £6,500, transmissible to the members' heirs! The Produce Exchange, held in a magnificent building, has 3,000 members, who deal in every kind of food. Then, again, there are the Cotton and Petroleum Exchanges, at all of which bustling, seething crowds, buzzing like so many bee-hives, or creating a noise and confusion resembling a veritable Bedlam, are speculating with the almighty dollar—that dollar which holds its own with such despotic sway!

Before leaving America and the many friends who have been so kind and courteous, and enlivened our visit with so much pleasure, a few remarks respecting the ladies who have locked hands in matrimony with so many Englishmen during the past few years would not be out of place. As soon as we enter the "Empire State" we cannot fail to observe that the looks, dress, and style of the women is notably better than those we have left behind. In New York itself this change is very perceptible. The height of fashion predominates, and it is nothing singular to see "sweet sixteen" in three or four different gowns during the day. The girls in their teens are not only very attractive in their attire, but piquant and fascinating in their manners and address. They can hold their own and queen it in their mothers' drawing-rooms in a way that outshines English girls of the same age; and what is more, their handsome faces, beaming with a lively expressiveness, and their conversation, sparkling with wit and repartee, far surpasses a like number of girls in any of our large centres of population. The American father will slave away at home in order that he may give his daughters a liberal education in accomplishments, backed by an expensive tour in Europe, while the girls in their turn get well posted up in all the passing news and popular literature of the day, and convey the information to their parent, who is too busy hunting up the dollars to spare much time for book-learning. In a word, the child becomes a kind of domestic encyclopædia to the father, who is often a self-made man, and has had few scholastic advantages.

Hearing that the White Star line of steamers were the largest, swiftest, and most admirably equipped of any crossing the Atlantic, we asked a friend known to the company to secure for us a passage in that splendid ship, the *Majestic*, 10,000 tons and 582 feet long, with twin screws revolving with little or no noise or thudding. Our cabin, called a " saloon " room, was 10 feet high, furnished with two berths soft and easy, delightful marble appliances for washing, with electric light and bells. We had, all told, 1,536 souls on board, but it can accommodate 2,136—quite a little town in itself!

Having ordered our heavy luggage from the Central Depôt to be sent down to the pier No. 45, where the steamer lay, we had nothing to do but to walk on board and take our places. Easier said than done. We were quite staggered to see such a crowd of people, friends of the passengers, who brought with them quantities of floral decorations in different designs, some of them worth £5 or more, notably two most beautiful little yachts, with the rigging covered with roses and geraniums, &c., and when placed on the saloon table at dinner-time were the centres of admiration. Indeed, the large saloon was literally overdone with the load of flowers, hiding, as they did, the gold and white gorgeous ornamentations of the room itself. After a good deal of handshaking and kissing, amid much arriving and departing of carriages, the pedlars shouting their wares, and all the hurry and skurry of departing friends, the bell rings, and the gangway is removed; then the truly majestic vessel swings itself out into the stream, amid the cheers and waving of handkerchiefs of the assembled crowd, and the answering shouts from the passengers. Then we have spare time and free space to scan and admire the splendid appointments of this magnificent floating hotel, its smoking, card, and retiring rooms, its well-stocked gratuitous library, its delicious writing- and reading-room, where one can quietly read and write in ease and comfort, for there is little noise or motion during the steaming of this great monster of the deep. The vessel being so unusually steady, a good deal of dancing was enjoyed by the young people on board. One would have supposed that this simple, innocent amusement could have been carried on without any reflections of a mercenary nature emanating from their elders, looking on, and apparently admiring the lithe figures and handsome dresses. Not so. Money calculations seem deeply engraved on the minds of fathers and mothers in general, and on those of the American in particular. Hence one was amused by the following remarks originating in the fertile brains of two financiers present, lost to all social sentiment, who were footing up the probable amount of capital which the parents of those dancing possessed:—" Now, I say, Nobbs; I calculate that there lot represents 200 million dollars. What think ye, old boy?" " Well, I should say that you are very near the mark."

"And I say again, Nobbs; if the M. girls" (these rich young ladies stood aloof) "had joined the others, then there would not have been a cent less than 250 millions." "Ah well," said his friend; "I guess you are about right now." So they turned on their heel and left the lively scene, perfectly satisfied that they had done a good stroke of business for future development on the stock market.

We reached Queenstown in six days and sixteen hours, and I saw no sickness on board. Our food was delicious, consisting of every conceivable luxury, as if we were on land. As to the attendance, well, we had a waiter to about every third chair, hence that department need not be praised. We reached Liverpool that night, and the docking of the huge steamer by the aid of two tugs was a sight worth seeing.

THE END.

The Gresham Press,
UNWIN BROTHERS,
CHILWORTH AND LONDON.

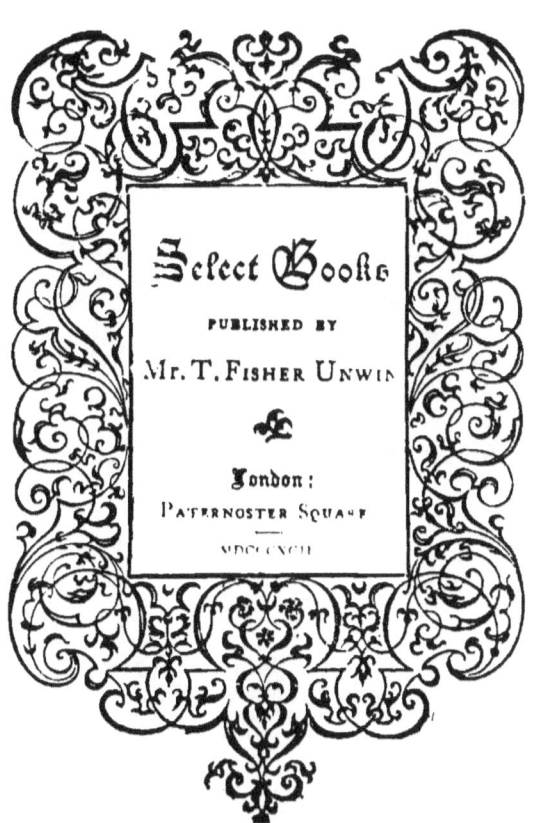

The Adventure Series.

Large crown 8vo., cloth, 5s. each, fully Illustrated.

I.
The Adventures of a Younger Son.
By E. J. TRELAWNY. With an Introduction by EDWARD GARNETT.
Illustrated with several Portraits of Trelawny.

II.
Robert Drury's Journal in Madagascar.
With Preface and Notes by CAPT. S. P. OLIVER, Author of "Madagascar."

III.
Memoirs of the Extraordinary Military Career of John Shipp.
With Introduction by H. MANNERS CHICHESTER.

IV.
The Adventures of Thomas Pellow, of Penryn, Mariner.
Written by Himself; and Edited, with an Introduction and Notes, by
DR. ROBERT BROWN.

V.
The Buccaneers and Marooners of America:
Being an account of certain notorious Freebooters of the Spanish Main.
Edited by HOWARD PYLE.

VI.
The Log of a Jack Tar; or, The Life of James Choyce, Master Mariner.
With O'Brien's Captivity in France.
Edited, with an Introduction and Notes, by V. LOVETT CAMERON, R.N.

VII.
The Voyages and Adventures of Ferdinand Mendez Pinto.
With an Introduction by ARMINIUS VAMBÉRY.

VIII.
The Story of the Filibusters.
By JAMES JEFFREY ROCHE.
To which is added The Life of COLONEL DAVID CROCKETT.

IX.
A Master Mariner:
Being the Life and Adventures of CAPT. ROBERT WILLIAM EASTWICK.
Edited by HERBERT COMPTON.

X.
Kolokotrones: Klepht and Warrior.
Translated from the Greek, and Prefaced with an Account of the Klephts, by MRS. EDMUNDS. With Introduction by M. J. GENNADIUS, Greek Minister Resident, London.

Catalogue of Select Books in Belles Lettres, History, Biography, Theology, Travel, Miscellaneous, and Books for Children.

Belles Lettres.

Pablo de Ségovie. By FRANCESCO DE QUEVEDO. Illustrated with Sixty Drawings by DANIEL VIERGE. With an Introduction on VIERGE and his Art by JOSEPH PENNELL, and a Critical Essay on QUEVEDO and his Writings by W. E. WATTS. Limited Edition only. Three Guineas nett. [1892.

A French Ambassador at the Court of Charles II. (LE COMTE DE COMINGES, 1662-1665). With many Portraits. By J. J. JUSSERAND. Demy 8vo., cloth gilt [1892.

Jules Bastien Lepage and his Art. A Memoir, by ANDRÉ THEURIET. With which is included Bastien Lepage as Artist, by GEORGE CLAUSEN, A.R.W.S.; An Essay on Modern Realism in Painting, by WALTER SICKERT, N.E.A.C.; and a Study of Marie Bashkirtseff, by MATHILDE BLIND. Illustrated by Reproductions of Bastien Lepage's Works. Royal 8vo., cloth, gilt tops, 10s. 6d.

The Women of the French Salons. A Series of Articles on the French Salons of the Seventeenth and Eighteenth Centuries. By AMELIA G. MASON. Profusely Illustrated. Foolscap folio, cloth, 25s.

These papers treat of the literary, political, and social influence of the women in France, during the two centuries following the foundation of the salons; including pen-portraits of many noted leaders of famous coteries, and giving numerous glimpses of the Society of this brilliant period.

The Real Japan. Studies of Contemporary Japanese Manners, Morals, Administrations, and Politics. By HENRY NORMAN. Illustrated with about 50 Photographs taken by the Author. Crown 8vo., cloth, 10s. 6d.

EXTRACT FROM PREFACE.—These essays constitute an attempt, *faute de mieux*, to place before the readers of the countries whence Japan is deriving her incentives and her ideas, an account of some of the chief aspects and institutions of Japanese life as it really is to-day.

The Stream of Pleasure. A Narrative of a Journey on the Thames from Oxford to London. By JOSEPH and ELIZABETH ROBINS PENNELL. Profusely Illustrated by JOSEPH PENNELL. Small Crown 4to., cloth, 7s. 6d.

"Mrs. Pennell is bright and amusing. Mr. Pennell's sketches of river-side bits and nooks are charming; and a useful practical chapter has been written by Mr. J. G. Legge. The book is an artistic treat."—*Scotsman*.

Gypsy Sorcery and Fortune Telling. Illustrated by numerous Incantations, Specimens of Medical Magic, Anecdotes and Tales, by CHARLES GODFREY LELAND ("Hans Breitmann"). Illustrations by the Author. Small 4to., cloth, 16s. Limited Edition of 150 Copies, price £1 11s. 6d. nett.

"The student of folk-lore will welcome it as one of the most valuable additions recently made to the literature of popular beliefs."—*Scotsman*.

Esther Pentreath, the Miller's Daughter: A Cornish Romance. By J. H. PEARCE, Author of "Bernice," &c. 6s.

Mr. LEONARD COURTNEY, M.P., in the *Nineteenth Century* for May, says it is "an idyll that captivates us by its tenderness, its grace, and its beauty. . . . In truth, the special distinction of 'Esther Pentreath' may be said to lie in the poetic gift of its author."

Main-travelled Roads. Six Mississippi-Valley Stories. By HAMLIN GARLAND. Crown 8vo., cloth, 3s. 6d.

"Main-travelled Roads" depicts the hard life of the average American Farmer and the farm hands. The author has lived the life he tells of, and he may be called a true realist in his art.

The English Novel in the Time of Shakespeare. By J. J. JUSSERAND, Author of "English Wayfaring Life." Translated by ELIZABETH LEE, Revised and Enlarged by the Author. Illustrated. Demy 8vo., cloth, 21s.

"M Jusserand's fascinating volume."—*Quarterly Review*.

English Wayfaring Life in the Middle
Ages (XIVth Century). By J. J. JUSSERAND. Translated from the French by LUCY A. TOULMIN SMITH. Illustrated. Fourth Edition. Crown 8vo., cloth, 7s. 6d.

" This is an extremely fascinating book, and it is surprising that several years should have elapsed before it was brought out in an English dress. However, we have lost nothing by waiting."—*Times.*

Dreams.
By OLIVE SCHREINER, Author of "The Story of an African Farm." With Portrait. Third Edition. Fcap. 8vo., buckram, gilt, 6s.

" They can be compared only with the painted allegories of Mr. Watts . . . The book is like nothing else in English. Probably it will have no successors as it has had no forerunners."—*Athenæum.*

Gottfried Keller:
A Selection of his Tales. Translated, with a Memoir, by KATE FREILIGRATH KROEKER, Translator of "Brentano's Fairy Tales." With Portrait. Crown 8vo., cloth, 6s.

" The English reader could not have a more representative collection of Keller's admirable stories."—*Saturday Review.*

The Trials of a Country Parson:
Some Fugitive Papers by Rev. A. JESSOPP, D.D., Author of "Arcady," "The Coming of the Friars," &c. Crown 8vo., cloth, 7s. 6d.

" Sparkles with fresh and unforced humour, and abounds in genial common-sense."—*Scotsman.*

The Coming of the Friars,
And other Mediæval Sketches. By the Rev. AUGUSTUS JESSOPP, D.D., Author of "Arcady: For Better, For Worse," &c. Third Edition. Crown 8vo., cloth, 7s. 6d.

" Always interesting and frequently fascinating."—*St. James's Gazette.*

Arcady:
For Better, For Worse. By AUGUSTUS JESSOPP, D.D., Author of "One Generation of a Norfolk House." Portrait. Popular Edition. Crown 8vo., cloth, 3s. 6d.

" A volume which is, to our minds, one of the most delightful ever published in English."—*Spectator.*

Robert Browning: Personal Notes.
Frontispiece. Small crown 8vo., parchment, 4s. 6d.

" Every lover of Browning will wish to possess this exquisitely-printed and as exquisitely-bound little volume."—*Yorkshire Daily Post.*

Old Chelsea. A Summer-Day's Stroll. By Dr. BENJAMIN ELLIS MARTIN. Illustrated by JOSEPH PENNELL. Third and Cheaper Edition. Square imperial 16mo., cloth, 3s. 6d.

"Dr. Martin has produced an interesting account of old Chelsea, and he has been well seconded by his conjutor."—*Athenæum.*

Euphorion: Studies of the Antique and the Mediæval in the Renaissance. By VERNON LEE. Cheap Edition, in one volume. Demy 8vo., cloth, 7s. 6d.

"It is the fruit, as every page testifies, of singularly wide reading and independent thought, and the style combines with much picturesqueness a certain largeness of volume, that reminds us more of our earlier writers than those of our own time."
Contemporary Review.

Studies of the Eighteenth Century in Italy. By VERNON LEE. Demy 8vo., cloth, 7s. 6d.

"These studies show a wide range of knowledge of the subject, precise investigation, abundant power of illustration, and hearty enthusiasm. . . . The style of writing is cultivated, neatly adjusted, and markedly clever."—*Saturday Review.*

Belcaro: Being Essays on Sundry Æsthetical Questions. By VERNON LEE. Crown 8vo., cloth, 5s.

Juvenilia: A Second Series of Essays on Sundry Æsthetical Questions. By VERNON LEE. Two vols. Small crown 8vo., cloth, 12s.

"To discuss it properly would require more space than a single number of 'The Academy' could afford."—*Academy.*

Baldwin: Dialogues on Views and Aspirations. By VERNON LEE. Demy 8vo., cloth, 12s.

"The dialogues are written with . . . an intellectual courage which shrinks from no logical conclusion."—*Scotsman.*

Ottilie: An Eighteenth Century Idyl. By VERNON LEE. Square 8vo., cloth extra, 3s. 6d.

"A graceful little sketch. . . . Drawn with full insight into the period described."—*Spectator.*

Introductory Studies in Greek Art. Delivered in the British Museum by JANE E. HARRISON. With Illustrations. Second Edition. Square imperial 16mo., 7s. 6d.

"The best work of its kind in English."—*Oxford Magazine.*

The Fleet: Its River, Prison, and Marriages. By JOHN ASHTON, Author of "Social Life in the Reign of Queen Anne," &c. With 70 Drawings by the Author from Original Pictures. Second and Cheaper Edition, cloth, 7s. 6d.

Romances of Chivalry: Told and Illustrated in Fac-simile by JOHN ASHTON. Forty-six Illustrations. New and Cheaper Edition. Crown 8vo., cloth, 7s. 6d.

"The result (of the reproduction of the wood blocks) is as creditable to his artistic, as the text is to his literary, ability."—*Guardian.*

The Dawn of the Nineteenth Century in England: A Social Sketch of the Times. By JOHN ASHTON. Cheaper Edition, in one vol. Illustrated. Large crown 8vo., 10s. 6d.

"The book is one continued source of pleasure and interest, and opens up a wide field for speculation and comment, and many of us will look upon it as an important contribution to contemporary history, not easily available to others than close students."—*Antiquary.*

The Temple: Sacred Poems and Private Ejaculations. By Mr. GEORGE HERBERT. New and Fourth Edition, with Introductory Essay by J. HENRY SHORTHOUSE. Small crown, sheep, 5s.
A fac-simile reprint of the Original Edition of 1633.

"This charming reprint has a fresh value added to it by the Introductory Essay of the Author of 'John Inglesant.'"—*Academy.*

Songs, Ballads, and A Garden Play. By A. MARY F. ROBINSON, Author of "An Italian Garden." With Frontispiece of Dürer's "Melancholia." Small crown 8vo., half bound, vellum, 5s.

"The romantic ballads have grace, movement, passion and strength."—*Spectator.*
"Marked by sweetness of melody and truth of colour."—*Academy.*

The Lazy Minstrel. By J. ASHBY-STERRY, Author of "Boudoir Ballads." Fourth and Popular Edition. Frontispiece by E. A. ABBEY. Fcap. 8vo., cloth, 2s. 6d.

"One of the lightest and brightest writers of vers de société."—*St. James's Gazette.*

History.

The Industrial and Commercial History of England. Lectures Delivered to the University of Oxford. By the late Professor JAMES E. THOROLD ROGERS. Edited by his Son, ARTHUR G. L. ROGERS. Demy 8vo., cloth, 16s.

Ten Years of Upper Canada, in Peace and War, 1805-1815. Being the Ridout Letters, with Annotations by MATILDA EDGAR. Also, an Appendix of the Narrative of the Captivity among the Shawanese Indians, in 1788, of Thomas Ridout, afterwards Surveyor-General of Upper Canada; and a Vocabulary compiled by him of the Shawanese Language. Frontispiece, Portrait, and Maps. Royal 8vo., cloth, bevelled edges, 10s. 6d.

"The volume is a noteworthy addition to the literature of **early Canadian history**."—*Athenæum*.

The Economic Interpretation of History. Lectures on Political Economy and Its History (delivered at Oxford by Professor J. E. THOROLD ROGERS). New and Cheaper Edition. Demy 8vo., cloth. 7s. 6d.

"A valuable storehouse of economic facts."—*Manchester Examiner*.

The Vikings in Western Christendom, A.D. 789—888. By C. F. KEARY, Author of "Outlines of Primitive Belief," "The Dawn of History," &c. With Map and Tables. Demy 8vo., cloth, 16s.

"As attractive and fascinating as it is scholarly and learned."—*St. James's Gazette*.

"In whichever aspect his volume is considered, it extorts in an equal degree our admiration.'—*Notes and Queries*.

Battles and Leaders of the American Civil
War. An Authoritative History, written by Distinguished Participants on both sides. Edited by ROBERT U. JOHNSON and CLARENCE C. BUEL, of the Editorial Staff of "The Century Magazine." Four Volumes, Royal 8vo., elegantly bound, £5 5s.

LORD WOLSELEY, in writing a series of articles in the *North American Review* on this work, says: "The Century Company has, in my judgment, done a great service to the soldiers of all armies by the publication of these records of the great War."

Diary of the Parnell Commission. Revised with Additions,
from *The Daily News*. By JOHN MACDONALD, M.A. Large crown 8vo., cloth, 6s.

"Mr. Macdonald has done his work well."—*Speaker*.

The End of the Middle Ages: Essays and Questions
in History. By A. MARY F. ROBINSON (Madame Darmesteter). Demy 8vo., cloth, 10s. 6d.

"We travel from convent to palace, find ourselves among all the goodness, the wisdom, the wildness, the wickedness, the worst and the best of that wonderful time. We meet with devoted saints and desperate sinners. . . We seem to have made many new acquaintances whom before we only knew by name among the names of history. . . We can heartily recommend this book to every one who cares for the study of history, especially in its most curious and fascinating period, the later middle age."—*Spectator*.

The Federalist: A Commentary in the Form of Essays on the United States Constitution.
By ALEXANDER HAMILTON, and others. Edited by HENRY CABOT LODGE. Demy 8vo., Roxburgh binding, 10s. 6d.

"The importance of the Essays can hardly be exaggerated."—*Glasgow Mail*.

The Story of the Nations.
Crown 8vo., Illustrated, and furnished with Maps and Indexes, each 5s.

"An admirable series."—*Spectator*.

"Each volume is written by one of the most foremost English authorities on the subject with which it deals. . . . It is almost impossible to over-estimate the value of a series of carefully prepared volumes, such as are the majority of those comprising this library."—*Guardian*.

32. Sicily (Phœnician, Greek, and Roman). By E. A. FREEMAN, D.C.L. [*January*.

31. The Byzantine Empire. By C. W. C. Oman, M.A. [*December.*

30. The Tuscan Republics and Genoa. By Bella Duffy. [*December.*

29. The Normans. By Sarah Orne Jewett.

28. Portugal. By H. Morse Stephens.

27. Mexico. By Susan Hale.

26. Switzerland. By Lina Hug and R. Stead.

25. Scotland. By John Macintosh, LL.D.

24. The Jews under the Roman Empire. By W. Douglas Morrison, M.A.

23. Russia. By W. R. Morfill, M.A.

22. The Barbary Corsairs. By Stanley Lane-Poole.

21. Early Britain. By Prof. A. J. Church, Author of "Carthage," &c.

20. The Hansa Towns. By Helen Zimmern.

19. Media. By Z. A. Ragozin.

18. Phœnicia. By Canon Rawlinson.

17. Persia. By S. G. W. Benjamin. Second Edition.

16. Mediæval France. By Gustave Masson. Second Edition.

15. Holland. By the late Professor Thorold Rogers. Second Edition.

14. **Turkey.** By STANLEY LANE-POOLE. Second Edition.

13. **Assyria.** By ZÉNAÏDE A. RAGOZIN, Author of "Chaldea," &c.

12. **The Goths.** By HENRY BRADLEY. Third Edition.

11. **Chaldea.** By Z. A. RAGOZIN, Author of "Assyria," &c. Second Edition.

10. **Ireland.** By the Hon. EMILY LAWLESS, Author of "Hurrish." Third Edition.

9. **The Saracens:** From the Earliest Times to the Fall of Bagdad. By ARTHUR GILMAN, M.A., Author of "Rome," &c.

8. **Hungary.** By Prof. ARMINIUS VAMBÉRY, Author of "Travels in Central Asia." Fourth Edition.

7. **Ancient Egypt.** By Canon RAWLINSON, Author of "The Five Great Monarchies of the World." Fifth Edition.

6. **The Moors in Spain.** By STANLEY LANE-POOLE, Author of "Studies in a Mosque." Fourth Edition.

5. **Alexander's Empire.** By Prof. J. P. MAHAFFY, Author of "Social Life in Greece." Fourth Edition.

4. **Carthage.** By Prof. ALFRED J. CHURCH, Author of "Stories from the Classics," &c. Fifth Edition.

3. **Germany.** By Rev. S. BARING-GOULD, Author of "Curious Myths of the Middle Ages," &c. Fourth Edition.

2. **The Jews.** In Ancient, Mediæval, and Modern Times. By Prof. J. K. HOSMER. Second Edition.

1. **Rome.** By ARTHUR GILMAN, M.A., Author of "A History of the American People," &c. Third Edition.

Biography.

The Life and Times of Niccolò Machiavelli. By Prof. PASQUALE VILLARI, Author of "The Life of Savonarola," &c. Translated by LINDA VILLARI. New and Revised Edition, in two vols., with New Preface and Two New Chapters. Containing four Copper-plate and 29 other Illustrations. Demy 8vo., cloth, 32s.

EXTRACT FROM PREFACE TO NEW EDITION.—This is the first complete English version of my book on "Machiavelli and his Times," the original translation, in four volumes, produced between the years 1878-83, having been considerably shortened to suit the convenience of its publisher. Whereas the two first volumes were issued intact with all the documents appertaining to them, the rest of the work was deprived of two entire chapters, and every document suppressed. One of the eliminated chapters treated of Art, and it was precisely in the Fine Arts that the Renaissance found is fullest and most distinctive expression.

Behramji M. Malabari: A Biographical Sketch. By DAYARAM GIDUMAL, LL.B., C.S., Acting District Judge, Shikarpur. With Introduction by FLORENCE NIGHTINGALE. Crown 8vo., cloth, 6s.

Life of John Boyle O'Reilly. By JAMES JEFFREY ROCHE. Together with his complete Poems and Speeches. Edited by Mrs. JOHN BOYLE O'REILLY. With Introduction by His Eminence James Cardinal GIBBONS, Archbishop of Baltimore. Portraits and Illustrations. Royal 8vo., cloth, 21s.

"Mr. Roche's book is most interesting. . . . We think the book will teach much to those who wish to know what manner of man an Irish rebel and conspirator may be."—*The Speaker.*

The Young Emperor: A Study in Character-Development on a Throne. By HAROLD FREDERIC, Author of "In the Valley," "The Lawton Girl," &c. With Portraits. Crown 8vo., cloth, 6s.

"As interesting as any novel, and is, moreover, an important contribution to the political history of the day."—*Pall Mall Gazette.*

The Autobiography of Joseph Jefferson

("Rip Van Winkle"). With many full-page Portraits and other Illustrations. Royal 8vo., 16s.

"It makes one of the most interesting and handsome gift-books of the season. It is a delightfully garrulous and chatty record of a long theatrical life, and full of amusing gossip about the 'traffic of the stage.' . . . It is really a rich gallery of stage portraits."—*Observer.*

Nelson:

The Public and Private Life of Horatio, Viscount Nelson. By G. Lathom Browne, Barrister-at-Law, Author of "Wellington," "Narratives of State Trials," &c. With Heliogravure frontispiece Portrait, 11 full-page Illustrations of portraits and relics of Nelson, hitherto unpublished, and 4 Maps. Demy 8vo., cloth, gilt tops, 18s.

Mr. Lathom Browne has had access to the documents and relics of Nelson in the possession of Earl Nelson and Viscount Bridport (Duke of Bronté); and by the thorough re-examination of all existing material has presented what has long been wanting—an impartial, exhaustive, and critical Life of Nelson, told largely from the point of view of his own letters and eye witnesses of his naval career.

Abraham Lincoln:

A History. By John G. Nicolay and John Hay. With many full-page Illustrations, Portraits, and Maps. Royal 8vo., complete in 10 vols., bound in cloth, price £6 the Set.

"The theme is a great one, and it has fallen into worthy hands. . . . We need hardly add that the work of Messrs. Nicolay and Hay is one which every public Library ought to possess."—*Speaker.*

Sir John Hawkwood (l'Acuto).

Story of a Condottiere. Translated from the Italian of John Temple-Leader and Guiseppe Marcotti, by Leader Scott. Illustrated. Royal 8vo., bound in buckram, gilt tops. Limited Edition.

"The career of such a man was well worth recording. . . . A valuable and interesting book."—*Glasgow Herald.*

The Life & Times of William Lloyd

Garrison. From 1840—1879. By His Children. Vols. III. and IV., completing the work. Portraits and Illustrations. Demy 8vo., cloth, 30s.

"There is something to be learnt in every page, and the diversity of subjects taken up by this strong, resolute nature, make it altogether a book of the age."
Daily Telegraph.

Life and Times of Girolamo Savonarola.

By PASQUALE VILLARI. Translated by LINDA VILLARI. Portraits and Illustrations. Two vols. Third Edition, with New Preface. Demy 8vo., cloth, 21s.

"We welcome the translation of this excellent work—which is all a translation ought to be."—*Spectator.*

Charles Dickens as I knew Him: The Story of the

Reading Tours in Great Britain and America (1866-1870). By GEORGE DOLBY. New and Cheaper Edition. Crown 8vo., 3s. 6d.

"It will be welcome to all lovers of Dickens for Dickens' own sake."—*Athenæum.*

The Lives of Robert and Mary Moffat.

By their Son, JOHN SMITH MOFFAT. Sixth Edition. Portraits, Illustrations, and Maps. Crown 8vo., cloth, 7s. 6d.; Popular Edition, crown 8vo., 3s. 6d.

"The biographer has done his work with reverent care, and in a straightforward unaffected style."—*Contemporary Review.*

The German Emperor and Empress:

The Late Frederick III. and Victoria. The Story of their Lives. By DOROTHEA ROBERTS. Portraits. Crown 8vo., cloth, 2s. 6d.

"A book sure to be popular in domestic circles."—*The Graphic.*

Arminius Vambéry: His Life and Adventures Written by Himself.

With Portrait and Fourteen Illustrations. Fifth and Popular Edition. Square Imperial 16mo., cloth extra, 6s.

"The work is written in a most captivating manner."—*Novoe Vremya, Moscow.*

Travel.

Twelve Months in Peru. By E. B. CLARK. With Eight Illustrations. Crown 8vo., cloth, 5s.

In this work the Author has endeavoured to give a brief outline of her novel experiences while sojourning in the Republic. The book is enriched with illustrations of local scenes.

Among the Holy Places: Travels in Palestine. By the Rev. JAMES KEAN, M.A., B.D. Illustrated. Demy 8vo., cloth, 7s. 6d.

"Mr. Kean endeavours to describe the Holy Land in such a clear and simple fashion as to enable the untravelled reader to realise what the country and people really are like, and he has been very successful."—*Catholic Times*.

Tahiti: The Garden of the Pacific. By DORA HORT. With Frontispiece. Demy 8vo., cloth, 10s. 6d.

"Presents a very enjoyable and entertaining picture. . . . Mrs. Hort's narrative has its tragedies, its romances, and its humours."—*Times*.

With Gordon in China: Letters from Lieut. Lyster. Edited by E. A. LYSTER. With Portrait. Large crown 8vo., cloth, 6s.

"Contains much that is valuable with regard to Gordon. . . . The volume has been edited with skill and care, and the letterpress is excellent."—*Irish Times*.

With the Beduins: A Narrative of Journeys to the East of the Jordan and Dead Sea, Palmyra, &c. By GRAY HILL. Numerous Illustrations and Map. Demy 8vo., cloth gilt, 15s.

"These Beduin tales are excellent reading, as indeed is the whole book."
Daily Telegraph.

Our Journey to the Hebrides. By Joseph Pennell and Elizabeth Robins Pennell. 43 Illustrations by Joseph Pennell. Crown 8vo., cloth, 7s. 6d.

"It will be easily understood that we could not plan a route out of our ignorance and prejudice. It remained to choose a guide, and our choice, I hardly know why, fell upon Dr. Johnson."—*Preface*.

Daily Life in India. By the Rev. W. J. Wilkins. Illustrated. Crown 8vo., cloth, 5s.

"A very able book."—*Guardian*.

Modern Hinduism: An Account of the Religion and Life of the Hindus in Northern India. By Rev. W. J. Wilkins. Demy 8vo., cloth, 16s.

"A valuable contribution to the study of a very difficult subject."—*Madras Mail*.

Central Asian Questions: Essays on Afghanistan, China, and Central Asia. By Demetrius C. Boulger. With Portrait and Three Maps. Demy 8vo., cloth, 18s.

"A mine of valuable information."—*Times*.

Tuscan Studies and Sketches. By Leader Scott, Author of "A Nook in the Apennines," "Messer Agnolo's Household," &c. Many Full-page and smaller Illustrations. Sq. imp. 16mo., cloth, 10s. 6d.

"The sketches are of that happy kind which appeal to the learned through their style, and to the simple through their subjects."—*Truth*.

Letters from Italy. By Emile de Laveleye. Translated by Mrs. Thorpe. Revised by the Author. Portrait of the Author. Crown 8vo., 6s.

"A most delightful volume."—*Nonconformist*.
"Every page is pleasantly and brightly written."—*Times*.

Theology and Philosophy.

The Sinless Conception of the Mother of God: A Theological Essay. By the Rev. FREDERICK GEORGE LEE, D.C.L. Demy 8vo., 7s. 6d.

"The statement and defence of the dogma is made with considerable fulness . . . and with large illustration of patristic and theological quotation."—*Dublin Review.*

My Note-Book. Fragmentary Studies in Theology and subjects adjacent thereto. By AUSTIN PHELPS, D.D , LL.D., Author of "My Study, and Other Essays," &c. With Portrait. Crown 8vo., cloth, 6s.

"Embodies the experience and reflection of an earnest and thoughtful mind."—*Times.*

The Two Spheres of Truth. Being a Revised and Amended version of "The Two Kinds of Truth." By T. E. S. T. Demy 8vo., cloth, 5s.

"The book is very readable."—*Spectator.*

Pharaohs of the Bondage and the Exodus. By Rev. CHAS. S. ROBINSON, D.D., LL.D. Seventh Edition. Large crown 8vo., cloth, 5s.

"They are the result of careful study, and are full of interest."—*Spectator.*

The House and Its Builder. With Other Discourses : A Book for the Doubtful. By the Rev. SAMUEL COX, D.D., Author of "Expositions," &c. Third and Cheaper Edition. Small crown 8vo., paper, 1s.

"The courage and sympathy which run through it are scarcely more conspicuous than the skill and originality."—*Leeds Mercury.*

The Risen Christ: The King of Men. By the late Rev. J. BALDWIN BROWN, M.A. Second and Cheaper Edition. Crown 8vo., cloth, 3s. 6d.

"We have again felt in reading these nervous, spiritual, and eloquent sermons how great a preacher has passed away."—*Nonconformist.*

The Wider Hope: Essays and Strictures on the Doctrine and Literature of a Future. By Numerous Writers, Lay and Clerical: Canon FARRAR, the late Principal TULLOCH, the late Rev. J. BALDWIN BROWN, and many others. Crown 8vo., cloth, 7s. 6d.

"A mass of material which will certainly prove useful to students of the subject. Here they will find a large body of valuable opinion on a topic perennially attractive."—*Globe.*

"Expositions." By the Rev. SAMUEL COX, D.D. In Four Vols., demy 8vo., cloth, price 7s. 6d. each.

"We have said enough to show our high opinion of Dr. Cox's volume. It is indeed full of suggestion. . . . A valuable volume."—*The Spectator.*

"Here, too, we have the clear exegetical insight, the lucid expository style, the chastened but effective eloquence, the high ethical standpoint, which secured for the earlier series a well-nigh unanimous award of commendation."—*Academy.*

"When we say that the volume possesses all the intellectual, moral, and spiritual characteristics which have won for its author so distinguished a place among the religious teachers of our time . . . what further recommendation can be necessary?"—*Nonconformist.*

Inspiration and the Bible: An Inquiry. By ROBERT HORTON, M.A., formerly Fellow of New College, Oxford. Fourth and Cheaper Edition. Crown 8vo., cloth, 3s. 6d.

"The work displays much earnest thought, and a sincere belief in, and love of the Bible."—*Morning Post.*

"It will be found to be a good summary, written in no iconoclastic spirit, but with perfect candour and fairness, of some of the more important results of recent Biblical criticism."—*Scotsman.*

Faint, yet Pursuing. By the Rev. E. J. HARDY, Author of "How to be Happy though Married." Sq. imp. 16mo., cloth, 6s. Cheaper Edition, 3s. 6d.

"One of the most practical and readable volumes of sermons ever published. They must have been eminently hearable."—*British Weekly.*

The Ethic of Freethought: A Selection of Essays and Lectures. By KARL PEARSON, M.A., formerly Fellow of King's College, Cambridge. Demy 8vo., cloth, 12s.

"Are characterised by much learning, much keen and forcible thinking, and a fearlessness of denunciation and exposition."—*Scotsman.*

Miscellaneous.

The Business of Life: A Book for Everyone. By the Rev. E. J. Hardy, Author of "How to be Happy though Married," &c. Square imp. 16mo., cloth, 6s.

CONTENTS.—The Business of Life.—To Be; To Do; To Do Without; To Depart.—The Dark Valley Lighted up.—Work and Rest.—Busy Idleness.—Idle Time not Idly Spent.—Ios.—Undecided Ones.—Bye-path Meadow; or, The Pitfalls of Life.—Fixing a Day.—Eyes Right.—Censoriousness.—The Science of Silence—Knocks on the Knuckles.—Stop Thief.—Never Young and Never Old.—Growing Old Gracefully.—Real and Amateur Gentlewomen—Disguised Blessings and Curses.—No Cross, No Crown.—Grace at Meals and Elsewhere.—Cultivate Small Pleasures.—Seeing, Reading, and Thinking.—Why do People wish to be Rich Before and After Marriage?—Wealth as a Profession.—The Ship of Duty.

Names; and their Meaning: A Book for the Curious. By Leopold Wagner. Large crown 8vo., cloth, 7s. 6d.

SOME OF THE CONTENTS.—The Countries of the World.—The Months and Days of the Week.—Creeds, Sects, and Denominations.—Tavern Signs.—Royal Surnames.—National Sobriquets and Nicknames.—Birds.—Religious Orders.—Paper and Printing.—Political Nicknames.—Flowers.—The Bible.—Wines.—Literary Sobriquets and Pseudonyms.—The Counties of England and Wales.—Carriages.—Dances.—Pigments and Dyes.—London Districts and Suburbs.—Battles.—Notable Days and Festivals.—Textiles, Embroideries, and Lace.—London Inns, Streets, Squares, and Gardens.—The Inns of Court.—Races.—London Churches and Buildings.—Class Names and Nicknames.—Malt Liquors.—Naval and Military Sobriquets.—Spirits.

The Principles of Strategy. Illustrated mainly from American Campaigns, by John Bigelow, Jun., First Lieutenant 10th Cavalry, U.S. Army. With 32 Maps. Fcap. folio, 21s.

"In this work we may welcome a valuable addition to military literature."
Standard.

Climbers' Guide to the Eastern Pennine Alps. By William Martin Conway. Describing the Mountain District between the Theodul Pass and the Simplon. Limp cloth, with pocket, flap and pencil, 10s.

"Deserves a place in every climber's pocket."—*Pall Mall Gazette.*

Climbers' Guide to the Central Pennine.
By WILLIAM MARTIN CONWAY.   32mo., limp cloth, with pocket, flap, and pencil, 10s.

Courts and Sovereigns of Europe.
By "POLITIKOS." Being Full Descriptions of the Home and Court life of the Reigning Families. With many Portraits. Crown 8vo., cloth, 10s. 6d.

"A most interesting and useful volume. . . . Lively and very readable chapters."—*Pall Mall Gazette.*

The Folks o' Carglen.
A Story. By ALEXANDER GORDON, Author of "What Cheer, O?" Crown 8vo., buckram, 6s.

"A series of sketches, slight in character, but admirably true to nature. . . . Bright and interesting."—*Scotsman.*

Hanging in Chains.
By ALBERT HARTSHORNE, F.S.A. With Eight Illustrations. Demy 12mo., parchment boards, gilt tops, 4s. 6d.

"Mr. Hartshorne illustrates his text by many curious and instructive plates, which form a specially interesting feature. He has done his work very thoroughly, and his book will be found not only very readable, but worthy of preservation."
Globe.

A Vindication of the Rights of Woman:
With Strictures on Political and other Subjects. By MARY WOLLSTONECRAFT. New Edition. With Introduction by Mrs. HENRY FAWCETT. Crown 8vo., cloth, 7s. 6d.

"Mrs. Fawcett's introduction is an admirable and perfectly dispassionate analysis of the main arguments of the book."—*Manchester Guardian.*

Emigration and Immigration:
A Study in Social Science. By RICHMOND M. SMITH, Professor of Political Economy and Social Science in Columbia College. Square imp. 16mo., cloth, 7s. 6d.

Prof. Smith's book is a popular examination of one of the most urgent of present-day problems from historical, statistical, and economic points of view the information being full and exact, and the author's style being a model of terseness and clearness.

How Men Propose. The Fateful Question and Its Answer. Love scenes from popular works of Fiction, collected by AGNES STEVENS. Square Imp. 16mo., cloth, 6s.; Presentation Edition, cloth elegant, bevelled boards, gilt edges, in box, 7s. 6d. Popular Edition, sm. 8vo., cloth, 3s. 6d. (Uniform with "How to be Happy Though Married.")
"A most entertaining book."—*Spectator.*

Sylvan Folk. Sketches of Bird and Animal Life in Britain. By JOHN WATSON, Author of "A Year in the Fields," &c. Crown 8vo., cloth, 3s. 6d.
"His descriptions are so fresh that they will give genuine pleasure to everyone who reads them. The book will be especially interesting to young readers."—*Nature.*

The Five Talents of Woman. A Book for Girls and Young Women. By the Rev. E. J. HARDY, Author of "How to be Happy though Married," &c. Sq. imperial 16mo., cloth, 6s.; Presentation Edition, bevelled boards, gilt edges, in box, 7s. 6d.
"Will be acceptable to all girls who are no longer 'children.'"—*Globe.*

How to be Happy though Married. Small crown 8vo., cloth, 3s. 6d. Bridal Gift Edition, white vellum cloth, extra gilt, bev. boards, gilt edges, in box, 7s. 6d.
"The Murray of Matrimony and the Baedeker of Bliss."—*Pall Mall Gazette.*

"Manners Makyth Man." By the Author of "How to be Happy though Married." Popular Edition, small crown 8vo., cloth, 3s. 6d.; imp. 16mo., cloth, 6s.

English as She is Taught. Genuine Answers to Examination Questions in our Public Schools. With a Commentary by MARK TWAIN. Demy 16mo., cloth, 1s.; paper, 6d.
MARK TWAIN says: "A darling literary curiosity. . . . This little book ought to set forty millions of people to thinking."

Books for Children.

The Children's Library.
Post 8vo., fancy cloth, marbled edges, 2s. 6d. each.

1. **The Brown Owl.** By Ford H. Hueffer. With Two Illustrations by Madox Brown.

2. **The China Cup, and Other Fairy Tales.** By Felix Volkhofsky. Illustrated by Malischeff.

3. **Stories from Fairyland.** By Georges Drosines. Illustrated by Thomas Riley.

4. **The Adventures of Pinocchio;** or, The Story of a Puppet. By C. Collodi. Translated from the Italian by M. A. Murray. Illustrated by C. Mazzanti.

5. **The Little Princess,** And Other Fairy Stories. By Lina Eckenstein.

6. **Tales from the Mabinogion.** By Meta Williams.

7. **Irish Tales.** Edited by W. B. Yeats. Illustrated by F. B. Yeats.

8. **The Little Glass Man,** And Other Stories from Hauff. Translated by various writers. With Introduction by Lina Eckenstein.

9. **A New Story.** By Mrs. Molesworth. [*March*, 1892.

Another Brownie Book. By Palmer Cox, Author of "The Brownies," &c. With many quaint pictures by the Author. Medium 4to., cloth gilt, 6s.

The first Brownie book was issued some years ago. The new book is like the first in size and style of binding, but a new cover design, printed in colors, has been made for it, and the contents are entirely new. It contains 150 large pages, describing in verse more adventures of the amusing Brownies.

Wild Nature Won by Kindness. By Mrs. BRIGHTWEN, Vice-President of the Selborne Society. With Illustrations by the Author, and F. CARRUTHERS GOULD. Second Edition. Small crown 8vo., cloth, 3s. 6d.; and, Cheaper Edition, paper boards, 1s.

The Brownies: Their Book. By PALMER COX. Reprinted from *St. Nicholas*, with many new Poems and Pictures. Third and Cheaper Edition. Medium 4to., cloth, gilt edges, 6s.

New Fairy Tales from Brentano. Told in English by KATE FREILIGRATH KROEKER, and Pictured by F. CARRUTHERS GOULD. Eight Full-page Coloured Illustrations. Square 8vo., illustrated, paper boards, cloth back, 5s.; cloth, gilt edges, 6s.

Fairy Tales from Brentano. Told in English by KATE FREILIGRATH KROEKER. Illustrated by F. CARRUTHERS GOULD. Popular Edition. Sq. imp. 16mo., 3s. 6d.

The Bird's Nest, and other Sermons for Children of all Ages. By the Rev. SAMUEL COX, D.D., Author of "Expositions," &c. Cheap and Popular Edition. Imp. 16mo., cloth, 3s. 6d.

Arminius Vambéry: His Life and Adventures. Written by Himself. With Introductory Chapter dedicated to the Boys of England. Portrait and Seventeen Illustrations. Crown 8vo., 5s.

Boys' Own Stories. By ASCOTT R. HOPE, Author of "Stories of Young Adventurers," "Stories out of School Time," &c. Eight Illustrations. Crown 8vo., cloth, 5s.

THE CAMEO SERIES.

Half-bound, price 3s. 6d. each.   Fine Edition, in parchment, 30 copies only printed.

1. **The Lady from the Sea.** By HENRIK IBSEN. Translated by ELEANOR MARX-AVELING.
2. **A London Plane-Tree,** and Other Poems. By AMY LEVY.
3. **Wordsworth's Grave,** and Other Poems. By WILLIAM WATSON.
4. **Iphigenia in Delphi,** With some Translations from the Greek, by RICHARD GARNETT, LL.D. Illust.
5. **Mireio: A Provencal Poem.** By FREDERIC MISTRAL. Translated by H. W. PRESTON. Frontispiece by JOSEPH PENNELL.
6. **Lyrics.** Selected from the Works of A. MARY F. ROBINSON (Mdme. Jas. Darmesteter). Frontispiece.
7. **A Minor Poet.** By AMY LEVY. Portrait. Second Edition.
8. **Concerning Cats.** A Book of Verses, by many Authors. Edited by Mrs. GRAHAM TOMSON. Illustrated.

THE PSEUDONYM LIBRARY.

Oblong 24mo.   Paper, 1s. 6d.; cloth, 2s. each.

1. **Mademoiselle Ixe.** By LANOE FALCONER. Seventh Edition.
2. **Eleanor Lambert.** By MAGDALEN BROOKE. Third Edition.
3. **A Mystery of the Campagna.** By VON DEGEN. Second Edition.
4. **The School of Art.** By ISABEL SNOW. Second Edition.
5. **Amaryllis.** By ΓΕΩΡΓΙΟΣ ΔΡΟΣΙΝΗΣ.
6. **The Hotel d'Angleterre.** By LANOE FALCONER. Third Edition.
7. **A Russian Priest.** By N. H. ПОТАПЕНКО. Third Edition.
8. **Some Emotions and a Moral.** By JOHN OLIVER HOBBES. Second Edition.
9. **European Relations.** By TASMAGE DALIN.
10. **John Sherman, and Dhoya.** By GANCONAGH.
11. **Macka's Dream,** and Other Stories from the Russian. By KAVOLGAR.

LONDON: T. FISHER UNWIN, PATERNOSTER SQUARE, E.C

www.ingramcontent.com/pod-product-compliance
Lightning Source LLC
Chambersburg PA
CBHW030809230426
43667CB00008B/1128